U 2

Tempo: A Rowman & Littlefield Music Series on Rock, Pop, and Culture
Series Editor: Scott Calhoun

Tempo: A Rowman & Littlefield Music Series on Rock, Pop, and Culture offers titles that explore rock and popular music through the lens of social and cultural history, revealing the dynamic relationship between musicians, music, and their milieu. Like other major art forms, rock and pop music comment on their cultural, political, and even economic situation, reflecting the technological advances, psychological concerns, religious feelings, and artistic trends of their times. Contributions to the Tempo series are the ideal introduction to major pop and rock artists and genres.

U2

Rock 'n' Roll to Change the World

Timothy D. Neufeld

ROWMAN & LITTLEFIELD
Lanham • Boulder • New York • London

Published by Rowman & Littlefield
A wholly owned subsidiary of The Rowman & Littlefield Publishing Group,
Inc.
4501 Forbes Boulevard, Suite 200, Lanham, Maryland 20706
www.rowman.com

Unit A, Whitacre Mews, 26-34 Stannary Street, London SE11 4AB

British Library Cataloguing in Publication Information Available

Library of Congress Cataloging-in-Publication Data

Names: Neufeld, Timothy D., 1963- author.
Title: U2 : rock 'n' roll to change the world / Timothy D. Neufeld.
Description: Lanham : Rowman & Littlefield, [2017] | Series: Tempo, a Rowman & Littlefield
    music series on rock, pop, and culture | Includes bibliographical references and index.
Identifiers: LCCN 2016036298 (print) | LCCN 2016037520 (ebook) | ISBN 9781442249394
    (cloth : alk. paper) | ISBN 9781442249400 (electronic)
Subjects: LCSH: U2 (Musical group) | Rock musicians—Ireland—Biography. | Rock musicians—
    Political activity.
Classification: LCC ML421.U2 N48 2017 (print) | LCC ML421.U2 (ebook) | DDC 782.42166092/
    2 [B] —dc23 LC record available at https://lccn.loc.gov/2016036298

Printed in the United States of America

To my sons:

Michael, "Every generation gets a chance to
change the world"
and Daniel, "Young, not dumb"

CONTENTS

FOREWORD

U2 is an icon now, in 2017, not just in the world of popular music or just in the worlds of celebrity entertainers, humanitarians, or political activists, but in *the world*. As in, U2 is a global icon. Some call U2 Ireland's greatest cultural ambassadors; more would agree it is Ireland's greatest commercial export, which is no small feat considering U2's hometown, Dublin, is also the home of Guinness. As with all exports with a global impact, U2 has its passionate devotees as well as its vociferous deriders, both of which attest to the fact that when U2 comes to stay, it changes the landscape and the lives connected to it.

Changing lives was sort of the point for the four teenagers who formed the band in 1976 and have remained the band's only lineup to this day. When Bono, Edge, Larry Mullen, Jr., and Adam Clayton met for their first practice, they were looking for a change in their own lives. They all knew the cultural tribulations of Ireland; Bono and Larry also had more personal trials to work through. Their sights were set on bands who inspired them: the already iconic Beatles, the Who, and the Rolling Stones, as well as the iconoclastic punk rockers from London to New York City, from the Clash to the Ramones, Television, Patti Smith, and the Velvet Underground. U2's stereoscopic vision put icons and iconoclasts into focus, into one point of view shared equally by four men. The vision in their heads convinced them that with effort, imagination, and ingenuity, a rock band could be a force for change; the dream in their hearts was fueled by faith, hope, and love, such that by starting a rock band it might be more than just fun, it could be a family, and whatever notes they played could take a sad world and make it better.

In the following pages, Timothy D. Neufeld presents one of the most considered examinations I have ever read of the multiple cultural forces that have shaped U2 and that, by engaging those same cultural conversations, U2 has shaped in return. Writing with a personal interest and working as a scholar to assemble the facts to guide inquiry and conclusions, Neufeld has written neither a biography nor catalog of U2's achievements but rather a spirited testament of the core trait in U2 that makes it grow more enigmatic, thematically, the closer one looks. U2 is a changing band. It is known for its sonic, performative, and business experimentations that turned into acclaimed innovations, but at a deeper level it is driven by the belief that there is something better in itself and in us; its discontents arise when it sees inequality and indignity, prompting it to want to change the conditions affecting the lives at stake. Being open to change has served U2 well, internally, and it has made its career based on entertaining everyone around it to accept disruption as a force for good.

While its detractors scoff at the notion, U2 is, in fact, more interested in what you can become than what it can achieve. U2 intended to be big, great, and influential—there was no shortage of ambition in those Dublin teens—but it didn't know back then how it would all turn out. The picture for the cover of this book is from January 2009, when U2 played in a preinauguration concert for US president-elect Barack Obama, staged in front of the Lincoln Memorial on the National Mall, in Washington, DC. As a central campaign motif of Obama's was change, it was fitting to have like-minded U2 help usher in his presidency by performing "Pride (in the Name of Love)," written to honor Dr. Martin Luther King, Jr., himself an incredible agent of change whose voice could be in the cultural conversations of the 1960s in part because of the courageous change President Lincoln himself enacted a hundred years prior. U2's involvement in the concert and its pose in front of the Lincoln Memorial reinforces a point about its own stature, but as charismatic performers still thrilling audiences with new music, the band hasn't yet joined a rock 'n' roll statuary hall. Contradictions in U2's career such as this have kept it interesting for fans and critics along the way, and U2 has always realized that the power for change is inherently embedded in a contradiction. What U2 couldn't see in 1976 was that it would get caught in the inevitable irony of success before it was done trying to change the world. All its effort, brains, artistry, and punk spirit worked, bringing the band a massive fan following that was, apparently, waiting for just this band's mix of music and message. The great irony of its career is that it is now iconic, while it still tries to operate within the principles of iconoclasm. "Smack in the middle of a contradiction is a good place to be," as Bono is fond of saying.

Scott Calhoun
Series Editor

TIME LINE

Cultural Events	U2's Career
1798: Irish peasants rise up against British rule in the United Irishmen Rebellion.	
January 1, 1801: Ireland and Great Britain merge into the United Kingdom of Great Britain and Ireland.	
1840s: The Great Famine in Ireland.	
1914–1920: The Home Rule Act allows for the creation of Northern Ireland and, eventually, the Republic of Ireland.	
November 21, 1920: Thirty-one people are killed in Dublin on a day that becomes known as the first Bloody Sunday.	
August 6 and 8, 1945: The United States drops atomic bombs on Hiroshima and Nagasaki, Japan.	

Cultural Events

1947: The Cold War begins and lasts until 1991.

1948: South Africa ushers in a new system of government called "apartheid."
Mohandas Gandhi is assassinated in New Delhi, India.

January 20, 1961: John F. Kennedy becomes president of the United States.

August 1961: Construction begins on the Berlin Wall, dividing East and West Berlin.

August 5, 1962: Nelson Mandela is arrested in South Africa and sentenced to life in prison.

1968: The Troubles, thirty years of conflict in Northern Ireland and areas of the Republic, begin and last until 1998.

U2's Career

August 19, 1950: Bob Hewson (Catholic) and Iris Rankin (Protestant) are married at St. John the Baptist Church of Ireland in Drumcondra, Dublin, in a ceremony that was considered scandalous.

March 13, 1960: Adam Clayton is born in Chinnor, Oxfordshire, England.

May 10, 1960: Paul "Bono" Hewson is born in Dublin, Ireland.

August 8, 1961: David "Edge" Evans is born in East London, England.

October 31, 1961: Larry Mullen, Jr. is born in Dublin, Ireland.

Cultural Events

April 4, 1968: Martin Luther King, Jr. is assassinated.

July 21, 1969: Neil Armstrong becomes the first human to walk on the Moon.

1972: Mount Temple Comprehensive School is established in Dublin.

January 30, 1972: Thirteen people are killed by British soldiers in Derry, Northern Ireland, on a day that becomes known as the second Bloody Sunday.

1974–1977: Disco rises to become mainstream.

May 17, 1974: A series of bombs explode in Dublin and Monaghan, Ireland, killing thirty-three civilians.

August 9, 1974: Richard Nixon resigns as president of the United States.

April 23, 1976: The Ramones release a self-titled debut album.

U2's Career

1973: Larry's sister dies at nine years old.

September 1974: Iris Hewson, Bono's mother, suffers a brain aneurysm at the graveside of her own father and dies four days later.

1976: Larry's mother is killed in a car accident.
Bono and a group of kids living around Cedarwood Road form a club they call Lypton Village.

September 25, 1976: Seven boys gather in Larry's home in response to a note he posted on a Mount

Cultural Events

U2's Career

Temple bulletin board about forming a band.

Fall 1976: Larry, Adam, Bono, Edge, and Edge's brother, Dik, form a band called Feedback and enter a talent contest at Mount Temple (Dik can't play at the talent show because he is too old).

January 14, 1977: David Bowie releases *Low*, recorded at Hansa Studio in collaboration with Brian Eno.

April 11, 1977: Feedback plays its first full concert at St. Fintan's School in Dublin, later changing its name to the Hype.

January 20, 1977: Jimmy Carter becomes president of the United States.

October 21, 1977: The Hype attend a concert by the Clash at Trinity College in Dublin.

April 8, 1977: The Clash releases a self-titled debut album.

June 1977: The music magazine *Hot Press* is founded in Dublin. Apple introduces the Apple II home computer.

October 14, 1977: David Bowie releases *Heroes*, recorded at Hansa Studio in collaboration with Brian Eno.

October 28, 1977: The Sex Pistols release the controversial *Never Mind the Bullocks*, a breakthrough for punk.

Spring 1978: The band has its first TV performances as the Hype for RTÉ's *Our Times* and a little later as U2 for RTÉ's *Youngline*.

Cultural Events	*U2's Career*
	March 1978: The Hype changes its name to U2, wins a talent contest in Limerick, and says farewell to Dik.
	May 1978: The band meets Paul McGuinness, who eventually becomes U2's manager.
	Mid-1978: Bono, Edge, and Larry join Shalom, a Christian commune.
	August 1978: U2 plays for two of its earliest charity gigs: the Contraception Action Campaign and Rock against Sexism.
November 4, 1979: Sixty-three Americans are taken hostage in Iran and held for fourteen months.	**Summer 1979:** U2 plays regularly at Dublin's Dandelion Market.
	September 1979: U2's first studio production, *U2-3*, is released in Ireland.
December 8, 1980: John Lennon is assassinated.	**March 23, 1980:** U2 secures a four-year, four-album deal with Island Records.
December 12, 1980: The Clash releases its fourth album, *Sandinista!* an eclectic three-record set.	**May 23, 1980:** "11 O'Clock Tick Tock" debuts as the band's first international single.
	October 20, 1980: *Boy*, U2's first full album, debuts.
January 20, 1981: Ronald Reagan enters his first of two terms as president of the United States.	**Summer 1981:** Larry, then Bono, then Edge leaves Shalom.

Cultural Events

May 11, 1981: Bob Marley dies of skin cancer.

August 1, 1981: MTV debuts in America.

August 12, 1981: IBM releases its first PC.

November 3, 1982: Michael Jackson releases *Thriller.*

March 27, 1984: Run-DMC releases its self-titled debut album, a breakthrough for hip-hop.

October 12, 1984: Five people die when the IRA attempts an assassination of Prime Minister Margaret Thatcher.

October 16, 1984: Bishop Desmond Tutu is awarded the Nobel Peace Prize for his opposition to apartheid.

January 20, 1985: Ronald Reagan enters his second of two

U2's Career

October 12, 1981: *October*, U2's second album, is released.

November 1981: U2 releases its first fan club magazine.

August 21, 1982: Bono and Alison Stewart are married in Dublin.

February 28, 1983: *War*, U2's third album, is released.

May 21, 1983: U2 tours the Chicago Peace Museum and sees *The Unforgettable Fire* exhibit.

June 5, 1983: At Red Rocks Amphitheatre, U2 films its first live concert.

October 1, 1984: *The Unforgettable Fire*, U2's fourth album, is released.

November 1984: Bono and Adam participate in Band Aid and record "Do They Know It's Christmas?"

December 3, 1984: U2 performs for Amnesty International's "Stop Torture Week" fund-raiser.

March 1985: *Rolling Stone* features U2 on its cover as "Our

Cultural Events	U2's Career
terms as president of the United States.	Choice: Band of the '80s."
February 28, 1885: The IRA launches a mortar attack on a police station in Newry, Northern Ireland.	**July 13, 1985:** U2 gives a career-defining performance at Live Aid.
March 7, 1985: The USA for Africa project releases "We Are the World."	**September–October 1985:** Bono and Ali Hewson volunteer in Ethiopia at a refugee camp.
	December 7, 1985: Bono appears on the release of *Sun City*, a collaborative effort protesting South African apartheid.
1986: Mikhail Gorbachev institutes glasnost in an effort to reform the USSR.	**May 17, 1986:** U2 plays at Self Aid benefit in Dublin, highlighting chronic unemployment.
January 28, 1986: The space shuttle *Challenger* explodes just after liftoff.	**July 1986:** Bono and Ali visit Nicaragua and El Salvador.
April 15, 1986: The United States bombs Libya.	**September 1986:** Edge's solo album, *Captive*, is released.
April 26, 1986: Chernobyl is the site of the worst nuclear power plant accident in history.	**November 1986:** U2 releases the first issue of *Propaganda*, a new fan club magazine.
1987: In the United States, the Iran-Contra scandal dominates the evening news.	**March 9, 1987:** *The Joshua Tree*, U2's fifth album, is released.
November 8, 1987: The IRA bombs a Remembrance Day parade in Enniskillen, Northern Ireland.	**April 7, 1987:** U2 appears on the cover of *Time* magazine as "Rock's Hottest Ticket."

Cultural Events	U2's Career
	April 30, 1987: U2's first time appearing as a headline act in a US stadium.
	September 20, 1987: U2's first use of a video screen in a stadium.
	November 1, 1987: U2 disguises itself as a country western band and opens its own show as the Dalton Brothers.
	November–December 1987: U2 records various concerts and the footage is used for the film *Rattle and Hum*.
	March 2, 1988: U2 wins its first two Grammy Awards, including Album of the Year for *The Joshua Tree*.
	October 1988: *Rattle and Hum*, U2's sixth album, and its companion theatrical film are released.
January 20, 1989: George H. W. Bush becomes president of the United States.	**December 30 and 31, 1989:** U2 plays Dublin's Point Depot, ushering in the new decade, and Bono talks about going away to "dream it all up again."
April–June 1989: Students protest in Beijing's Tiananmen Square.	
July 20, 1989: The first house arrest of Aung San Suu Kyi begins.	
November 1989: Border crossings on the Berlin Wall are opened.	

Cultural Events

February 1990: Nelson Mandela is released from a South African prison.

April 10, 1990: Public Enemy releases *Fear of a Black Planet*, reflecting the mainstream culture of hip-hop.

June 1990: Demolition of the Berlin Wall begins.

October 3, 1990: Unification of East and West Germany is complete.

January–February 1991: A US-led coalition attacks Iraqi forces in Operation Desert Storm.

March 1991: The Yugoslav Wars begin with the Croatian War of Independence, initiating the breakup of Yugoslavia.

June 1991: The Slovenian Independence War begins.

July 1991: Boris Yeltsin resigns as the president of Russia.

October 14, 1991: Aung San Suu Kyi wins the Nobel Peace Prize while remaining under house arrest in Myanmar (Burma).

April 1992: The Bosnian War begins.

April–May 1992: Los Angeles explodes in riots when a jury acquits four police officers after the beating of Rodney King.

U2's Career

October 3, 1990: U2 arrives in West Berlin to begin recording at the famous Hansa Studios.

November 19, 1991: *Achtung Baby*, U2's seventh album is released.

June 20, 1992: U2 participates in a Greenpeace protest of the Sellafield nuclear power plant.

Cultural Events

January 20, 1993: Bill Clinton enters his first of two terms as president of the United States.

December 10, 1993: Nelson Mandela and F. W. de Klerk receive the Nobel Peace Prize.

1994: Apartheid officially ends in South Africa, and Nelson Mandela is elected as the country's first black president.

January 20, 1997: Bill Clinton enters his second of two terms as president of the United States.

November 22, 1997: Michael Hutchence, lead singer for INXS, commits suicide.

March 1998: The Kosovo War begins.

U2's Career

1993: U2 partners with Bill Carter to satellite link the bombed-out city of Sarajevo during concerts.

February 24, 1993: U2 wins a Grammy Award for *Achtung Baby*.

July 5, 1993: *Zooropa*, U2's eighth album, is released.

March 1, 1994: U2 wins a Grammy Award for *Zooropa*.

June 5, 1995: U2 releases the single, "Hold Me, Thrill Me, Kiss Me, Kill Me," which is written for the movie *Batman Forever*.

November 7, 1995: The release of "GoldenEye," sung by Tina Turner and written by Bono and Edge.

May 14, 1996: The release of "Theme from *Mission: Impossible*," recorded by Larry and Adam.

March 3, 1997: *Pop*, U2's ninth album, is released.

September 3, 1997: U2 keeps a promise made in 1993 and plays Sarajevo.

May 19, 1998: U2 plays at the Yes Campaign in Belfast in

Cultural Events	*U2's Career*
	support of the Good Friday Agreement.
August 7, 1998: US embassies in Tanzania and Kenya are bombed by al-Qaeda.	
December 2, 1998: The Good Friday Agreement is enacted, officially ending the Troubles.	
	1999: Bono works aggressively on behalf of Jubilee 2000.
	September 23, 1999: Bono meets with Pope John Paul II to discuss Third World debt relief, and exchanges a pair of his sunglasses for a rosary.
October 12, 2000: The USS *Cole* is bombed by al-Qaeda while harboring in a Yemeni port.	**February 2000:** *The Million Dollar Hotel*, a film Bono helped write and produce, is released.
	March 2000: The soundtrack from *The Million Dollar Hotel* is released, featuring songs by U2 and friends.
	July 2000: U2.com, the band's first official website, is launched.
	October 30, 2000: *All That You Can't Leave Behind*, U2's tenth album, is released.
January 20, 2001: George W. Bush becomes president of the United States.	**February 21, 2001:** U2 wins two Grammy Awards for "Beautiful Day."
September 11, 2001: Using commercial airliners in four separate attacks, terrorists bring	**October 2001:** U2 plays an emotional set of three concerts at Madison Square Garden, just

Cultural Events	*U2's Career*
down the two World Trade Center buildings, damage the Pentagon, and crash an airplane in a Pennsylvania field.	three miles away from the World Trade Center and six weeks after the attacks.

January 2002: Bono and Bobby Shriver launch DATA (Debt, AIDS, Trade, Africa).

February 3, 2002: U2 reproduces its Madison Square Garden tribute to 9/11 victims during halftime at the Super Bowl.

February 27, 2002: U2 wins a Grammy Award for *All That You Can't Leave Behind*.

2003: President George W. Bush establishes the President's Emergency Plan for AIDS Relief (PEPFAR).

March 20, 2003: The Iraq War begins as the United States leads a coalition of forces to topple Saddam Hussein.

February 2004: Facebook launches.

May 16, 2004: Bono helps launch ONE, an advocacy organization that seeks the elimination of extreme poverty, especially in Africa.

October–November 2004: Apple features U2's "Vertigo" in its iPod commercial, introduces the U2 Special Edition iPod, and releases a digital box set called *The Complete U2*.

Cultural Events

August 29, 2005: Hurricane Katrina causes massive flooding and catastrophic damage in New Orleans, resulting in over 1,000 deaths.

July 2006: Twitter launches.

U2's Career

November 22, 2004: *How to Dismantle an Atomic Bomb*, U2's eleventh album, is released.

2005: Bono and Ali found Edun, a global fashion brand that seeks to encourage trade in Africa.

February 13, 2005: U2 wins three Grammy Awards for "Vertigo."

March 14, 2005: U2 is inducted into the Rock and Roll Hall of Fame.

November 2005: Edge cofounds and launches Music Rising.

December 2005: Bono is named "Person of the Year" by *Time* magazine, along with Bill and Melinda Gates.

2006: U2 faces heavy criticism for moving a portion of its business to the Netherlands to avoid taxes in Ireland.

January 26, 2006: Bono and Bobby Shriver launch (RED), a new business model to generate revenue in the fight against AIDS in Africa.

February 2, 2006: Bono gives the keynote address at the National Prayer Breakfast in Washington, DC.

Cultural Events	*U2's Career*
	February 8, 2006: U2 wins a Grammy Award for *How to Dismantle an Atomic Bomb*.
	September 25, 2006: U2 performs a cover of the Skids' "The Saints Are Coming" with Green Day during a pregame show at the reopening of the Louisiana Superdome after Hurricane Katrina.
June 2007: Apple releases the iPhone.	
	January 23, 2008: The film *U2 3D* is released, featuring the Vertigo tour in the first live-action 3D concert movie.
January 20, 2009: Barack Obama enters his first of two terms as president of the United States.	**January 18, 2009:** U2 performs for the inauguration of Barack Obama.
June 2009: Hundreds of thousands of Iranians are met with violence by government forces as they protest election results in a period of civil unrest known as the Green Movement.	**February 27, 2009:** *No Line on the Horizon*, U2's twelfth album, is released.
	September 15, 2009: Blackberry announces a revolutionary new "U2 Mobile Album" meant to enhance the 360° tour experience.
	October 25, 2009: U2 films *U2: 360°* while performing at the Rose Bowl in Pasadena, California, and broadcasts the concert live on YouTube.

Cultural Events

November 13, 2010: Aung San Suu Kyi is released from fifteen years of house arrest.

January 8, 2011: Congresswoman Gabby Giffords survives an assassination attempt in Tucson, Arizona.

May 16, 2011: Mark Kelly, husband of Gabby Giffords, commands the final flight of the space shuttle *Endeavour*, from which he records a greeting that is used during the introduction to U2's "Beautiful Day" in concert.

February 26, 2012: Treyvon Martin, an African American teen living in Miami, is fatally shot by George Zimmerman.

2013: The #BlackLivesMatter movement coalesces around the acquittal of George Zimmerman in the shooting death of Treyvon Martin.

January 20, 2013: Barack Obama enters his second of two terms as president of the United States.

July 17, 2014: Eric Garner, an African American male, dies after a New York City police officer detains him with a chokehold and while repeating the words, "I can't breathe."

U2's Career

May 21, 2010: Bono has emergency back surgery, postponing the 360° tour.

June 14, 2011: Bono and Edge's *Spider-Man: Turn Off the Dark* officially opens on Broadway.

March 2012: Adam helps launch Walk in My Shoes, an initiative to create awareness about mental illness.

November 29, 2013: U2 releases "Ordinary Love," a song honoring Nelson Mandela and written for the film *Mandela: Long Walk to Freedom.*

February 2, 2014: U2 releases "Invisible," which debuts during the Super Bowl and generates funds for (RED).

Cultural Events

August 9, 2014: Michael Brown, an African American teen living in Ferguson, Missouri, is shot and killed by Darren Wilson, a white police officer.

February 2015: The streaming app Meerkat is released.

March 2015: The streaming app Periscope is released.

April 4, 2015: Walter Scott, an African American male, is fatally shot by Michael Slager, a white North Charleston police officer.

April 12, 2015: Freddie Gray, an African American male, dies from injuries while in the custody of the Baltimore Police Department.

May 22, 2015: Ireland becomes the first country to legalize same-sex marriage by a popular vote.

Summer 2015: The influx of Syrian, Afghan, and Iraqi refugees arriving in Greece reaches a critical level, creating tension and civil unrest throughout Europe.

U2's Career

September 9, 2014: *Songs of Innocence*, U2's thirteenth album, is released digitally at an Apple press conference.

November 16, 2014: Bono is involved in a high-impact bicycle accident that leaves him with numerous serious injuries.

February 21, 2015: Longtime friend and spiritual advisor to the band Jack Heaslip passes away.

May 27, 2015: Dennis Sheehan, U2's first and only tour manager, dies from a heart attack while on tour.

September 20, 2015: For the first time ever, U2 cancels a concert (Stockholm) due to a security breach.

October 26, 2015: U2's "Song for Someone" is released via the Vrse app as a state-of-the-art, interactive, 360-degree virtual reality video.

November 13, 2015: U2 cancels its Paris concert as a series of deadly terrorist attacks happen throughout the city.

December 7, 2015: U2 returns to Paris for a rescheduled show—the last of its 2015 I+E tour—a concert that is broadcast later that day on HBO.

Cultural Events	*U2's Career*
September 2, 2015: The body of three-year-old Alan (Aylan) Kurdi, a Kurdish refugee, washes up on a Mediterranean beach in Turkey. The photograph captures the attention of the world and highlights the European crisis.	
	April 12, 2016: Bono testifies before a US Senate subcommittee about foreign aid, Africa, and the international refugee crisis.

ACKNOWLEDGMENTS

In the vernacular of U2, I would like to thank "all the stolen voices" that contributed to this book (see "The Miracle [of Joey Ramone]"). I'm indebted to quite a number of authors, colleagues, and friends who have helped shape my writing, and I hope that through it, the ideas and gestures of kindness "will one day be returned."

First and foremost, a book like this would have been much harder to write without the fantastically rich archive of @U2 (www.atu2.com), the longest-running U2 fansite on the web, as well as Matt McGee, the site's founder and author of *U2: A Diary*. Across a myriad of Google searches, these two resources have been at the top of the list more often than I can count. I also offer thanks to a number of others associated with this site (where I, too, am a news writer). Tassoula Kokkoris, Sherry Lawrence, and Karen Lindell are brilliant researchers, writers, and editors who have directly influenced my work over and over. As a professor, I have valued the insight of other academics, especially Arlan Hess and Christopher Endrinal, who are U2 scholars in their own right and never leave me wanting of meaningful conversation. There's not enough room here to list a cadre of other names related to the @U2 website, but all have had an impact on me through their articles and conversations (including ceremonial midnight pizza runs in downtown Manhattan).

Beth Maynard, a coauthor of *Get Up Off Your Knees: Preaching the U2 Catalog* and the one who found my first blog post about U2 in 2006 and introduced me to a whole online community of thoughtful U2 fans, and Angela Pancella, an inspiring author and director of an urban non-profit, continue to challenge and nuance my theological notions of the band. The crew of U2Songs.com, specifically Christopher Jenkins and Aaron J. Sams, have also been great sources for the tiniest U2-related details along the way.

Scott Calhoun, editor of Rowman & Littlefield's Tempo series, got more than he bargained for by picking me up as one of his writers. Not only an excellent editor, he is one of the most scholarly voices I know on the topic of U2, and I am grateful beyond words for his patient and gracious coaching throughout this project, as well as to Natalie Mand-ziuk and all the other kind and resourceful people at Rowman & Little-field who gave guidance and helped me make decisions along the way. Recognition also goes to my colleagues in the biblical and religious studies department at Fresno Pacific University where I teach, who put up with my incessant rambling about this band and have kindly allowed me to occasionally skirt my duties as department chair while preparing this manuscript. I'm grateful to my office assistant Sara Martin, a stellar senior student who I trusted to proofread all of these words. Several deans have allowed me freedom and time to write this book and to teach a very unique class called Theology, Culture, and U2—thanks to Dr. Will Friesen for initial permission, Dr. Kevin Reimer for encouragement, and Dr. Ron Herms for helping see this project through to the end.

Finally, a grateful, heartfelt thanks to the global U2 community. I have intimate friends all over the world because of this band, though I've never met most of them. "Hugs before handshakes" we like to say. And special appreciation goes to the Crystal Ballroom, a social media community I lead on Periscope, where I've tested many of the ideas and stories that follow. One of the points I try to make in this book is that U2 is much bigger than four men. I'm grateful to Larry, Adam, Edge, and Bono, but I'm equally thankful to the amazing fraternity that surrounds them. I've never met the band, gotten an autograph, or stood in line on a curb to snap a photo, but I have talked or corresponded with enough of the U2 crew to know that these people are the real deal. This isn't just a business, it's a craft—a lifelong endeavor of love. Many artists, technicians, and support staff are mentioned in this text, but space prohibits me from citing many of the others I wish I could have called attention to. One of the great lessons of this forty-year-long case study is watching the development of an inspiring U2 family.

And I can't complete my acknowledgments without mentioning my own family. Tracy, my wife (Mrs. Crystal Ballroom), deserves credit for reading along as I wrote but more importantly, for hauling our two boys around to music lessons and school and church and so many other activities while I spent late nights in my office researching and writing or while I was off on a U2 excursion. And I'm grateful for the patience of Michael and Daniel, who asked me, "Dad, when are you going to be through with your book?" more than once. "A house doesn't make a home," but you three do.

INTRODUCTION

My world changed on November 18, 1987. Sitting at the top of the Los Angeles Memorial Coliseum, I was ambushed by a phenomenon that was greater than the sum of its four parts. It was a synergy of music, words, images, lights, and decibels. Lots of decibels. But the magnitude of volume wasn't limited to just sound. That night there was an explosion of passion, mood, and spirit. It started big and only got bigger. Out of the darkness came the hymn-like strains of an organ, slowly growing in intensity. As U2 took the stage, the Olympic torch on the Coliseum burst into flame. Then came the unmistakable 6/8 rhythm of Edge's guitar intro, the pounding of Larry's kick drum and toms, Adam's driving quarter notes, and a blinding flash of white light that flooded the audience. By the time Bono sang "I want to run," the opening line of "Where the Streets Have No Name," we were higher than the stadium itself. It was the first time I'd heard a seventy-thousand-voice choir, and I almost believed the band had come to see us perform rather than the other way around. I became a follower.

My fascination with U2 began in 1985 with a simple record—a mini-album that bore a sticker advertising a reduced price. *Under a Blood Red Sky* (1983) contained eight live songs and only cost a few bucks. It was a great deal and a great introduction to U2, encapsulating much of what the band had come to stand for during the first five years of its career. Every song demonstrated a passionate live performance, each carrying the emotion of a full concert on its own. The themes articulated on this small album were varied yet all engaging: conflict, war, suf-

fering, peace, celebration, unconditional love, and even a little bit of
Latin liturgy. This was complex stuff, the kind of catchy rock 'n' roll that
could be listened to while driving home from a long day of work and
also meaty enough to provide ample conversation with thoughtful
friends well into the night. But most fascinating to me was this post-
punk Irish band's use of scripture—both the opening and closing tracks
referenced the ancient book of Psalms. "Gloria" kicked the album off
with the chorus "Gloria in te Domine / Gloria exultate" (loosely translated from Latin: "Glory in you, Lord / Glory, exalt him"), and "40" concluded the record with the crowd chanting a three-thousand-year-old
refrain of "How long, to sing this song?" I was mesmerized.

In the pre-Internet era of my first U2 album, I really didn't know
much about the band. There was an occasional article or a conversation
with another fan who had heard a random rumor about the group, but
all I really had was the primary text of the songs. I began to dissect the
lyrics, analyzing each and every line. U2's first three albums, *Boy*
(1980), *October* (1981), and *War* (1983), had slipped by me, except for
a few popular songs that made it onto American radio stations; I eventually went back and picked those albums up. After *Blood Red Sky* came
The Unforgettable Fire (1984), a very odd-sounding album with an almost ambient, ethereal quality; *The Joshua Tree* (1987), a must-have,
trendsetting record of the 1980s; and then *Rattle and Hum* (1988),
which appeared both as an album and a movie. I'll never forget leaving
the theater after watching it—what had I just seen? Was it a documentary? A concert video? A feature film? Were these guys righteous activists or just sanctimonious celebrities? I wasn't quite sure, but I was
definitely intrigued all the more.

And then I abandoned the group for a while. I wasn't alone. Many
fans who had come to rely on U2's straightforward approach to music
and activism were confounded by the next series of albums. I loved
Achtung Baby (1991), but the sensual language felt carnal and foreign.
And when band members dressed in drag for the album cover, it
seemed like a reversal of their squeaky-clean, choir-boy lifestyles. There
was a lot to love about the record (the first U2 I'd purchased on CD),
including its fervent spirit and creative production, but the unambiguous sensuality left me confused. And here's a confession I'm hesitant to
make as the author of a book in which I claim to be a fan: I didn't even
purchase the experimental-sounding *Zooropa* (1993) and the dance-

themed *Pop* (1997), the band's next two albums. As I saw it (along with many others), U2 had become the band of press conferences in a Kmart lingerie department (which they actually did!). The group appeared to have sold out. I eventually learned it was all part of an elaborate, calculated commentary on culture by a band that was immersing itself in the milieu it was attempting to critique. I was the unwitting victim of a very intentional, brilliant hoax. Though I ultimately bought the albums (and loved them), U2's grand experiment in irony and misdirection, apparently, had worked a little too well, resulting in low sales and less loyalty from fans.

In 2000, U2 began releasing another set of albums that won a lot of fans back, primarily because the new records reflected the earlier, more accessible sounds and themes of a younger U2, but this time with the seasoned voice of experience and age. *All That You Can't Leave Behind* (2000) marked the beginning of a new millennium with a fresh spirit of hope and joy. It took on even deeper meaning when terrorists brought down the World Trade Center buildings in New York, prompting the band to become an agent of healing in a climate of chaos and fear. *How to Dismantle an Atomic Bomb* (2004) continued building on themes of peace, faith, and reconciliation and ushered in a new generation of U2 fans with the punk-influenced riffs of "Vertigo" and a call to take action against senseless global poverty. It felt like the band had returned to its musical and ideological roots. *No Line on the Horizon* (2009) represented fresh sonic territory for the group. It was filled with lavish sounds and compelling stories, and though the album underperformed in sales, it captured the hearts and souls of faithful listeners through its personal narratives of pain and conflict, as well as those of joy and grace. As the members of U2 moved into their fifties—their fourth decade of making music together—they faced a bit of an identity crisis, resulting in their longest gap between records. The outcome, eventually, was *Songs of Innocence* (2014), a retrospective album focusing on the group's earliest years as it navigated the turbulent waters of a violent Dublin. Creating one of its most intimate and emotive supporting tours, U2 demonstrated it could still generate relevant, artistic, and popular content. The band had transcended stereotypes characteristic of other legacy acts in the music industry and had migrated to undiscovered territory. No rock 'n' roll group had survived this long while maintaining the ability to create new, critically acclaimed material with all the original members intact. U2 had become a one-of-a-kind supergroup.

U2 is a quartet of men who came together as teens in a time when their world—Ireland—was plagued with violence and religious sectarianism. They formally joined forces in 1976 in response to a note posted on the school bulletin board by a young novice drummer hoping to start his own band. Larry Mullen, Jr., the author of the note, was just fourteen years old when he and a handful of classmates from Mount Temple Comprehensive gathered around a drum set that filled the kitchen in his small Dublin home one Saturday in September. Adam Clayton showed up that day and brought his own bass guitar. At sixteen years old, he also had a sense of rock 'n' roll swagger that immediately caught the others' attention. Dave Evans, a nerdy fifteen-year-old who had built his own guitar, also responded. Later he would be rechristened "Edge" (also "the Edge") by his artsy friends. Sixteen-year-old Paul Hewson tried to play guitar but didn't do so with much proficiency. He did, however, have lots of charisma and energy and loved to sing. Taking the name "Bono," he quickly became the lead singer and front man of the new band.

The early years were filled with lots of trial and error for this quirky group of teens who had more soul than talent. Known first as Feedback, then the Hype, and finally as U2, the band experimented with different configurations of vocals and instruments, finally settling on a solid combo of drums, bass guitar, electric guitar, and lead singer. Relentlessly pursuing their new passion, the four boys endured personal hardships, overcame youthful inexperience, and blazed new territory as a rock band in the middle of a repressive Irish context, accepting any and every opportunity to perform. Indeed, it was their live performances that quickly set them apart from a flurry of other groups emerging around the same time. Almost by chance, the adolescent band discovered a love for the stage but, even more so, loved the connections that were made with audiences it performed to from the stage. Very early on, U2 became well known for impassioned, spirited, and aggressive concerts that often overshadowed unrefined ability.

In addition to an engaging stage presence, U2 also anchored its formative period in a set of values that looked oddly counter to the rock 'n' roll environment of its day. Inescapably impacted by the violence of religious sectarianism so prominent in Ireland, the band cultivated a spirit of reconciliation and hospitality in the middle of a deeply divided culture and rejected dominant religious institutional frameworks. Still—and perhaps as an alternate to the austerity of organized Christianity—three of U2's members became profoundly committed to a "born-again" Christian communal movement, preferring Bible studies in the back of the tour bus to raucous parties after concerts. Eventually, all four of U2's members would claim a less rigid form of Christianity as a foundational component of the group. Also in response to Ireland's repressive Catholic culture, U2 infused its music with a rare blend of activism. Inspired by difficult social conditions and topics that were considered taboo in the church, the band championed equality, justice, and peace and sought to infuse concerts with meaningful content. Another early value was U2's commitment to community, as it both built a fan base and fostered a relational component not often seen in the cutthroat music industry. Despite being in its musical infancy, U2 emphasized live performance, maximum engagement with audiences, social activism, spirituality, and community. Though these core values were intuitive to the young band, they continued to evolve in ways that later helped shape a forty-year career and launched the four neophytes on a mission to change the world.

My purpose in writing this book is to demonstrate that U2 provides a unique case study for understanding how popular musicians both have the opportunity to influence culture and are themselves conversely shaped by the culture they inhabit, revealing a dynamic and vibrant, ever-changing interplay of artistic expression and social engagement. Coming together as teens in 1976, Adam, Larry, Bono, and Edge were unaware that they were about to embark on a decades-long global adventure. While they certainly had lofty aspirations, the formation of a band was more of an experiment than a calculated strategic assault on rock 'n' roll. U2 became an icon through hard work as well as by being in the right places at the right times, surrounded by the right people. At every step of the band's development, its members acted out of instinct and mission while also responding and adapting to the context of its day. Now, U2 serves as a powerful and relevant model for understanding how artists and culture shape one another.

The trajectory of this book moves from the youthful idealism of a band barely able to play instruments, through multiple phases of artistic expression and cultural engagement, to an examination of faith and activism as consistent expressions evidenced over the band's entire career. Chapter 1 examines the complicated interplay of Ireland's political, social, and religious history, including a violent period known as the Troubles. U2 formed in a context that directly led to the group's unique vision and mission to transform the world around it. Dublin in the 1970s provided the impetus, and Mount Temple Comprehensive offered a safe space for the members to discover and develop a love for the arts while living in the middle of a gloomy context of drugs, poverty, and violence.

Chapter 2 traces the growth of the young band, specifically through the production of the first three albums. Full of hope and idealism, U2's optimistic spirit compelled the members to seek out and offer alternatives to the banal world around them. Three of the four teens even became members of an outlying religious community, an experience that would later influence the entire band. The young group also quickly came to realize the power of technology and media and embraced an upstart cable channel called MTV in this era. Chapter 3 follows the development of a much more experienced U2 as the band exploded in popularity and rose to conquer the music industry. With America as its backdrop in the 1980s, U2 played to massive venues and both enjoyed and wrestled with newfound fame while consistently offering a blend of rock music and brazen social conscience.

Chapter 4 delineates a bold period of satire and irony in which the band made a radical shift away from overt political and social statements, instead opting for a progressive, experimental style through which it engaged its own internal demons. Inspired by the rapidly changing landscape of post–Cold War Europe in the 1990s, U2 mystified and thrilled fans with grand staging and theatrics while tackling the taboo subjects of ego, pride, greed, sexuality, and more. As it examined its own soul, the band challenged the world to do the same. Chapter 5 marks yet another shift in the musical and thematic style of U2. Searching to redefine itself on the cusp of a new millennium, the group discarded the artsy and introspective approach of the previous decade, replacing it with intimacy and authenticity in a post-9/11 era of Middle Eastern conflict and global terrorism. Staging for live performances became an experiment in community, and marketing turned to partnerships with monstrous corporations. As seasoned veterans of the music industry, Adam, Larry, Bono, and Edge celebrated family and career with a graceful message of love. Chapter 6 examines the most recent period of a long career and traces U2's movement into new and uncharted territory as a band with unparalleled fame, fortune, and success. Resisting the temptation to become a top-hits legacy act, U2 and its formidable franchise pressed on to create state-of-the-art tours while also searching, once again, for relevancy in an age of new media and technology.

The final two chapters veer away from a strict chronological investigation to a discussion of underpinning foundational values of U2. Chapter 7 gives an overview of how U2 both has been shaped by spiritual faith and also has contributed to a unique understanding and application of that faith. Through an integration of Christianity and the arts, U2 has blazed a trail across religious institutionalism in a way that has brought both the favor and disdain of organized Christianity, transcending common approaches to religious music. Chapter 8 closes the book with a look at U2's—and specifically Bono's—commitment to social activism by examining the causes the group has supported through albums, concerts, and special projects. Learning lessons from experiments such as Live Aid early on in its career, the band helped pioneer a new form of philanthropy, consistently engaged cultural issues, and challenged audiences—all signature pieces of a forty-year career.

U2 has always sought to disrupt culture; a desire to challenge listeners and operate differently as an organization has been part of the band's DNA. At the same time, it has played by, and indeed mastered, the rules of a ferocious and daunting music industry. The result is a complex portrait of a musical act that has consistently spoken with a countercultural voice against the injustices facing a global village but has also used every modern, corporate, and commercial agency at its disposal to advance its own cause. U2 is really a study in contradictions: in one decade, fighting against synth pop but in another using it as a musical anchor; at one point, prank calling the White House and ten years later being warmly invited into the Oval Office; in one era, ranting about the evils of American conservatism but in a more recent one championing the virtues of corporate capitalism; early on, rejecting organized religion but later catering to megachurches. Certainly, some of U2's movement across social, religious, economic, and political spectrums can be chalked up to developmental issues—maturity, experience, wisdom, family. But more importantly, the long and very public career of U2 provides an opportunity to examine the dynamism and fluidity of a group of artists whose beliefs and practices have been and continue to be in progress.

U2 is remarkably self-aware regarding its apparent contradictions over the years. As the wealthy, established, and successful lead singer flies around the world, speaking in front of global leaders, it seems impossible that he wouldn't remember the disdain he had for such people as his band was being formed. This type of contradiction was brilliantly demonstrated on the Innocence + Experience tour in 2015 when Bono would talk to his younger self during a reflective, almost painfully introspective moment of prose in "Bullet the Blue Sky":

> So this boy comes up to me, his face red like a rose on a thorn bush, like all the colors of a royal flush, a young man with a young man's blush. And this boy, he looks a whole lot like me. He stuck his face into my face, and he asked me, "Have you forgotten who you are? Have you forgotten where you come from? You're Irish, but here you are, smiling, and making out with the powerful, like you're really there for the powerless." (*U2: Innocence + Experience*)

Bono continued the argument with his adolescent self later in the song:

> Now the boy is behind a police line. And I'm on the other side of a barricade to myself, age 19. Other side of the barricade now, other side of the barricade. The boy keeps shouting, shouting, "We don't want you in our revolution. You're part of the problem, not the solution!" (*U2: Innocence + Experience*)

The rant is an amazing admission: speaking and acting on behalf of U2, Bono understands the paradox of becoming something he once railed against—the very thing that a teenage version of himself would have detested—but is still invested in the same core issues. With the album *Songs of Innocence*, U2 comes full circle to its simple beginnings, again emphasizing an activism that leads to engagement with the world around. But rather than standing in the exact same place it had once been, simply mimicking the opinions of forty years ago, the band has spiraled up and now stands over and above the original place with new experiences, reinterpreting old memories and adapting original beliefs in fresh ways. The result is a deeper, more refined understanding of the interplay between art and culture.

On U2's second album, *October*, Bono sang, "I *can't* change the world / But I *can* change the world in me." As the young, self-aware idealist entered his twenties, he knew that changing the world would be difficult, if not impossible, but found inner transformation more hopeful. In 2015, on the band's thirteenth studio album, *Songs of Innocence*, the fifty-plus-year-old veteran front man offered a revised perspective and a new variant of the old lyric, this time in "Lucifer's Hands": "I *can* change the world / But I *can't* change the world in me." Having spent decades pursuing an activist agenda and experiencing significant victories in the battle against global poverty along the way, Bono and his band had learned that, ultimately, changing the world is actually easier than changing the self. On the Innocence + Experience tour, he would often comment that external enemies are much easier to identify than internal ones.

Every culturally relevant artist faces at least two worlds when confronting the reality he or she seeks to critique: the inner and the outer. Even a young U2 was able to recognize the tension between internal idealism and external forces. During an interview with Dave Fanning in 1979, the nineteen-year-old Bono was articulate and insightful about U2's approach to the music business:

> It's a big industry. There's a lot of people trying to stand on us. . . . Rather than pretending that it's not there . . . we'd like to join that race, and in fact, beat the people that are involved, and make use of it rather than just go talking against it. We are teenagers, we are young. There is the big chance that we will be exploited, but we hope we're not stupid. (Bono, "Audio. Bono, August 1979, RTÉ Radio, Ireland")

U2 was already caught between its artistic desire and what an industry required, being told by promoters to play traditional Irish music and cover popular tunes. Bono was emphatic in his opposition to this as the band toured Ireland, even before recording its first album:

> Because we play an original set, we have certain difficulties. . . .
> We're expected [by promoters] to treat [fans] like simple people. . . .
> This is not true of us. There's people in those towns who want to hear
> what [we] have to say. . . . They're really smart. (Bono, "Audio. Bono,
> August 1979, RTÉ Radio, Ireland")

Neither U2 nor the rapidly growing and increasingly loyal fan base
would settle for the typical fare of an average band. Bono, Edge, Adam,
and Larry were on a quest for something bigger, and they welcomed
their fans to join. Speaking with Fanning, Bono reiterated,

> The reason we joined up in the first place was not just to be part of
> any one movement . . . but was basically disillusionment with the
> crap that was going on in the top thirty, and we thought we'd have
> something to say. That's what we're about and we're trying to put
> what we have to say on a record. That's our ambition. (Bono, "Audio.
> Bono, August 1979, RTÉ Radio, Ireland")

Nearly four decades later, Bono again reflected on his band's mission and purpose. Commenting on a phrase often attributed to St.
Francis of Assisi—"Go into all the world to preach the gospel, and if
necessary, use words"—Bono said, "I love that one. Actions, actions,
actions. It's about being useful, and that's what I want to be" (McGirt,
"Bono").

Conscious of its ability to *say* something and *do* something, U2 continues pursuing an arduous balance of the internal and external, seeking
to both unsettle as well as adapt to a rapidly changing culture. Some will
judge the mission of U2 as successful; some not. And though critics
might disagree about the end product, there is little doubt that the
members of U2 have, at minimum, changed their own worlds and at
best made a virtuous mark on a global scale, all while being shaped and
nuanced by the very culture they have sought to disrupt.

I

GROWING UP IN IRELAND

Imagining a world without U2 is difficult because—unlike any other band—this Irish quartet, featuring Bono (lead vocal), Edge (guitar), Adam Clayton (bass), and Larry Mullen, Jr. (drums), has both thoroughly shaped and been shaped by the culture it has inhabited over a forty-year journey. Indeed, interaction with the world, including political, social, and spiritual connecting points, is such a key part of U2's art and mission that fans consider it normal, appropriate, and desirable. The band's sense of community, activism, and faith has resulted in a global fraternity filled with faithful disciples, each drawn to a super-group that has been as much a force on its environment as it has been a consequence of that environment. On the surface, it may seem that this well-oiled twenty-first-century megafranchise carefully crafts a product and hones its message, but in subtle ways—and sometimes glaringly obvious ones—the events and circumstances of the band members' childhoods, as well as the war-torn history of the island where they formed, play an even greater part in shaping its message. Simply put, the band's story is inseparable from Ireland's story. This give and take with culture is part of a creative process that has characterized U2's work for four decades, and it is why so many fans across the planet are intrigued—and even compelled—to listen and learn from U2.

Ireland's early history is an interplay of political conflict and religious friction. Ultimately, competing ideologies on this small island collided in an eruption of anger and violence, giving way to the twentieth-century conflict known as the Troubles. Additionally, U2's hometown of

Dublin, unlike any other city in Ireland, provided the progressive environment the band needed for discovering its creative heart and soul. Here, members of U2, even in the throngs of the Troubles, were able to break through traditional sectarianism by befriending both Protestants and Catholics, attend an experimental high school free from the constraints of religious indoctrination, and foster lifelong friendships with other growing artists and musicians. On the one hand, mid-twentieth-century Dublin was a wild hub of poverty, drugs, anger, and street gangs, but on the other, and perhaps as a result of it, the capital city of Ireland provided the context for reflection and limitless opportunities in artistic formation. The historical and cultural milieu in which U2 formed was the result of centuries of Irish history, as well as the last few decades of modern events leading up to the 1970s.

Ironically, *Songs of Innocence*, the band's thirteenth and most recent studio album, is the place to start for hearing U2 comment on its own prehistory. Filled with memories and reflections about childhood, the album functions as an anthology of sorts and provides ample content for addressing the earliest years of the foursome. In the lead track, "The Miracle (of Joey Ramone)," Bono sings, "We were pilgrims on our way." Therein lies the irony: after forty years of collaboration, culminating with the oft-declared title of "world's greatest band," the members of U2 can now look back with perspective to see themselves as young teens, better understanding how individual pieces of the past shape a much broader picture in the present.

THE TROUBLES ANTICIPATED

U2 formed in the 1970s amid the turmoil of religious sectarianism, political conflict, economic hardship, and cultural isolation, some of which dates back to earliest days of Irish civilization. Ireland's patron saint, Patrick, is credited with bringing Christianity to the island's inhabitants in the fifth century, ushering in the Catholic faith, and by the beginning of the seventh century, a high kingship emerged, loosely uniting a jumbled assortment of smaller kingdoms. For three hundred years, the Irish experienced relative peace and stability, but that all changed as waves of Viking invaders set their sights on this new kingdom.

In the second half of the twelfth century, largely in an effort to unify Ireland and bring the church back into alignment with Roman Catholicism, an alliance between Henry II, king of England, and the English pope Adrian IV led to the successful conquering of the island, inaugurating an era of English rule. Henry II quickly became sovereign and forced the submission of the Irish kings and lords. Additionally, English peasants were sent to Ireland to settle and work there, a tactic still used throughout the world as a means of transforming a foreign territory by displacing an indigenous culture with the language, law, and customs of the invading power. The struggle between Ireland's native culture and English rule continued for centuries.

Henry VIII successfully reasserted the English Crown's authority in the sixteenth century and once again united the hodgepodge of Irish territories. His method of colonization, however, was brutal. Many Irish peasants suffered and died due to a combination of war, famine, disease, and dislocation. Henry imposed English law, restricted nationals, and punished dissenters. Promoting his newly authorized Church of England—a symbol of defiance against the increasingly aggressive Catholic Church in Rome—the king closed Irish monasteries, confiscated lands, and established a Protestant "Church of Ireland" in 1537. During this period, religious and political sectarianism reached new and dangerous heights for the Irish people.

Throughout the seventeenth and eighteenth centuries, the English government continued to confiscate land and deny rights and political offices to Irish Catholics. Dissatisfaction with British rule culminated in 1798 as angry peasants rebelled, attempting to create an Ireland free and independent from England. The revolt was unsuccessful but highlighted the need for autonomy and revitalized the Irish spirit. With the turn of the century, British and Irish Parliaments negotiated to create a new structure of governance, and on January 1, 1801, Ireland and Great Britain merged to form the United Kingdom of Great Britain and Ireland.

It wasn't just politics and religion that threatened the peace of Ireland. Environmental issues also worked to destabilize the country in massive proportions. In the 1840s, the Great Famine, also known as the Irish Potato Famine, devastated Ireland as blight ravaged potato crops. More than one million people died, and a million more fled to the United States. Ireland's population has never fully recovered. The famine also exacerbated already tense sectarianism. Poor Irish Catholics, who relied on the potato as a food staple, were affected in far greater proportions than the English, who had privilege, wealth, and, most importantly, land ownership. To the Irish people, the British government seemed disinterested in their suffering, and many suspected that England, the world's most prosperous empire, was using the famine for political advantage. When Ireland emerged from the Great Famine, the majority language had changed from Irish to English, indicating a clear cultural shift on the island.

Irish nationals who had not fled to new lands found themselves at increasing odds with the British government and progressively more divided among themselves over possible responses. The "Home Rule" movement dominated political conversation from the 1870s through the turn of the century. Home Rulers sought self-rule, believing that Ireland should be a free country, completely separate and unobstructed by British oversight. This demand for Irish autonomy was formally authorized in a limited sense by the British Parliament in 1914. However, the Home Rule legislation allowed for six counties in the north to remain under the rule of England. These six counties later became Northern Ireland, while the rest of the country took the name Republic of Ireland. Nevertheless, skirmishes with the British, guerilla activity, and even a civil war continued to destabilize the island in the early twentieth century, and the newly formed Irish Republican Army (IRA) became a militant voice for complete independence. A treaty in 1921 with the British government secured total autonomy for Ireland proper but also confirmed Northern Ireland as a permanent ward of the United Kingdom. This arrangement officially became known as the partition of Ireland.

Though Ireland continued to divide along geopolitical lines, one of the most drastic distinctions, and one that bears significantly on any discussion of U2, is seen in the religious segregation that continued to compartmentalize the island. The dominant religion of Ireland has always been Christianity, but Northern Ireland favored Protestantism, keeping a tight association with the Church of England, while the rest of the island leaned toward Roman Catholicism. The religious schism dividing the country pitted those who followed the pope against those who were faithful to the king. This distinction cannot be overstated. By the mid-twentieth century, the people of Northern Ireland had more resources, were more Protestant, and had a higher regard for the British Empire than those who lived elsewhere. Catholics, on the other hand, were discriminated against, opposed the partitioning of Ireland, and rejected British rule.

Despite the partitioning of Ireland, divisions continued to intensify as violence and paramilitary activities propelled the country toward decades of conflict and fear. The IRA emerged in several forms as a terrorist organization seeking the reunification of Ireland, resulting in fierce clashes with British forces and with Northern Ireland Protestants. While the IRA fought for a united and autonomous Ireland, the unionists stood in opposition. Unionists, and the more violent loyalists, favored alliance with the British and actively worked to retain Northern Ireland's integration with the United Kingdom. Many unionists were landowners and feared that separation from England might ruin them, potentially curtailing their own rights and threatening their financial interests. Most of the conflict occurred in the north, but fighting also took place in Dublin and London. Amid a backdrop of religious, political, and economic contention, the era would become infamously known as the Troubles.

THE TROUBLES REALIZED

Centuries of fighting and disagreement between Irish nationals and the British government had taken its toll, and a perfect storm began to form as competing interests and ideologies converged on an island smaller than the state of Indiana. Lasting from the late 1960s through the late 1990s, the Troubles marked thirty years of violence for both Northern Ireland and the Republic of Ireland, occasionally spilling over into England and mainland Europe. During this time, thirty-six hundred people were killed and thousands more injured. The northern cities of Belfast and Derry were hardest hit by the conflict and were the sites of repeated violent confrontation between three aggressive ideologies: Catholic nationalists, Protestant unionists/loyalists, and the British military.

In the mid-1960s, civil rights issues gained attention in Ireland and highlighted the plight of the Catholic population. Nationalists in Northern Ireland, unfairly treated for centuries, actively sought the end of job and housing segregation, equal voting rights for those who did own property (Protestants) and those who did not (Catholics), and reform of the Protestant-controlled police force. Unionists, who controlled the northern government and allied closely with Britain, feared a shift in power. Tensions continued to rise as violent groups on both sides fanned the fires of discontent, leading to riots, bombings, and other paramilitary activities.

In 1972, just about the time the members of U2 were entering adolescence, nearly five hundred people were killed, most of them civilians. Belfast was a war zone, filled with British troops and heavily restricted by curfews. As the city spiraled into chaos, the British government suspended the ability of Northern Ireland's parliament to rule itself, thus pitting nationalists, unionists, and the British army against each other in a three-way tug-of-war for control. Wave after wave of explosions, ambushes, and incursions in Belfast, Derry, and Dublin to the south left the island's inhabitants dejected and war weary.

As U2 recorded its first set of albums in the early 1980s, violence continued, often in an almost predictable pattern including terrorist bombings, executions by authorities, and retaliatory attacks, while paramilitary groups secured the support of international governments and acquired illegal munitions. Several infamous dates live on in Ireland's memory, all instigated by the IRA and ending in significant loss of life and injuries. On October 12, 1984, the terrorist group set off a bomb in a Brighton hotel where Prime Minister Margaret Thatcher and other politicians were staying. In Newry, on February 28, 1985, a police station was attacked with mortar fire. And most notably, on November 8, 1987, at a Remembrance Day parade honoring military veterans in Enniskillen, an explosion killed eleven people and injured sixty-three others. The incident occurred just hours before a concert in Denver during *The Joshua Tree* tour and deeply affected the band, prompting a highly charged and emotional rant from Bono about the violence in Ireland during "Sunday Bloody Sunday," which later appeared in the film *Rattle and Hum*.

Bombings and executions continued in the 1990s, and though ceasefires were occasionally put in place, they had limited effect as both nationalist and unionist paramilitary groups fought each other. Finally, in 1998 the main political parties of Northern Ireland met together and negotiated a truce known as the Good Friday Agreement, which allowed for a multiparty political structure and defined the relationship between the Irish and British governments. The agreement found widespread acceptance across the north and south and officially ended the violence of three decades. Without a doubt, the era of the Troubles shaped the mission of U2, both consciously and unconsciously, and found its way into the group's music, performances, and activism.

DUBLIN IN THE 1970s

Dublin today is a trophy city, a shining symbol of Ireland's tenacious ability to rise above its troubled past. Settled more than a thousand years ago during the Viking Age, this capital city is now recognized as a world-class urban center and is known for industry, finance, education, and art. But Dublin's warm and inviting reputation is fairly newfound. By many accounts, Ireland in the 1970s was a repressive environment. The heavy-handed, conservative nature of the Catholic Church tended to stifle creative expression, favoring temperance and conformity. Music journalist Neil McCormick says, "Officially there was no homosexuality in Ireland. Along with no contraception, no divorce, no abortion and (if the Catholic church had its way) no sex for any unmarried person not engaged in the procreation of good Catholic babies" (McCormick, *Killing Bono*, 66). Living in the republic was a monocultural, monochromatic, monotonous experience.

Dreary and bleak conditions in Dublin in the 1970s only accentuated the banality of life in the southern part of the island. Four decades prior to U2's formation, the city more closely reflected the gloomy nature of its Irish name, *Dubhlind*: the "black/dark" (*dubh*) "pool" (*lind*) on the River Liffey. Along with waves of emigration that drained the country of its uninspired citizenry, musical artists found themselves a part of the exodus. A host of bands that called Ireland home escaped as quickly as their fame would provide for passage to another world. Van Morrison, Rory Gallagher, Thin Lizzy, and Bob Geldof and the Boomtown Rats all set sail for more creative ports. With high unemployment and low expectations, the island was a place to leave, not embrace.

The Dublin of U2's childhood, though nestled in the heart of the republic, was not isolated from the violence of the north. As the Troubles spilled over onto the streets of the city, the blood of the dead and wounded seeped into the consciousness of its youth. Riots in 1972,

protesting the shooting of twenty-six unarmed civilians by British soldiers up north in Derry (an event which would later be known as the
infamous Bloody Sunday massacre and immortalized in U2's song of the
same name), culminated in the burning of the British embassy in Dublin. Multiple bombings in the city center throughout 1972 and 1973 left
another wake of dead and injured. But the worst of the bombings happened close to where Bono and his friends lived and left a permanent
impression.

May 17, 1974, found expression four decades later on U2's album
Songs of Innocence in "Raised by Wolves." Filled with anger and despair, the song is a retelling of the day's events. "Wolves" is a snapshot
of what Bono remembers as four car bombs were detonated, killing
thirty-three people. In the album's liner notes, Bono recalls, "On May
17th I rode my bike to school that day and dodged one of the bloodiest
moments in a history that divided an island." Written from the perspective of a best friend, Andy Rowen, the song commemorates the Talbot
Street explosion, which Andy and his father saw as they drove by in
their family van. In a *Rolling Stone* interview, Bono says, "The bomb
tore apart the street. I escaped but one of my mates was around the
corner with his father, and it was a very hard thing for him to witness
and I'm not sure he really got over it" ("U2's 'Songs of Innocence'").
Bono relives the tragedy in "Wolves," singing, "I'm in a white van as a
red sea covers the ground," and "5:30 on a Friday night / 33 good
people cut down."

The horrific event scarred Rowen and became a catalyst for his
heroin addiction. As Bono explained in the album notes, "The scene
never left him, he turned to one of the world's great pain killers to deal
with it, we wrote about him in our song, 'Bad.' Andy says, 'Heroin is a
great pain killer until it kills you.'" Pain, despair, and heartache experienced in their hometown affected the members of U2 even before they
were a band and shaped a corporate conscience within them that would
later be the impetus for addressing strife and injustice around the
world.

Alongside the Troubles, Dublin also faced pressure from another
sector. Throughout the city's conflicted history, it had suffered the effects of an extensive succession of slums and tenement encampments.
In the 1960s, city planners began a very active campaign to reduce the
severity of these conditions and to move the city's urban poor into

modern housing. Tens of thousands of people were relocated out of the slums into the suburbs at the outskirts of the city. Though this solved the problem of unwanted and unsightly pockets of poverty throughout the heart of Dublin, the planning was shortsighted and produced unintended results as huge populations of people were displaced and then moved to new communities. Bono lived on the edge of Ballymun, one of the new suburbs. Far from being the progressive solutions they were touted to be, these untried experiments in social engineering became stagnate pools of crime, drug abuse, and unemployment.

As a child, Bono watched the new suburbs being built around his family. Though he lived on Cedarwood Road, a decent street with kind residents and open fields behind his small home, the project to relocate urban families drastically changed his neighborhood. At first, the highrise apartments seemed bold and modern, but there were inadvertent negative outcomes. Bono remembers, "They took people out of the inner city and forced them to live there and broke up communities and there was a lot of unhappiness and trouble. The towers housed some very heavy gangs, so even though we lived on a nice little road we had two fairly rough neighbourhoods on either side of us" (U2 and McCormick, *U2 by U2*, 16). The projects, including the seven towers, West Finglas, and Ballymun, were dangerous places. In an interview with journalist Michka Assayas, Bono recalls,

> Violence, as I told you, is the thing I remember the most from my teenage years and earlier. . . . [The projects] started very quickly to descend into a dangerous place. Lifts would break down. People'd get very upset that you'd have to walk up the stairs. I remember walking up the stairs to see my friends, it was piss coming down the stairs, and stink. These were really nice families, good families, living next to people who were sociophobes, who were feeling freaked out about their new address. So when we used to go for a walk in the fields, we could come across the gangs from the Seven Towers, and that was the jungle. (Assayas, *Bono*, 112)

Amid the fervor to rebuild Dublin, the communities that became home to tens of thousands of residents lacked shops, gas stations, transportation, and other amenities. Nothing more than huge warehouses for people, these compounds of sterile, cookie-cutter housing units were breeding grounds for vice and crime, leaving packs of teens without purpose or ambition to wander a jungle of cement wastelands.

In addition to the violence, these new housing projects triggered another unplanned consequence: heroin. From the late 1970s into the 1990s, Dublin suffered the destructive effects of drug addiction and crime. Compounded with poor housing and poverty, heroin became commonplace and brought with it uncontrollable waves of vice, including muggings, robberies, and organized crime. Bono recalls,

> The drugs came in, round 1978. There was very cheap heroin. The people who were smoking dope ended up smoking heroin, as they gave it to them for nothing. And then when people were really strung out, that became an unbelievably violent place. (Assayas, *Bono*, 112–13)

It was in this Dublin—a black, murky pool of poverty, unemployment, crime, drug addiction, and poor housing—that four teens began to find their own voices as they placed themselves, whether intentionally or by chance, into a much larger story than each of them could experience on their own. And it was four influences in particular that shaped them into a singularly unique set of artists. First, each had a specific family situation—sometimes supportive and nurturing, other times filled with pain and disappointment—that affected their development. A second influence was the educational experience they shared at Mount Temple, where they all discovered their love for music and for each other. Friends, a third influence, also contributed to their formation, often being the catalyst for creative endeavors and unexpected connections. Finally, musical role models and mentors provided the impetus for the content and style of their young yet visionary artistic journey. Under the constant sway of these cultural influences, four teens began to discover an identity and mission for life.

THE INFLUENCE OF FAMILY

Psychologists and therapists often use the term *family of origin* to talk about the family in which someone grew up, including parents, siblings, and any other relatives that occupied a childhood home. All of these relational networks strongly influence how a person develops from child to adolescent and on to adulthood. Like the slow and steady flow of a mighty river carving out a canyon, a family's influence is inescapable, gradually shaping and forming the lives of each member. Bono, Edge, Adam, and Larry, all from unique and different families of origin, for good or for bad, have been affected in deep and profound ways by the presence of—and the absence of—immediate family members.

Of all the families in U2, Bono's is the most unusual, even scandalous. The marriage of Iris Rankin, a Protestant, to Bob Hewson, a Catholic, in 1950 was unthinkable considering the religious divisions that had consumed Ireland for centuries. Adding to the salacious nature of their union, the wedding took place in a Protestant church. Iris continued breaking with traditional notions of childrearing by taking Bono and his brother, Norman (eight years older), to a Protestant worship service every Sunday while Bob would wait outside or go to Mass. Years later, Bono reflected on the significance of his parents' unconventional marriage, especially as it related to Irish sectarianism: "Both my mother and my father didn't take religion seriously, they saw the absurdity of the fuss made over their union. . . . One of the things that I picked up from my father and my mother was the sense that religion often gets in the way of God" (Assayas, *Bono*, 31). From the beginning, the unconventional nature of the Hewson family seemed to foreshadow the defiant, zealous spirit of its youngest son.

The family's progressive view of faith shaped Bono's understanding of life early on, but no single influence was greater than the loss he experienced at the age of fourteen. Iris, at the graveside of her own father (who had unexpectedly passed away), suffered a cerebral aneurysm, collapsed, and died four days later. Bono was distraught as he watched his mother being disconnected from life support systems in the hospital. He remembers,

> My mother died and then there were just three men living on their own in a house. That is all it was then, it ceased being a home. It was just a house, with three men killing each other slowly, not knowing what to do with our sense of loss and just taking it out on each other. (U2 and McCormick, *U2 by U2*, 18)

Iris was never spoken of again. Anger and rage filled the void, with intermittent lulls of silence and denial. Fights were common—fights with Norman and fights with Dad. Amid the awkwardness of normal adolescence, the boy, now thrown into manhood, was overcome by grief, doubt, fear, and hopelessness. Bono sings in "Mofo" as a grown man continuing to deal with the loss, "Mother, am I still your son? / You know I've waited for so long to hear you say so." More recently, in a song bearing her name, he offers a similar sentiment, "Hold me close / Hold me close and don't let me go." After his father's death, Bono made peace with Bob, resolving years of anger and trauma: "In this little church, on Easter morning, I just got down on my knees, and I let go of whatever anger I had against my father. And I thanked God for him being my father, and for the gifts that I have been given through him. . . . I wept, and I felt rid of it" (Assayas, *Bono*, 23).

Bono was not the only member of U2 influenced by the devastating loss of a family member. "Everything about my life was pretty normal for a while," says Larry, but then tragedy struck. "My sister died in 1973 and then my mother died in 1976. In some ways, both events defined the kind of person I've become. My mother's death certainly catapulted me in the band's direction" (U2 and McCormick, *U2 by U2*, 25). Today, Bono and Larry recognize their losses as part of the bond each shares with the other. "The thing that stuck us together," Bono recalls, "was that I had this experience of bereavement. I had lost my mother when I was fourteen and he had lost his when he was sixteen, and . . . we both ran away with the circus" (Assayas, *Bono*, 50).

Bono and Larry shared not only the loss of mothers in their teen years but also the unsettled and dysfunctional atmosphere of a grief-stricken, single-father home. Both of their fathers were strict disciplinarians and thought the boys were wasting time pursuing something as frivolous as rock 'n' roll. Though family situations were similar, the teens reacted differently—Bono raged and acted out his anger, while Larry retreated into his personal space, quietly forging on. In either case, both the extrovert and the introvert suffered a tragedy that eventually propelled them to passionately embrace music as a catharsis for pain. The loss they shared isn't lost on Bono, who reflects,

> The mother is so, so important in rock music. Show me a great singer and I'll show you someone who lost their mother early on. There's Paul McCartney, there's John Lennon. Look at Bob Geldof and what happened to his mother. In hip hop, by contrast, it's all about the father—being abandoned by the father and being brought up by a single mother. But for me it's all about the mother. I had rage and

grief for my mother. I still have rage and grief for my mother. I channeled those emotions in music, and I still do. (Boyd, "Bono's Dublin")

Family situations were much different for U2's guitar and bass players. For Edge and Adam, parents were more supportive and families had strong and positive relationships. However, none of their parents were, in fact, Irish. Edge's folks were Welsh but lived in London when Edge was born and then moved to Dublin when he was just a year old. Edge, who obviously has no memory of England, today considers himself fully Irish in every aspect. He, his older brother, Dik, and their younger sister, Gillian, were given a great deal of freedom to explore life, be inquisitive, and engage new opportunities. As a child, Edge was happy and supported.

This sense of freedom certainly fostered Edge's own desire to ask questions and test ideas through experimentation, even when the results were less than desirable. More than once his escapades involved homemade explosives, raging bonfires, or mischievous outings with his brother. "It was the combination of curiosity, wildness, lack of strict parental control, and access to a fully stocked school chemistry lab that led to our experiments, anything really to break the tedium of the Dublin suburbs of the 1970s" (U2 and McCormick, *U2 by U2*, 23). A garden shed in their backyard would later become the rehearsal room for U2, but early on it was also the site of an explosion gone wrong that left Dik with a scar. Fascinated with gadgets and electronics (their father was an engineer), the two brothers spent hours dismantling and building things. Eventually, they built a guitar from plans found in an electronics magazine. The Evans home, nestled safe and sound in the Malahide suburb of Dublin, was idyllic compared to the gale-force storms that raged through Bono and Larry's families.

Adam was born in his grandmother's home in England in 1960, an event that came to characterize his entire family experience—full of close relatives, though mostly women. His father, a pilot, was often traveling and not around much. Adam was left at home with a mother, a grandmother, and a great-grandmother. "I was the first child, a boy, fussed over by this group of women," says Adam (U2 and McCormick, *U2 by U2*, 11). Two sisters soon followed, adding further to the feminine mystique of the home. At age four, the family moved to Kenya, where his dad found work as a commercial pilot. After only a year, Adam's father relocated the family again, this time to Malahide (coincidentally, the suburb outside of Dublin where Edge lived). Even through a number of living transitions, Adam's experience with parents and siblings was closer to that of Edge's than Bono's or Larry's, and he was always well taken care of, encouraged to develop his creative nature, and surrounded by music.

THE INFLUENCE OF SCHOOL

Each of U2's four members had varying experiences with education, starting in different contexts, but, in the end, connecting and thriving because of the remarkable school they attended together as teens. Adam, more so than any of the others, experienced an erratic education. When he first moved to Dublin, he went to the local national school, saying,

> [T]hat was pretty much where it stopped making sense for me. I arrived into an Ireland that was subtly repressive. The sky was grey and grim and at school there was a lot of instruction in Irish, a language I didn't understand. I found it difficult to fit into that system. (U2 and McCormick, *U2 by U2*, 11)

Even though it was frustrating and inhibiting, it was here that Adam met Edge and the Evans family, though that friendship wouldn't blossom fully till several years later.

When he was eight years old, Adam's parents sent him to a boarding school designed to mimic the English system on the opposite side of Dublin. It was equally negative, and Adam kept a low profile there. At thirteen, he changed schools again, this time moving to an Irish public boarding school, and though he still didn't do well academically, he was delighted to make friends with another boy who had cassette tapes of the latest rock 'n' roll notables. Adam recalls of his early teen years, "I was getting pretty turned on to music and it always seemed to change my mood; it somehow made it bearable to be in that school situation" (U2 and McCormick, *U2 by U2*, 13). When his parents eventually succumbed to his pleas and bought him a bass guitar, he formed a band and even started writing an Irish rock opera, finally enjoying school.

Then came what seemed to be a fatal blow—his parents withdrew him from his expensive private education due to bad grades. "I thought that was it, the musical career was over," he recalls, "and so I was dispatched to Mount Temple, a comprehensive school in north Dublin, which was not a place where I felt comfortable at all" (U2 and McCormick, *U2 by U2*, 13). He might not have been so depressed about the move had he known what an important place this school would eventually be for him and three other boys.

Bono's experience with education didn't fare much better—he got in a fight his very first day of school, an event that foreshadowed the years to come. At the Inkwell, a Protestant school for children, he was a mischievous, energetic, high-spirited boy who was as eager to kick the ball over the fence and into the river as he was to boot it into the goal— never one to miss the chance of a grand adventure, chasing the ball down the cascading rapids for miles. He also went to St. Patrick's Grammar School, where the antics and pranks continued. Still not happy, he was asked to leave after only a year because he threw dog poop at a teacher. From there, Bono transferred to Mount Temple. This was a very different place with a completely new philosophy of education. "The moment I arrived I felt alive," says Bono (U2 and McCormick, *U2 by U2*, 18).

Edge's family life was a bit more stable and so was his schooling. Just a five-minute walk from his home, St. Andrews National was the school he and his brother and sister attended, though he didn't live up to the academic reputation of his siblings. "I was just restless and always seemed to be doing stupid things," he remembers (U2 and McCormick, *U2 by U2*, 24). One day he was so distracted that he took out a knife and carved his name into a desk, somewhat surprised when the teacher was easily able to deduce who it was who committed the offense. Though he ended up faring better in his early years, he, like Bono and Adam, found something different when he graduated into Mount Temple, a place not at all like the small village school he had previously attended.

Larry, too, had little motivation to excel academically, though his father pushed for application into two of the area's best Catholic schools. Larry took the exams required for enrollment but was unhappy because each school emphasized academics and sports, neither of which interested him. When his younger sister died, his father relinquished, and Larry enrolled in a less prestigious public school that was close by. It was a new, experimental school at which Larry found a fresh aptitude for education. And it was here, at Mount Temple, that lifelong friendships were made—friendships that would eventually shape the destiny of so many.

It really is a remarkable story: four boys, all disinterested in school, easily distracted, and prone to mischief, none of whom were friends when they entered, serendipitously found their way to a school unlike any other in the Dublin area and once there discovered the support, nurture, and encouragement needed for remarkable artistic and personal development. Mount Temple Comprehensive School, established in 1972 as an experiment in secondary schooling, was less rigid and authoritarian, with teachers and counselors who inspired students to explore, discuss, and question life—curiosity was encouraged, not suppressed! It differed from traditional Irish schools in a number of other ways as well: it was coeducational instead of segregated by sex; it was open to the public regardless of denomination, accepting both Protestants and Catholics; the staff encouraged individuality rather than conformity; there were smaller classes with greater attention to students' needs. The emphasis wasn't just on academics but also included development of the whole person, giving special attention to spiritual nurture and formation. Through religious education courses, the Christian Movement (a Bible club for students), and the counsel of trusted teachers who also served as mentors, students experienced a very different kind of faith, not at all bound by common institutional religious structures. Though they didn't know much of one another, each of the four boys immediately embraced and thrived in this new, progressive model of education, Bono arriving in 1972, Edge in 1973, Larry in 1974, and Adam in 1976. (Bono and Adam were in the same class, Edge was one year behind them, and Larry was another year behind Edge.) As an experimental school, Mount Temple was unique in all of Ireland.

THE INFLUENCE OF FRIENDS

While Mount Temple became a significant space for personal formation, the boys also found identity, solace, and purpose among friendships. Adam and Edge were the first to meet. Both from the same suburb, they had briefly attended primary school together and were already acquaintances. Adam was quite well known at Mount Temple, not because he was overly social but because no one could miss his hippie-like wardrobe—he wore a long sheepskin Afghan coat, had a huge, bushy Afro hairdo, and sported a pair of sunglasses! Bono was also very popular but in a different way. Known by all, he was an extrovert who flirted with the girls, started a drama club, and early on filled the role of a front man, carrying around a guitar he could barely play. Edge had his brother, Dik, and the two were inseparable, often found exploring and experimenting or, worse, blowing something up. Larry, the lesser known of the four on campus and by far the most introverted, was serious-minded about music, retreating into a world where his drums were his close confidants. Nonetheless, it was Larry, prompted by his father, who put out the call for musicians in an effort to form the Larry Mullen Band.

Apart from Mount Temple, the neighborhood was another place for mates to test creative ideas; the asphalt street was a garden nursery for rich relationships, giving birth to networks of friendships, many of which still exist today. Along with Bono, two childhood pals lived on Cedarwood Road in the north part of Dublin. At three years old, long before he took the name Bono, Paul Hewson discovered Derek Rowen, a boy just a year older. The two played at each other's homes and became lifelong friends. In their teens, they met and befriended another resident of Cedarwood Road, Fionan Hanvey. These three kindred spirits became a kind of incubator for creativity, pushing imagination to the limits in a land of dull banality. This cadre of friends reacted to the neighborhood violence by creating their own club, a gang of sorts that was completely unique to them. Very active in their teen years, they often met in Bono's garage, a place of sanctuary from the outside world. This group of misfits huddled around the arts and in time came to be known as "Lypton Village."

Though no one can recall why that name was chosen, naming was an important exercise for the gang; naming was a creative act in and of itself, offering an opportunity to reframe each of their lives. In this imaginary society, Derek Rowen was renamed "Guggi," Fionan Hanvey took the name "Gavin Friday," and Paul Hewson became "Bono" (though the nickname had many iterations, including "Bonavox" and "Bono Vox"). Lypton Village eventually expanded, embracing other cultural malcontents in search of artistic freedom, including "Strongman"

Trevor Rowen, "Guck Pants Delany" Andy Rowen, "Dave-iD" David Watson, "Pod" Anthony Murphy, "Bad Dog" Reggie Manuel, and "Clivejive." Later in an unofficial capacity, Dave Evans was named "Edge/the Edge," while Larry received "Jamjar," and Adam was dubbed "Sparky" and "Mrs. Burns," among other nicknames (though Larry and Adam's monikers don't stick like Dave's). Dick Evans, Edge's brother, was also renamed "Dik."

"There are a lot of odd and unique elements to the U2 story," notes Neil McCormick, "but the existence of Lypton Village is among the most extraordinary" (McCormick, "Boy to Man," 19). The Village provided a strange and remarkable escape from the political, religious, and ideological conservatism of Dublin. Bono remembers,

> [T]he alcohol level in our neighborhood was so high, people going to the pubs a lot, and we were young, arrogant, and probably very annoying kids, but we didn't wanna go that route. The pub looked like a trapdoor to somewhere very predictable, so we wouldn't drink. We used to watch *Monty Python*. We invented our own language, gave each other names, and we'd dress differently. (Assayas, *Bono*, 114)

This artsy, surrealist rabble of rejects stood defiantly against the established culture, "an indication," says McCormick, "of just how bold and original Bono's response to the world was, before he even became a rock singer" (McCormick, "Boy to Man," 19).

Painting and playing music were common activities in the early days but soon progressed to performance art with bananas, drills, ladders, and impromptu installations using anything available for props. Their stage could be street corner or city bus, it was all the same. Irony reigned. As a middle-aged adult, Bono reflected on the experience with what in retrospect might be seen as a mission statement for Lypton Village: "Humour was our best weapon, followed eventually by music. . . . Your enemies define you, so choose them carefully. Never pick an obvious fight" (Bono, "Bono's Teenage Kicks"). The list of Village members who went on to make a living in the arts is astounding and worth noting. In addition to U2, Gavin Friday, Guggi, Dik Evans, Strongman, and Pod formed the Virgin Prunes, a band that matured alongside U2 and enjoyed a prominent though much briefer career. Guggi later found success as an avant-garde artist. Gavin Friday continued in music and has had a meaningful career as a singer-songwriter, actor, and poet. Other friends and schoolmates, though not formal members of Lypton Village, also found careers in the arts: Peter Rowen, Guggi's brother, became a professional photographer; Neil McCormick set out on a very successful career in music journalism; Steve Averill formed the Radiators from Space, one of the first punk bands in Ireland, and became a highly acclaimed graphic designer who has designed or supervised every U2 album cover; Christopher Nolan, a paraplegic student at Mount Temple, went on to be a notable and influential author and poet; and last but not least, Alison Stewart, Bono's eventual wife, became an activist and businesswoman, cofounding EDUN, a fashion brand promoting fair trade in Africa. The legacy of artists from Mount Temple and the Cedarwood Road area is certainly not coincidental. A product of their times, this tribe of witty, creative adolescents, never satisfied with the status quo, sought out and prompted one another to defy common assumptions of their monochrome culture and moved out in force through the power of their own imaginations to change their world.

THE INFLUENCE OF MUSIC

While families, schools, and friends all played a significant part in shaping the four members of U2, there were many musical influences as well. All the boys grew up in homes that appreciated music. Adam has said that the two dictating forces of his life are women and music, each of which was powerfully present in his family. His grandma was a pianist in a dance band, and his aunts played contemporary music on reel-to-reel tapes and records. He tried piano lessons but didn't have the aptitude of his grandmother, so he soon quit. Bono's grandmother had a piano that he would experiment with, and she also introduced him to traditional Irish music. His father, on the other hand, filled the house with opera, often conducting an invisible ensemble of instruments and vocalists, waving knitting needles through the air, lost in a world of librettos. Bono calls it the "heavy metal" of his childhood. His brother had a reel-to-reel player, so the two would listen to current rock tunes of the day. Edge's home was filled with music as well. His mom, an alto, and his dad, a tenor, sang in the church choir and encouraged the children to sing and play instruments. When he was seven years old, his mom bought him a little toy guitar, and though he knew nothing about tuning or fingering chords, he'd wave it around and pretend he could play. A couple of years later, she purchased his first real guitar at a yard sale for a pound. Larry's mother was a concert pianist and started him with piano lessons when he was eight, though he wasn't interested in learning scales and theory and quickly gave it up. At nine, he began drum lessons with Joe Bonnie, a well-known Irish drummer. Larry especially liked the military-style drumming, later joining the Post Office Workers Band, which focused on orchestra and marching band standards. He loved being in uniform, marching down the street with a snare strapped to his side. Though still unaware of each other, all of U2's members mention a very similar set of rock 'n' roll influences during their early teen years, listening to musical heroes such as the Rolling Stones, David Bowie, the Eagles, the Beatles, Jimi Hendrix, Elvis, Bob Dylan, Bob Marley, and Led Zeppelin. Their choice of music was sophisticated for their age, not the stuff of 1970s pop or disco.

Although the band's families valued and encouraged music, Ireland's culturally conservative ethos didn't allow for much musical creativity or expression, and the country's isolationism kept it fairly secluded from the arts and media of Britain and Europe. Dublin, however, did offer a small oasis of global inspiration. In the late 1970s, a new form of music—indeed, a complete new culture of discontent—was making its way from London, across the Irish Sea, and washing up on the shores of Dublin. Rather than try to restrain the oncoming wave, as most of conservative Ireland would prefer, Adam, Larry, Edge, and Bono could see that this new style called punk was a force to be harnessed, like a surfer on a board atop a swelling wave.

The first outside sounds of punk were coming in bits and pieces from the Ramones, the Sex Pistols, and the Clash, bands that demonstrated not so much a mastery of their instruments but, more importantly, a passion for the music they were playing, including a very theatrical and engrossing stage presence. The first homegrown punk bands—though Irish punk didn't carry the full weight of its British counterpart, again due to the island's isolation—included Bob Geldof's Boomtown Rats, the Radiators from Space, and, in Belfast, Stiff Little Fingers and the Undertones (both more known for their commentary on the Troubles than the Dublin bands). Additional influences on U2 from this period include Television, XTC, Patti Smith, the Buzzcocks, and other local Irish rock legends such as Rory Gallagher and his band Taste, Phil Lynott, Thin Lizzy, and the Horslips.

One final note could be made here about musical influences: the inspiration did not always come from other bands or singers but often from the limited music-related media musicians were able to receive. While much of Ireland had very restricted and often censored forms of television (RTÉ) and theater, Dublin was able to receive the BBC from across the sea, which gave musicians access to *Top of the Pops*, a weekly program featuring live performances of popular bands. The British also produced *NME* (*New Musical Express*), a popular music magazine, and *Sounds*, a weekly pop/rock newspaper. Not readily available in Ireland, these imports were cherished by young music visionaries. But most notably, Dublin's own *Hot Press*, a music magazine founded in 1977, played a significant role in the development of the country's rock scene and particularly in the growth of U2. Specifically, two men from *Hot Press* had a formative impact on U2: Niall Stokes, the magazine's founding editor, and Bill Graham, a music journalist often credited with discovering the band. Each championed U2, closely following their development, publishing reviews, and offering advice to the rising stars.

Through these four major influences—family, schooling, friendships, and musical heroes—Bono, Edge, Adam, and Larry began to find meaning and purpose, being shaped by the consistent, often unconscious forces permeating a complex and dynamic urban center in the 1970s. Dublin was the perfect place at the perfect time for the emergence of U2, a band like no other before. Neil McCormick has said of U2 in this critical era, "They don't have to be the best musicians. They just have to be the right musicians" (McCormick, "Boy to Man," 14). So true. They were, indeed, the right musicians, with an abundance of passion, an all-engaging presence, and enough spirit to share with anyone who would listen. Musical ability would soon follow. And so would the albums.

2

INNOCENCE AND IDEALISM

Larry was the one to post the announcement. The flyer on the Mount Temple bulletin board in the fall of 1976 read: "Drummer looking for musicians to form band. Contact Larry Mullen, third year." A few days later, on Saturday, September 25, seven boys crowded into Larry's tiny house on an afternoon that, whether by fate or divine design, would shape the destinies of the four who survived the audition. It became their first and—as Bono likes to say from the perspective of a fifty-year-old veteran—their only job.

From the beginning, U2 used music to express a hopeful view of the world, taking the rage and anger of a punk scene rapidly bursting the confines of London and turning it into a new kind of creative energy. Maintaining the zeal and passion of other influential punk artists, U2 sought an alternate message. Adolescents themselves, their music contrasted the innocence of youth with the dark reality of global war and interpersonal conflict. With unswerving commitment to this ideal, three of the four band members embarked on a spiritual pilgrimage that included membership in a Christian commune. This experience was both positive and negative, at first offering a core of beliefs and values but later creating a dilemma that challenged their artistic integrity. In the end, the group emerged, choosing a unique posture of engagement with culture rather than rejection of it. Free of constraints, U2 began a love affair with technology and media—specifically with a brand-new cable channel called MTV—and set out to conquer the world. In the early 1980s, members of U2 honed their craft, deepened their faith, and refined their message for a global audience.

FIRSTS

Larry's bulletin board announcement led to the first meeting of what he presumed might be the Larry Mullen Band, but any notion he had of fronting the group quickly faded. Bono, unable to play guitar very well and untried as a singer, took the lead and immediately became the guiding personality and energy of the bunch. Edge showed up with his brother, Dik, and an electric guitar they had built. Adam brought a bass guitar and plenty of rock 'n' roll swagger, though he had little skill on his instrument. And Larry, the most formally trained, sat behind a drum kit that barely fit into his kitchen. The other hopefuls were Ivan McCormick, a thirteen-year-old with a good guitar (and brother of Neil McCormick, who today is an author and music critic), and Peter Martin, who supposed he could be the band's manager since he didn't have any musical ability. It wasn't long before the group narrowed itself down to a quartet—Ivan was dismissed because of his age and later formed a band with another Mount Temple student, and Dik, a graduate of high school, wasn't allowed to play at Mount Temple gigs because he was too old. With Larry laying down a solid rhythmic foundation for the group, Adam picking up the bass in earnest, Edge beginning wild experiments with guitar sounds, and Bono taking the helm as front man, the boys set off into virgin territory, never to look back.

Before the foursome could even imagine the musical destiny that awaited them, the group took the name Feedback. Having had no experience with rock 'n' roll, they simply thought this technical term sounded cool. Now a proper band with a name, the group began rehearsing, setting its sights on a Mount Temple talent show scheduled for the end of the fall term in 1976. The boys fumbled through rehearsals, sometimes meeting in Edge's backyard garden shed or Adam's house or a school classroom, trying to gain some sense of their instruments and roles within a band. At just an hour a week, the practices didn't produce much, but it was enough to craft a ten-minute set for the school talent show. Armed with only three songs, an unlikely collection including the Bay City Rollers' "Bye Bye Baby," a Beach Boys medley, and Peter Frampton's "Show Me the Way," the teens commandeered the stage as amps buzzed and classmates shouted for more.

"Bye Bye Baby" was performed more as a joke than a serious number; it was a simple piece they knew the girls would love. But something happened when they played "Show Me the Way." The live performance became more than the sum of its rehearsals. As the quartet performed, they discovered a new energy, an intangible sense that they'd never experienced. Bono recalls, "Because of everything I was going through, I turned this pop song into a prayer. . . . I was starting to use music as a way of really expressing what was going on in my head" (U2 and McCormick, *U2 by U2*, 31). "I want you to show me the way" wasn't just a lyric about a girl, it was a spiritual experience—the result of four new friends collaborating and rising in some sort of transcendent way to a place none of them had been before. The talent show was a hit, and the band members, through all their nervousness and anxiety, found something more meaningful than they had expected. Edge remembers,

> What was surprising to me was getting up there and playing "Show Me the Way," which was really a fairly simple tune, and suddenly something happened. . . . There was something about it that really worked between us, that even as inept as we were, when we hit it, stuff went off in a very visceral and very primitive way. If the performance bug is contagious, we definitely caught it that day. (U2 and McCormick, *U2 by U2*, 32)

"After that," says Larry, "I think we were a band" (U2 and McCormick, *U2 by U2*, 32).

Blissfully unaware of their nearly complete lack of ability, the boys continued to practice, adding Saturday rehearsals into the mix. And though he was still a beginner on his own instrument, Adam had the best rock 'n' roll image, with lots of panache and style as he talked about "gigs" while sipping his coffee, eyes masked by cool oversized shades. Effectively, he was the band's first manager, securing Feedback's second show—the band's first paid performance—at St. Fintan's, another school in North Dublin, in the spring of 1977. Here they added two female backup singers and a flute, but from the band's perspective, it all went very poorly. The audience booed and laughed as the group covered "Nights in White Satin." Embarrassed and humiliated, Feedback limped its way home. The boys continued languishing as they tried to reproduce other seemingly impossible popular songs, but in doing so they made another discovery: they could write their own music, which was much simpler to play than the covers they had been attempting. From then on, their thirst for original songs was insatiable. Larry reflects, "Once we had written the first song, we spent the rest of our time trying to write better songs and drop the covers from our set" (U2 and McCormick, *U2 by U2*, 35). Feedback, rising beyond its failure—a theme that would manifest itself repeatedly in the future—were exploring a new frontier.

Soon after, the group, which still often included Dik Evans on guitar (though the background singers were cut), decided to rename itself the Hype, thinking it to be a much cooler name. Naive, and largely operating on their own, they spent hours developing original material while continuing to cover popular hits, gradually becoming more aware of the London punk scene and incorporating songs by the Sex Pistols, the Ramones, the Clash, and others. These bands left a significant impression on the guys, especially Bono, because the aggressive music of the punks was more complex than pop. Each song was a social statement, commenting on some aspect of culture, politics, economics, justice, and life. Two concerts in particular loomed large in the memories of the band. After watching the Clash at Trinity College in Dublin, the boys found a new vision for what could happen in a live performance. Bono remembers the shift that took place in the way he and the others thought about being a band, saying, "Lots of bands around us were much better-looking, better players, better songwriters—they had everything. But we had the 'it'—whatever 'it' might be—and we built around that. That idea comes from the Clash" (Bono and John, "Bono, Elton John & Chuck D"). Another show, this one by the Ramones, also had a lasting impact on the young band. Bono reflects on that concert in the *Songs of Innocence* album notes: "The world stopped long enough for us to get on it. Even though we only saw half the show, it became one of the great nights of our life." In "The Miracle (of Joey Ramone)," Bono memorializes the evening, singing, "I woke up at the moment when the miracle occurred / Heard a song that makes some sense out of the world." On the Innocence + Experience tour in 2015, U2 continued paying tribute to both the Clash and the Ramones for the impact each band left on U2's formative years.

If there is a formal birth date for U2, it would have to be the spring of 1978, a season in which several things happened to solidify the band's persona and commitment. First, in a seemingly inconsequential event, Adam got kicked out of Mount Temple. But it was this unfortunate incident that gave him time to focus more on managing the band. As he began to foster connections with other musicians and artists in his spare time, he alone promoted the band using any means possible, including a fake advertisement in *NME* and, later, simple business cards that read, "Phone Adam Clayton to book U2." Through a relentless pursuit of music insiders and media representatives, he built a relationship with Steve Averill, a graphic designer and founder of the punk band Radiators from Space. While an important relationship at the time, there is no way that Adam could have foreseen its potential for the future. The fledgling bassist asked Averill for some advice about naming his newly formed band, signaling that he really liked group names like XTC and INXS. Averill suggested the name U2 because it had meaning on many different levels: it was a notable spy plane, a popular cassette deck, a German sub, and a ubiquitous expression ("you too"). But most importantly, Averill thought the ambiguous name would be visually bold with significant graphic potential, easily transferable to a worldwide audience. The band agreed, and an icon was born. Averill continued as a significant presence with U2, supervising the thoughtful and artistic graphic design of every U2 studio album to come. Without a doubt, Averill is one of the chief architects of U2's global and iconic image and an important influence in helping the band think conceptually about its craft, often linking U2's music and mission to the larger culture.

Several other things happened at this point that helped propel the young U2 forward. Amid heavy local competition, the band won the top spot at a contest in Limerick, which quickly brought them into the national spotlight. Also at this time, at another concert in Howth, the foursome formally said good-bye to their on-again-off-again guitar player Dik Evans. That night, the band, with Dik present, took the stage as the Hype. But when Dik played his last song and walked off in an intentionally choreographed stunt, Bono emerged after a break, re-introducing the four-piece as U2. With a solid image and a newfound national following, the boys realized an urgent need for a capable manager. It didn't take long—Adam's persistent contact work again paid off—and the band was introduced to Paul McGuinness, another soon-to-be lifelong and influential relationship.

While the members of U2 were in their late teens, McGuinness, just a decade older, needed only one listen of a cassette demo to know that he should see them in concert. In May of 1978, he attended his first U2 show, following it up with an invitation to meet the band in a nearby bar after the concert. Already having experience directing plays, editing a magazine, working in film production, and managing a folk-rock group, McGuinness was the multifaceted visionary that U2 needed at this early stage in its career. Even before the band had recorded its first album, the new manager was conspiring to move the message and music of the energetic, charismatic teens beyond Ireland. McGuinness astutely realized that the typical path to musical success often ended in London, a music scene that was critical and patronizing of Irish bands. His vision was much more ambitious, paying little attention to the UK market and heading for an America filled with Irish expatriates. Neil McCormick appropriately notes, "McGuinness didn't just take U2 out of Ireland; he brought the band to the world" (McCormick, "Boy to Man," 21). Often referred to as the "fifth member of U2," McGuinness's influence is not lost on Bono, who recalls, "More than anyone in my life, he is a person who believed in me and gave me the confidence to realize my potential as an artist. He has an enormous and sharp intellect, and mine was very unschooled and haphazard" (Assayas, *Bono*, 53).

As the upcoming band's new manager, McGuinness worked diligently to promote the group and look out for the members' best interests. His intuition for shrewd business negotiations can be seen from the beginning, as he chose to operate outside the normal conventions and standard practices of the late 1970s music industry. Early on, U2 and McGuinness decided to keep all of the legal rights and ownerships of their own music rather than sign these over to a record company as was typical. McGuinness also routinely fought for U2's place in festival or concert lineups, challenging an organizer's notion that the band should play at the least desirable times because they were unknown. In a particularly controversial movement, the Dublin music magazine *Heat* published an article accusing McGuinness of fraud and manipulation in managing U2. McGuinness fought back with a lawsuit, eventually ruining the publication and causing it to close. This was especially awkward because one of the magazine's founders was Steve Averill, close friend and consultant for the band. For good or for bad, McGuinness had proven himself a no-nonsense, sharp-witted, and cunning business partner, capable of defending his young clients against the mainstream practices of a music industry known for taking advantage of artists.

The late 1970s were formative years for Adam, Larry, Bono, and Edge, filled with "firsts" that would build a foundation for superstardom. The first rehearsals, a succession of band names, early concerts and competitions (both successes and failures), fledgling attempts to manage themselves, and initial business negotiations all set the stage for patterns and practices that would come to define a forty-year franchise. In hindsight, much of what we know and see of U2 today can be traced back to their earliest years.

NEITHER HIPPIES NOR PUNKS

Early on, U2 determined that its music would be different than anything else available in the market of its day. Mainstream pop and Irish folk were easily accessible but were primarily forms of entertainment that provided very little passion and commentary on current issues. Two other options left the band members wanting as well. Hippie culture, imported from America and Britain, could be found throughout Ireland in the 1970s in small yet substantial ways. Several publications promoted anarchism; one in Belfast was called *Outta Control* (curiously, it was also in the late 1970s that the Clash promoted its Get Out of Control tour and, in response, U2 wrote the song "Out of Control"). But this revolution of free love and anarchy seemed empty to the band. While John Lennon's "Imagine" was a noble picture of an ideal world, and a song (and album) Bono says was influential at the age of eleven, Lennon's message stopped short of helping people achieve the ideal it was presenting. Bono says of Lennon's accomplishments, "[I]magining wasn't one of them. I'm more of a doing, more of an actions, more of a building [person], and dreaming to me is a thing of the '60s. Doing is a thing that we have to be a part of." ("Bono," *Charlie Rose*). The flowery, idealistic, passive form of love that hippies were promoting wasn't an answer to the problems both at home in Ireland and around the world and thus was not inspiring for the band.

Not content with traditional Irish music or with the hippie movement's nebulous idealism, U2 might have been tempted by a second option: the punk scene. But here, too, the movement came up short as a mission for the young band. On one hand, punk differed greatly from the free love that hippies offered and, in essence, emerged as a reaction to it. Punk musicians were aggressive, unafraid to take on social issues, and undeterred by the status quo, channeling rage and anger into their music. On the other hand, punk, though very different in style, ended up in the same place as hippies, with no outcome and no product to show for the art form. Where one group used love, the other used anger, but neither had the means to inspire change in the world. U2, always breaking with conventional means, began a career hopeful that its message could make a difference, rejecting both the blissful ignorance of hippies and the pointless anger of punks.

At a one-of-a-kind event in January of 1981, Bono, speaking to a small group of musicians, acknowledged that punks and hippies had a valid assessment of Western culture, but he expressed dissatisfaction with these movements because they didn't address the treatment of society's problems and shortcomings. Then twenty years old, he spoke of his own band's mission, saying, "In U2, we're an aggressive band, we're an emotional band, we're a live band. I think we have a love and an emotion without flowers in our hair, and I think we have an aggression without the safety pins in our noses" (*U2's Vision*). And although "punk opened the door," according to Adam, Larry consistently insisted that they should not become a punk band (U2 and McCormick, *U2 by U2*, 35). As a musical style, punk was limited. As a philosophy, it was a dead end. From the start, U2 recognized that neither the escapism of a drug-based hippie culture nor the anger of a hate-filled punk scene was enough to sustain them.

One way individual members of U2 began to work out the dilemmas of purpose and mission came through increased engagement in Christianity, at least for three of them—Bono was the first to explore his faith, Edge followed at Bono's urging, and Larry committed after his mother's death; Adam and manager Paul McGuiness had no interest. For the three Christians, the journey to faith was gradual, starting at Mount Temple with religion class and lunchtime Bible studies and progressing to weekly meetings with Guggi (Derek Rowan) and others, some of whom were members of Lypton Village. They also attended a

Protestant church where Guggi's father was a preacher—a real "Bible-basher" according to Bono.

Such religious fervor was not uncommon. During the mid- to late 1970s, a charismatic wave of Christianity was sweeping through America and Europe, and many teens and young adults were finding profound and life-changing experiences within the renewed church. The movement focused on worship through music and passionate corporate gatherings, preferring spontaneity, spirit-led prayer, and energetic Bible preaching rather than the formality of the Church of Ireland or Roman Catholicism. Perceived as fresh and new, the charismatic gatherings appealed to those in late adolescence who were looking for purpose and meaning beyond the emptiness of hippies and punks. In reality, joining the charismatic movement was an action of defiance against the status quo—both the violent street gangs and the established church. The greatest act of rebellion for Bono, Edge, and Larry was their commitment to a vibrant "born-again" religious experience.

By 1978, the three Christian members of U2 had discovered another way to enrich and express their faith. While roaming around Dublin with their Village friends, they met a deeply spiritual man named Dennis Sheedy. In turn, Sheedy introduced them to Pastor Chris Rowe, the leader of Shalom, a Christian commune patterned after the early church as it is recorded in the biblical book of Acts. This separatist community practiced a modern form of asceticism, promoting denial of the self, social justice, equality, and other values that were attractive to the guys. The three members of U2 found a home with these people and dedicated themselves to the gathering's strict code. Bono recalls, "I lived with no possessions. We were part of a community. Everyone helped each other out sharing what little money we had. . . . It was like a church that was really committed to changing the world" (Assayas, *Bono*, 145–46). By 1980, Bono, Edge, and Larry increased their commitment to this radical community, devoting themselves to its teaching, sharing money they made, and attending meetings and retreats routinely.

But tensions rose as U2 became more successful. The boys respected Shalom because of its commitment to simplicity, faith, and a countercultural way of living, but the group's leaders increasingly pressured the musicians to give up their career in service to God. Bono, Edge, and Larry were told that they could not be committed Christians and have a career in rock music unless they sang Christian songs and performed for church audiences. For the Shalom leaders, "good Christians" did not engage in secular practices; the two ideas were incompatible. This tension created a very real and threatening controversy for U2. As the three Christians were being compelled to commit to the commune, even to the point of giving up the band, Adam and Paul McGuinness countered with equal pressure. The very core of U2's existence was at stake. After an intense period of soul searching, one by one, the band members withdrew from Shalom—Larry first, then Bono, and finally, after almost leaving the band, Edge abandoned the spiritual gathering. Shalom had nearly became the band's undoing. By 1981, U2 had reconciled both relationships and mission, and the three Christians graciously and amicably parted ways with the commune, though still agreeing that Shalom and its leaders had been a strong and formative spiritual presence in their lives.

The importance of Shalom in the formation of U2 cannot be overlooked. As the band members bade farewell to their teen years, the controversy forced them to confront intense and serious questions of life and faith. The few years they spent with Shalom reinforced a set of values—compassion, global awareness, self-control, vulnerability, hospitality, Christian commitment—that has influenced every album and tour. But the experience also sharpened their criticism of organized religion, coercion, separatism, and militant dogma. As they exited the Shalom era, what remained was a message of love, acceptance, transparency, and surrender.

Along with their reluctance toward hippies, punks, and organized religion came an increased interest in activism, especially in the area of social justice. Issues both at home and abroad captured their attention and influenced not only their music but on a more essential level, the very way the band perceived the world. In Ireland, the Troubles was a defining period in which Protestantism and Catholicism collided in the most violent of ways, at precisely the time U2 was taking shape. The religious sectarianism so common to the island became, at least in part, the impetus for Bono, Edge, and Larry's movement toward the Shalom community. They longed for a place that emphasized the unity of Christian believers rather than the bitter intolerance they had experienced growing up. U2's formation was an active response to the religious conflict in Ireland. Neither Protestant nor Catholic, the band intentionally sought to transcend those categories.

In the beginning, U2 was more of an idea than a band. While still discovering the rudimentary skills needed to play music, the group was inspired by those who had social or political messages. On this point, the Clash was more than a musical role model. Joe Strummer, the band's front man, was a revolutionary, directly leading to Bono's own sense of activist destiny. Particularly influential was Strummer's ability to cross and combine musical genres, incorporating rock, punk, rap, hip-hop, and reggae in a way that respected and elevated other forms and artists, pushing boundaries and breaking through conventional barriers of culture and race. This was the kind of rebel that filled Bono's imagination. He recalls, "[Joe] was speaking about things he saw in his life—the things right in front of his face that none wanted to talk about—and taking his message around the world" (Bono and John, "Bono, Elton John & Chuck D"). But it was the Clash's 1980 album *Sandinista!* that really provoked Bono, spurring his interest in Nicaragua and Central America and prompting a visit in 1986. The experience was later venerated in one of U2's defining songs, "Bullet the Blue Sky."

As U2 recorded its second album, *October*, in 1981, the band members were also conscious of and impacted by events happening across the globe. Throughout the late 1970s, Cambodia was the site of genocide—the systematic extermination of an ethnic group. At the hands of the Khmer Rouge, as many as three million Vietnamese and other minority populations were brutally murdered, while others were conscripted into forced labor. Known as the Killing Fields, the cities and towns of Cambodia, then referenced as Kampuchea by their Communist oppressors, suffered unimaginable atrocities, while the United States and other nations did nothing to help.

Even as U2 recorded its next single, "Fire," a heated discussion broke out among the band about the violence happening on a distant continent. Paul McGuinness, frustrated by the amount of time and money being spent on the recording, suggested that it wasn't morally right to spend thousands of pounds on a single track while people were starving and dying in Kampuchea. Bono, equally concerned with the devastating conflict, had a different perspective, signaling the impact of Shalom (which they had just left), saying, "The same Satan that is evident in Kampuchea, in the starving people there, is the same Satan who

is working in the Marquee clubs, through drugs right here in this country" (*U2's Vision*). Using apocalyptic language that both reflected immediate concerns and a theological interpretation of the future, U2
recorded the lyrics "The sun is burning black," "The moon is running
red," and "The stars are falling down" (all direct reference to Revelation
6:12–13). The lyrics of "Fire" conveyed both remorse and a hope that
such despair caused by the situation in Kampuchea would not be un-
ending.

   Also during this period, the band became keenly aware—and skeptical—of the American Christian subculture. In 1980, the United States
experienced a new partisan phenomenon that shook up its political
system and shifted the balance of presidential power. Opposing the
election of Democratic Jimmy Carter to the White House, Jerry Falwell, the pastor of a successful Baptist church and the founder of Liber-
ty University, both in Lynchburg, Virginia, actively endorsed and financially supported Ronald Reagan for president. With the establishment
of his political organization, the Moral Majority, Falwell used his influence with the Christian Right to help secure Reagan's two-term election. Falwell was also famous for his church's TV production, *The Old-
Time Gospel Hour*, a venue he routinely used in the 1960s to feature
segregationist politicians and to openly speak against civil rights leader
Dr. Martin Luther King, Jr. Falwell was particularly suspicious of
King's nonviolent strategies.

   As an outsider, Bono became fascinated with and disturbed by the
constant fund-raising and campaigning that he saw in Falwell's organizations, which he believed was representative of the American church
as a whole. At the time, he commented to a group of young musicians in
England, "When I see Christians getting involved in politics to the
extent of making their hour, which is supposed to be dedicated to
Christ . . . which gets involved in the politics in America (which we
know is completely crazy—I mean they really do get on with it—all the
flags and everything), I see a real danger" (*U2's Vision*). Bono could not
accept the idea that the American church preached a message of love
yet was also intolerant and partisan. Years later, again in "Bullet the
Blue Sky," he would lament the situation in a musical bridge, ranting, "I
can't tell the difference between *ABC News*, *Hill Street Blues*, and a
preacher on the *Old-Time Gospel Hour* stealing money from the sick
and the old. Well the God I believe in isn't short of cash, mister" (*U2:*

Rattle and Hum). During the Zoo TV tour, Bono took on the character of Mirror Ball Man, a questionable American televangelist with a heavy southern accent, an obvious jab at Falwell's practices.

Even starting out, the social conscience of the band was often evident, as the young U2 played diverse charity events, such as the Contraception Action Campaign (1978), Rock against Sexism (1978), and the National Milk Run (1980). Throughout their formation, the four teens, along with their manager, advocated for an ethical and moral high ground not characteristic of the music business of their day. Indeed, just a few years later, in 1984, Paul McGuinness founded Principle Management, choosing the name because he wanted to build a company that operated with a strong set of principles, one that would run counter to accepted practices. As the band matured, its members continually challenged, prodded, and questioned themselves, as well as the industry they set out to dominate.

A MUSICAL LEGACY IS BORN

If U2's sense of activism was the first driving force behind the band's unique approach to a sterile music industry, then the infectious energy of its stage presence was the second. Though fairly rough and untried, U2's ability to convey an emotional message through its live performances was unlike any other of its day. The band played every opportunity offered, quickly attracting the attention of young fans and music critics alike. Having said goodbye to Dik Evans as the Hype in 1978, the reinvented quartet overcame their youthful inexperience by filling the stage with passion and conviction. It didn't matter that they couldn't play their instruments well—this band brought something much more than a musical performance to each show.

While attending Mount Temple, the boys primarily performed at schools, churches, and talent contests. But a shift came in the second half of 1978 as the band, free from the demands of a rigorous educational system, redoubled its efforts. One of the favorite local venues to gig was McGonagles. Throughout the late 1970s, the boys played the famous club, at first as the Hype and then as U2 (often written "U-2" in the early days), opening for Revolver and then moving on to become the headline act (often following the support band Frankie Corpse &

the Undertakers, which included Ivan McCormick). Over the course of at least twenty shows at McGonagles, the band honed the ability to not merely perform but to redefine the stage through a youthful passion, artistic creativity, and heightened relationship with the audience. Ivan McCormick recalls in a *Hot Press* interview, "[W]e used to play gigs in McGonagles with them. They had mime sections in their act, all sorts of theatrical stuff. I remember that polo neck with the nipples cut out that Bono used to wear. That was strange" ("Stories about Boys").

But the McGonagles venue also provided a much deeper and richer cultural context for the young band than is immediately apparent. For the four young men, it was a place of historical significance. First known as the Crystal Ballroom, this dance hall was the place Bono's parents went when they were courting; it was here that Bob Hewson and Iris Rankin danced and fell in love. And it is this older venue that U2 commemorates in the 2015 single "The Crystal Ballroom," a rarely performed but often requested song from the Innocence + Experience tour. Bono has acknowledged the significance of the club, saying,

> A whole generation of Dubliners would go to the Crystal Ballroom for dances, and many couples first met there. My mother and father used to dance together in the Crystal Ballroom, so that song . . . is me imagining I'm on the stage of McGonagles with this new band I'm in called U2—and we did play a lot of our important early gigs there. And I look out into the audience and I see my mother and father dancing romantically together to U2 on the stage. (Boyd, "Bono's Dublin")

On the deluxe version of *Songs of Innocence*, Bono solemnly sings in the song bearing the club's name, "In the ballroom of the crystal lights / Everyone's here with me tonight / Everyone but you." Undoubtedly, the historical importance of the venue energized and deepened the band's performances.

The McGonagles gigs also caught the attention, as well as the affection, of Bill Graham, one of the first writers for *Hot Press*. As early as 1978, he saw something unique in U2's passion and appetite for the live performance and after one McGonagles performance wrote, "Standing apart from this year's new bands in a suss and willingness to learn that will soon end any technical faults, U2 profit from the fact that they've an identity that needs little alteration" (Graham, "Revolver, U2"). Graham believed the band had enormous potential, even as they were being overlooked by locals and overshadowed by other bands. Commenting on two important concerts at McGonagles, he notes in a 1979 article that though U2 didn't receive any favorable print reviews, "they were simply the most exhilarating performances by a local band I've witnessed in the last twelve months" (Graham, "Trinity Buttery & McGonagles Matinee"). Graham championed the new spirit he saw in U2 for many years to come and would often be credited with helping the band find the success they deserved. For U2, playing at McGonagles was a foundational experience in an important venue.

Throughout 1978 and 1979, U2 earned rave revues from local music critics, primarily for its live performances. Coincidentally, and certainly to the band's advantage, *Hot Press* magazine was in its infancy at precisely the same time U2 began to capture the hearts and imaginations of audiences throughout Ireland. Based in Dublin, the publication mirrored *Rolling Stone* in America, examining music, pop culture, politics, and current news of the day. In addition to Graham's numerous articles, founding editor Niall Stokes and music critic Declan Lynch also praised U2 for fresh and exhilarating concerts. Both Graham and Stokes would go on to author numerous articles and books on the band, chronicling the power of the group's stage presence. During the late 1970s and early 1980s, U2 also received lavish revues from other print publications, including the British music newspapers and magazines *Sounds*, *Record Mirror*, *Melody Maker*, and *NME*, consistently praising the upstart band for a unique sound, original songs, and passionate performances that left audiences in awe. Likewise, with the release of U2's first album, *Boy*, music critic Jim Henke from *Rolling Stone* became an ardent champion of the band, a relationship that has lasted for decades.

Particularly compelling was Bono's ability to improvise on stage, often using grand theatrics but still always being aware of the temperament of a room, reacting to fans and hecklers alike with an engaging and captivating presence. Many of the venues U2 played were dark and dingy clubs, filled with punks and discontents. It wasn't uncommon for fights or scuffles to break out, though not because U2's music elicited a violent response. The aggressive nature of concertgoers was more a consequence of uncertain times, volatile emotions, and problematic venues. Still, U2 seemed to be at home in this kind of unruly environment, where Bono excelled at playing mediator, breaking up bar fights, calming disorderly crowds, and nurturing community in the midnight hours of restless dance floors. Charming and charismatic, he treated everyone as if they were his best friends, listening, interacting, and making each person feel like each individual was the only member in the audience. The young front man exuded authenticity and warmth through impassioned performances and caring interactions.

For Bono, an unruly audience—and there were many of them, especially as U2 opened for other punk bands that often had their own set of aggressive fans—was simply another challenge for the band to overcome. At one particularly hostile show, an impatient fan yelled to Bono, calling him a "poser." With ever a quick wit, the lead singer gladly consented and then turned the insult into an accolade. "Course I'm a poser. You're a poser, we're all posers" (Graham, "Battling through a Hail of Spittle," 41). In that instant, Bono removed any barriers with the audience and disarmed his critics; everyone in the room became his friend. This wasn't a show. This was the real Paul Hewson, fighting back from the edge of despair after his mother's death, desperately attempting to fill a gaping hole through music and friends while living out his life on the stage.

As U2 continued reinventing the art of the live performance, the band also set out to grow a fan base through media appearances. In the spring of 1978, the Hype had its first recording for TV, performing "The Fool" on RTÉ's *Our Times*. Bono sang, "I break all the rules / They call me a fool," signaling his unconventional nature. Soon after, the band appeared again, this time as U2, on RTÉ's *Youngline* performing "Street Mission," the song's title subtly hinting at three of the members' intentions to embed Christian faith in their earliest original tunes. At the time of these appearances, Adam was just eighteen years old, Bono and Edge were seventeen, and Larry was a mere sixteen. These broadcasts on Ireland's national television were important moments for U2, revealing the band's charismatic stage presence, especially for a young teenage audience that wasn't old enough to attend U2's concerts in bars and clubs.

RTÉ also began to feature U2 on its radio outlets. One of the band's most opportune moments came with an appearance on Dave Fanning's show in the fall of 1979, during which the host interviewed each member of the group on a separate night and played three tracks that had just been recorded at the famous Windmill Lane Studios. Fanning praised the boys' youthfulness, zeal, and distinctiveness. As is the case with many of U2's interviewers, Fanning became an avid supporter and lifelong friend of the band, so much so that for three decades U2 granted the music journalist exclusive interviews and debut airplay of new singles.

U2's journey into fame also coincided with a brand-new, innovative medium unlike any before. On August 1, 1981, a cable television station, featuring a groundbreaking music-video format, debuted in America. It didn't take long for U2 to recognize the potential of this pioneering technology. With the release of their second album, *October*, the band filmed its first music video, an artistic interpretation and performance of the hit "Gloria." Shot just two months after MTV's launch, the video featured the group performing on a barge in Dublin's Grand Canal Basin while onlookers danced and cheered. "Gloria" was U2's big break on the fledgling network and received heavy airplay. Thus began a love affair between U2 and MTV, a relationship that would propel each well into the twenty-first century.

For U2, the live performance was complemented and accentuated by media appearances. And whether it came through traditional sources such as print and radio or the innovative technologies of television and MTV, the band set out from the beginning to harness the power of every tool available on their quest not only to dominate the music industry but to stand as an alternative to it. Unflinching in the face of interviewers, a growing expanse of cameras and microphones became as important as their own instruments along the way.

As the band continued developing its stage and media presence, it also spent time in the studio. Through a series of recording sessions, sometimes quite contentious yet always energetic and creative, U2 released a demo and its first trio of records, proving its ability to craft engaging and original material and eventually finding an international audience.

In 1979, the group partnered with producer Chas de Whalley at Windmill Lane Studios, recording three songs in one all-night, tension-filled session. It was there that the band members experienced firsthand the pressure of working with time constraints, arranging music, recording individual tracks, appeasing engineers, and meeting deadlines. The collaborative process was not only tedious, it was stressful and quarrelsome. But it was also a further indication that from the beginning, the four young men held themselves to a high standard, unwilling to settle for something less than they knew they were capable of. After a disagreement with de Whalley about the postproduction mix of their new recordings, Paul McGuinness solicited the help of others, searching for the perfect sound. The final product was U2-3 (or *Three*), a three-track record distributed throughout Ireland by CBS Records. The order of the tracks came about in a unique way that demonstrated the band's love and admiration for its fan base, further breaking the mold of the status quo industry. While being interviewed by Dave Fanning over the course of a week, U2 let the show's listeners comment and vote on the arrangement of tracks on the new album. This lively and creative dialogue resulted in fans picking "Out of Control" for the A-side and "Boy/Girl" and "Stories for Boys" on the flip side. The album, primarily sold to local fans and used for radio promotions, was a hit, and a tour in support of the record ensued, taking U2 across the channel to England for their first exposure.

After *U2-3*, the band worked hard, playing gigs, promoting their demo album, and trying to secure a legitimate record deal. The group's big break came while touring London in early 1980, when it gained the attention of Island Records. After one particularly successful show, the label, recognizing U2's originality, creativity, and charisma, scrambled to bring the band on board. The best part about the deal they negotiated was that U2 received a four-album contract, guaranteeing the ability to tour as well as record. Just a month after signing, U2 cut its first single with Island Records, "11 O'Clock Tick Tock," aided by Joy Division producer Martin Hannett. Quickly proving to be a successful venture, the deal fostered a partnership that was beneficial for both U2 and the record company over the next twenty years.

With contract in hand, the band moved back into Windmill Lane Studios to record a full debut album, this time with the wildly creative and often unconventional producer Steve Lillywhite. Far more than a one-shot all-nighter, U2 gained complete access to the studio and its amenities. Always looking for imaginative and nontraditional approaches while recording, the musicians used a variety of unusual percussive instruments, including a glockenspiel, bottles suspended from strings, broken glass, and even the spokes of a bicycle wheel. And though Edge was limited to one guitar, his classic Gibson Explorer (a model he still uses), he was also experimenting with fresh sounds and effects. Using his new Electro Harmonix Deluxe Memory Man echo unit, the guitarist invented tones and textures that would, in a very short time, become his signature sound. Ignoring the standard note bends, whammy bars, and traditional chord progressions of other rock guitarists, Edge applied his love of math to music, building his solos and background rhythm work around a series of echoed and delayed notes. In a calculated way, the young guitarist used his effects box to create syncopated rhythms, generating patterns and phrases that would not have been possible otherwise. The result, precise loops of notes providing a chiming-like quality layered with rich harmonics, eventually became a style sought after and emulated by bands across Europe and North America. Just as Bono was making a name for himself through passionate and charismatic stage performances, Edge was getting attention for his innovative technology and new guitar stylings.

The final product of their creative time in the studio was *Boy* (1980), an album exploring the innocence of childhood contrasted with the complexity of adolescence. Being teens themselves, the topic seemed an appropriate investigation for a band that was just coming of age, often through heartbreaking loss, and a fitting topic for a debut record. In keeping with the theme, the album cover featured a black-and-white photograph of a young, shirtless boy. The model, Peter Rowen, brother to Guggi, Trevor, and Andy, depicted the simplicity and purity of childhood but not without controversy. The provocative image also had overtones of pedophilia for some, though that was never the intent of Steve Averill, the artistic director for the project. For that reason, the cover of the North American pressing was altered to feature a distorted picture of the band members. A bold and creative project, *Boy* was welcomed by critics and fans alike and produced U2's first hit single, "I Will Follow," a song about the unconditional love of a mother for her child but also containing a subtle message about the group's own journey toward the Christian faith. The album was considered a success, solidifying U2's presence in the United Kingdom and introducing the young band to North America through supporting tours in 1980 and 1981.

While the recording of *Boy* was an exciting, joyful, and successful experience, the production of U2's second album would nearly be their demise. With mixed reviews and little radio play, *October* (1981) was heavily themed with spiritual imagery, reflecting Bono, Edge, and Larry's involvement in the Christian commune Shalom. Lyrics for the album seemed weak to critics, focusing on the band's religious experience rather than issues that mattered to a broader audience. Peppered with sentiments like "Rejoice," a powerful antipunk notion of Bono's that went unacknowledged by reviewers, weighty Latin phrases from church liturgy in "Gloria, in te Domine," and direct quotes about the apocalypse from Revelation 6:12–13 in "Fire," the content felt preachy and paternal to many.

To complicate the matter, just before the band began recording in a Minneapolis studio, Bono's briefcase containing the lyrics for *October* went missing from backstage at a show in Portland, Oregon. The pressure to improvise and write new songs on the fly created an undue burden on the crew as Lillywhite filled the role of producer once again. Also at this time, the three members of Shalom were struggling to understand their place as artists, wondering if their greatest service to God might be met by surrendering the band. In the end, Bono, Edge, and Larry left the commune and gave themselves to their music, what they believed was an equally valid expression of Christian faith. The same notion permeated the 2015 Innocence + Experience tour, when Bono, on behalf of his bandmates, routinely told audiences, "We surrender to you. We surrender to the music. We surrender to the God who made the music."

But though *October* seemed an irrelevant album to critics, its themes were significant and important to the band and reflect an ongoing growth in its ideology. Still discontent with the shortcomings of the hippies and punks, U2 was committed to a much more positive outlook. "October is an image," said Bono in a 1982 interview before a concert in Hattem, Netherlands,

> We've been through a time when things were in full bloom. We had fridges and cars and we sent people to the moon, and everybody thought how great mankind was. But now it's gone through the seventies and through the eighties and it's a colder time of year . . . and the "trees are stripped bare," and we finally realize maybe we weren't so smart after all . . . now that we've used the technology we've been blessed with to build bombs for war machines. (U2, "U2 *October* Interview" 1982)

U2 considered itself an alternate voice to the pessimism that faced an increasingly fractured Dublin. "This band stamps on pessimism.

We're anti-cynics. *October* is an optimistic record, because through it
there's a joy" (U2, "U2 *October* Interview" 1982). While other bands
were repeating the mantras of unemployment and despair, Bono countered, "Fight it. Rejoice. Don't let it bring you down" (U2, "U2 *October*
Interview" 1982). And perhaps that's the message U2 repeated to itself
as its second album, essentially a record about God, found only margi-
nal success, ultimately disappointing the band. Fortunately, the members, undaunted by their limited success, learned to turn their failures
around and forge ahead.

Their next project, *War* (1983), did just that. While *Boy* dealt with
the theme of innocence and *October* with spirituality, U2's third album
was much more black and white, focusing on the less nebulous concept
of warfare. Turning outward, the band began an examination of global
issues, including peace, aggression, and the human condition, subject
matter that would fuel U2 through the 1980s. Once again, Lillywhite
was at the helm as producer, helping the band craft an iconic record
that conveyed both the physical and emotional consequences of violence, by setting aside the ethereal gimmicks of the first two albums in
favor of raw, stripped-down instruments and tracks. Peter Rowen, the
child who appeared on *Boy*, was the subject of this album's cover again,
but this time the boy looked seasoned, as if he himself had been the
victim of a difficult life.

The album's first track, "Sunday Bloody Sunday," has become one of
U2's most famous. Often interpreted as a protest song, its inspiration
comes from three separate events. First, the song provides a nod to
Sunday, January 30, 1972, a day when the British military killed thirteen
unarmed Irish civil rights protestors and wounded thirteen others,
deepening the conflict of the Troubles in Derry, Northern Ireland.
Second, the song references a much older event on Sunday, November
21, 1920, in Dublin, when the Irish Republican Army (IRA) assassinated fourteen British agents, later resulting in the killing of fourteen
civilians by British forces during a soccer match at Croke Park. Finally,
the concluding line of the song, "To claim the victory Jesus won on
Sunday Bloody Sunday," was meant to be a reflection on the redeeming
nature of the first Easter Sunday. Though much less overt than *October*, Bono's lyric suggested that the way of Christ could provide a peaceful path through the world's conflicts.

War also produced other popular hits. "New Year's Day" has been a standard in concert for over thirty years, and "40" combined a series of Psalms (6, 40, and 140) and became the closing concert number in the early 1980s, during which the foursome would walk off the stage one by one while the audience repeated the ancient poetic phrase, "How long, to sing this song?" (a theme also found in "Sunday Bloody Sunday"). Overall, *War* was U2's first number-one album in the United Kingdom, even displacing Michael Jackson's wildly popular *Thriller*. Through the band's third album, accompanied by an ambitious supporting tour, U2 had solidified its place as a popular European band that was here to stay.

Over the course of the late 1970s and early 1980s, the Irish quartet, first known as Feedback, then the Hype, and finally U2, embraced adolescence. Moving from schools to clubs to international tours, the band navigated the music industry with a fresh ideology, a new business model, engaging stage performances, passionate activism, pioneering technologies, and a reinvigorated faith. Though certainly not without difficulties, especially with regard to song writing and integration of at least three members' Christianity, the fledgling group overcame every obstacle. But perhaps the most outstanding quality of U2 was its ability to connect with an audience. Not satisfied with the mindless fodder of popular culture, this young band considered its listeners more intelligent than average concertgoers, capable of hearing content that went deeper than the status quo. In a sense, U2's audience had grown and matured right alongside the band.

Reflecting on seeing U2 for the first time in 1980, music critic Jim Henke wrote,

> U2 was special. It didn't matter where the concert was taking place. Their sheer power and passion, coupled with Bono's ability to break down the barrier between the stage and audience, completely knocked me out. I thought they were amazing. (Henke, "Here Comes the Next Big Thing")

Having gained a firm foothold in Ireland and the United Kingdom, many bands might have rested on their accomplishments. Not U2. The first three albums and associated tours were just warm-ups for the next big stage in the band's career. And though they had made forays across the Atlantic many times, they soon set out in earnest to conquer a new frontier. Armed with powerful performances and compelling messages, U2 embraced a new image and style and ran headlong and whole-heartedly into the arms of America.

3

INTO THE ARMS OF AMERICA

With the next set of albums—*Under a Blood Red Sky*, *The Unforgettable Fire*, *The Joshua Tree*, and *Rattle and Hum*—U2 firmly positioned itself as an international band. The group's foray into the American music scene progressed from being well received in the early 1980s to smashingly successful by the end of the decade, but not without controversy. U2's attention to global crises, along with a love-hate thematic approach to American politics and culture, earned it the praise of some and the scorn of others. On the one hand, U2 was a welcomed musical alternative to the mediocrity of 1980s pop and glam rock. But on the other hand, newfound fame brought special challenges as the band experienced chart-topping hits, award-winning albums, and a burgeoning fan base, as well as a growing cadre of critics. For some listeners, the band's message, a carefully crafted commentary on affairs of the day, began feeling too grandiose for a culture wallowing in overindulgence.

On the stage, something unique was happening in their shows—as they played to larger and larger venues, they engaged audiences and connected with listeners in ways that most music fans hadn't previously experienced. U2's pioneering spirit, evident both in the studio and on the stage, transcended expectations and industry standards and inspired the group to make innovative leaps in music, media, and technology. Along with a growing social conscience, a message of global peace found its way into the band's catalog and concerts as it paid tribute to Martin Luther King, Jr., exposed US subterfuge in Central America, informed listeners about South African apartheid, and ignited a longing in the hearts of fans for something bigger than themselves. Armed with keen intellect, fresh imagination, and refined skill, U2 stormed the decade, building a franchise—and the start of a brand—that would earn the quartet supergroup status.

STORMING AMERICA

Under a Blood Red Sky was a pivotal album for U2 in 1983. Recorded at three different venues, including the Red Rocks Amphitheatre outside of Denver, Colorado, the album, along with its companion concert film, *U2 Live at Red Rocks: Under a Blood Red Sky*, propelled the band into the American music scene. Recorded on a US leg of the *War* tour, the collection of songs perfectly represented the musical creativity and raw passion of U2's live performances, introducing a whole new audience to "Sunday Bloody Sunday," "I Will Follow," "New Year's Day," and "40," all destined to become trademarks of the band's musical legacy. The record went platinum around the globe, selling the most copies—an astonishing three million—in America. But while the album was a crucial component of U2's move into the United States, it was the concert video that captured and altered the musical consciousness of its new followers.

    U2 Live at Red Rocks broke ground and influenced the industry in multiple ways—but it almost didn't happen. Like many artists, the band had dreamed of playing at the historic Red Rocks Amphitheatre. Eventually, through a complex set of partnerships involving promoters and international radio and TV broadcasters, Principle Management negotiated a deal and contracted a summer date. As support teams prepared for the show, no one could have predicted that its eventual success would be due to the culmination of a perfect storm—literally! On June 5, 1983, the day of the concert, the Rocky Mountains venue was overwhelmed by an ominous weather system, resulting in torrential rain and flash flood warnings. Most of the crew assumed the show would be canceled. Despite the storm, Bono, staying true to his character, visited rain-drenched fans who had waited hours in inclement weather, and the band continued with preparations. Crew members wrapped cables, covered cameras, and mopped up water from the stage. As show's start time approached, the storm broke and settled into a much less menacing mist. Combined with ambient lighting featuring the outdoor venue's natural beauty, the receding storm gave way to a surreal landscape that surpassed any staging the concert's producers could have planned.

At the show, two significant moments helped define U2's image as an unparalleled live band, an unstoppable force of passion and energy. First, the band gave one of the best performances of its career during "Sunday Bloody Sunday." While introducing the song, Bono explained that it was not meant to be a protest (either for or against the Irish Republican Army), as some had assumed, saying, "This song is not a rebel song. This song is 'Sunday Bloody Sunday.'" In the middle of the performance, Bono marched across the stage brandishing a large white flag, a symbol of the band's commitment to peace and a defining icon that would be used for years to come. The zeal of the band, the verve of the crowd, and the mystique of the environment coalesced in what *Rolling Stone* called one of the "50 Moments That Changed the History of Rock and Roll." Second, in an instant that was both exhilarating and terrifying, Bono climbed to the top of a tall, slippery lighting rig to wave his white flag during "The Electric Co.," a seemingly appropriate name for a song during which there was a very real possibility of electrocution. In the end, he made it down safely, and the image was immortalized as the cover photo for the video's packaging.

U2's maiden effort at concert video production was a wild success, earning the universal approval of both music and film critics. *U2 Live at Red Rocks* also presented an opportunity for the band to continue its infatuation with media, through which it gained even greater access to an American audience. Soon after recording, a portion of the concert was broadcast on the upstart Showtime network, while other clips received heavy rotation on a very young MTV. In 1986, the entire concert was televised throughout the United States. As U2's pioneering release into the home video market, the film was made available in VHS, Betamax, and the state-of-the-art LaserDisc formats. Red Rocks was both a defining and a transitional moment for U2 because it documented the group's compelling live performances while engaging the hearts and minds of music fans who were tired of the predictable, overly sanitized, and heavily commercialized pop, new wave, and rock of the early 1980s. But just as U2 was finding a productive niche in an otherwise sterile industry, and in spite of its enormously successful *War* tour, the band risked everything, heading again into virgin territory with a new trio of albums.

AN AMERICAN TRILOGY

If U2's first three albums chronicled the journey of four Irish lads becoming a band, then the next three after *Under a Blood Red Sky* documented both its fascination with and critique of America. The first trilogy, including *Boy*, *October*, and *War*, focused largely on the innocence of adolescent musicians finding identity, the trauma of growing up in the Troubles, and the role of faith while navigating a conflicted world. The sentiments found in this series were Irish, and the content was primarily Ireland bound. But the next trilogy, comprising *The Unforgettable Fire*, *The Joshua Tree*, and *Rattle and Hum*, took the band into very new space, picking up themes of global concern, including social justice, military conflict, poverty, and violence. Sonically, this set of albums buried the earlier recordings and redefined rock 'n' roll. Solidly in charge of their instruments, the band and crew left behind the glockenspiels of their musical childhood in favor of lush and complex musical landscapes, partnered with rich and multifaceted lyrics.

Breaking with conventional wisdom, U2 abandoned the tried and true rock formula perfected with *War*, choosing instead to push into experimental territory. In search of a new sound, the band moved into Slane Castle, a three-hundred-year-old residence that doubles as a concert venue. There they spent months in 1984 testing, writing, and recording with producers Brian Eno and Daniel Lanois. Both accomplished musicians themselves, Eno and Lanois brought their considerable talent in ambient and experimental music to the sessions, resulting in rich textures, ethereal strings, and complex backgrounds. Fully immersed in the ethos of both a historic castle and cutting-edge technology, the band said good-bye to the clean-cut, hard-hitting beats of their previous albums, favoring a looser, more progressive sound. Bono's vocals were smooth and glassy, his lyrics poetic. Edge focused on melodic lead lines and looped patterns; Adam's bass softened, and Larry functioned less as the band's metronome and more as its quiet yet steady conscience.

The resulting album, 1984's *The Unforgettable Fire*, introduced a sophisticated U2 to America. Nuanced with European influences, the record's musical understatement paralleled its audacious subject matter. More artsy, and thus open to multiple levels of interpretation, even the album's title reflected several layers of meaning. Primarily, *The Unforgettable Fire*—both the title of the album and a track on the record—refers to a dark moment in American-Japanese relations and reflects the inspiration U2 received from an art exhibition of the same name commemorating the bombing of Hiroshima and Nagasaki in 1945. Having experienced the exhibit in Chicago in 1983, U2 was deeply impacted by stories and visuals of the blasts. Especially moving was the artwork of children who had survived. The destruction of these two cities in Japan was a singular event—never before and never again have nuclear weapons been used in a combat situation. The results were catastrophic: At least eighty thousand people were killed instantly in Hiroshima, forty thousand in Nagasaki. Tens of thousands died later of burns and radiation exposure; hundreds of thousands suffered injury, including nausea, bleeding, and loss of hair, many eventually succumbing to multiple types of cancers. Two-thirds of the buildings in Hiroshima were destroyed, and over 90 percent of its doctors and nurses were killed as hospitals collapsed. In Nagasaki, a heavy industrial center, factories, along with the workers who filled them, were flattened. In a flash, schools, churches, and historical landmarks were obliterated.

It was this dark side of the American story that U2 discovered while attending the Chicago peace exhibit in 1983. In an interview after the album's release, Bono spoke of touring the exhibition: "The images from the paintings and some of the writings stained me, I couldn't get rid of them" (King, "The Fire Within"). In the album's opening song, "A Sort of Homecoming," Bono sang, "The city walls are all come down / The dust a smokescreen all around." And it's hard not to think of Nagasaki, a city nestled between two mountain ranges, when hearing the next verse: "And we live by the side of the road / On the side of a hill as the valley explodes / Dislocated, suffocated, the land grows weary of its own." Through "Homecoming" and other songs on *Fire*, U2 painted a musical picture as meaningful as the exhibit itself.

It's also on this record that U2's compositional skills began to show depth and maturity, especially as they considered alternate interpretations for the notion of fire. Not just a reference to the literal bombings of Hiroshima and Nagasaki, the idea of flames and explosions became a metaphor in other ways. Bono reflected on his lyric-writing process, saying,

> I realized as the album was moving on, that this image of "the unforgettable fire" applied not only to the nuclear winterscape of "A Sort of Homecoming," but also the unforgettable fire of a man like Martin Luther King, or the consuming fire which is heroin. So it became a multi-purpose image for me, but it derived from that exhibition. (King, "The Fire Within")

The seventh track on the album, "Bad," is an impassioned plea to a lifelong friend of the band, Andy Rowen, a victim of Dublin's raging heroin scene who nearly lost his life due to an overdose. All of the pain and grief of that experience seemed to coalesce in and then pour through the music and lyrics of "Bad," serving as an anthem for anyone who had suffered crippling defeats in his or her own life. Played live, the song became a central moment in U2's concerts, acting almost as an altar call as Bono sang, "Surrender, dislocate . . . let it go."

In many ways, U2's call to surrender was perfectly timed for an America that was consumed with itself. Politically, Ronald Reagan's presidency (1981–1989) championed an aggressive brand of neoconservatism, promoting a strong military buildup, a provocative foreign policy, and a hard-hitting approach to Communism, all of which reinvigorated the Republican Party. The country turned right with economic policy too, implementing supply-side strategies (deemed "Reaganomics") that reduced taxes, deregulated industry, and downsized government services, a scheme that favored the wealthy and increased the disparity between rich and poor. This neoconservatism in politics and economics directly correlated to a renewed religious fervor as well. The Baptist pastor Jerry Falwell's "Moral Majority" had over four million members and mobilized the Evangelical Christian Right in support of conservative politicians and legislation. But the surge in political, economic, and social conservatism also coincided with an age of decadence, as materialism and consumerism began to define the American dream. With more expendable income, a new class of "yuppie" emerged, reflecting a young, well-paid urban professional who indulged in life's luxuries. Pop culture and entertainment exploded with slick images of Wall Street, Southern California "Valley Girls," designer clothes, and exotic vacation destinations. When Bono encouraged the audience to "let it go," it was as if he were singing past the heroin epidemic of Dublin and right into the heart of a bloated, repressed, and self-absorbed American populace.

While on tour in support of *The Unforgettable Fire*, "Bad" became more than a song. It was a communal experience and part of a larger motif. With a significant catalog of songs at its disposal, U2 began to shape set lists into something that resembled a liturgical experience, not just a collection of top hits. In this era, the band learned to skillfully and intentionally map out an emotional journey for concertgoers, starting with upbeat standards, moving to thoughtful reflection, and culminating in corporate celebration. Usually performed about two-thirds through the show, "Bad" was itself a movement within a larger symphony, beginning with the hypnotic and percussive tones of sequencers (a first for U2), Edge's echoing guitar, and Bono's hauntingly simple vocals sung directly to the audience. As the song developed, Larry matched Adam's ascending bass line with a full set of drums, while Bono moved into the power of his upper register, only to quiet again and then repeat the whole progression. With the final chorus, Bono invited the audience into a crescendoed exclamation, nearly screaming "Let it go!" Then, calmly, and ever so adroitly, the front man escorted the crowd back to terrestrial soil, gently singing, "Come on down," repeatedly. Right on cue, without any verbal instruction given, the willing concertgoers would join the chorus, as if they had become members of the band themselves. And in an almost ritualistic way, the crowd's melodic response of "Come on down" functioned as a collective release, a kind of tribal invitation to the divine and to each other. The experience was replicated night after night, in city after city, throughout the United States in late 1984 and the first half of 1985. America, it seemed, was ready for the participatory, confessional, and cathartic release of "Bad." And U2 was eager and willing to provide.

While the darkness of Dublin's heroin culture, along with America's nuclear bombings, provided material for U2's exploration of a despairing world, "fire" also had another meaning, a more positive one, demonstrated in two songs honoring the efficacious spirit of Dr. Martin Luther King, Jr. In King, the band found a model for dealing with the Troubles and the terrorism of the Irish Republican Army. Bono remembers, "America had had its own troubles with race relations in the sixties. We started to see similarities with the civil rights movement. We became students of nonviolence, of Martin Luther King's thinking" (Assayas, *Bono*, 170). Other similar influences also came from Mohandas Gandhi in India, Nelson Mandela in South Africa, and the biblical Jesus, all rooted in active resistance through nonviolence.

"Pride (in the Name of Love)," one of U2's most recognizable hits, captured King's spirit of peaceful activism. With sweeping dynamics, a strong progressive guitar background, and a soaring yet singable refrain, the song quickly became a standard, an anthem in which Bono and the audience called back and forth to one another in a chorus of *ohs*, a pattern that soon became a regular feature of U2's concerts. Talking about the writing process, Bono recounts, "We looked for a subject big enough to demand this level of emotion that was coming out. We had discovered nonviolence and Martin Luther King, not just in relation to his use of the Scriptures and his church background, but also as a solution to the Irish problems" (Bono, "*Rolling Stone* Interview"). With "Pride," U2 combined strong song writing, powerful content, and maximum audience engagement, all inspired by King's peaceful activism. *The Unforgettable Fire* came to a close with another song honoring King, this one a sweet, understated lullaby. In "MLK," the album's benediction, Bono offered the tranquil blessing, "Sleep, sleep tonight / And may your dreams be realized." For those who didn't know of King's legacy, the song was ambiguous enough to still be a simple but effective word of hope and encouragement. But for those who had studied the activist's life, the song was a powerful and challenging reminder of King's mission.

The Unforgettable Fire was far more than a mere follow-up to a successful trio of albums. Through *Fire*, U2 rejected the typical rock formula and reinvented themselves, combining experimental music with bold content and raw emotion, giving attention to cultural critique and subjects that captured the hearts of its listeners. The accompanying tour took the band into sold-out arenas across the United States, as well as to a record number of international venues. Eventually selling seven million copies worldwide, *Fire* landed a number-one spot on the UK charts, while in the United States it hit number twelve, with "Pride" becoming the group's first single to break into the Top 40. In 1985, as they traveled across America, *Rolling Stone* put U2 on the cover of the March issue with the caption, "Our Choice: Band of the '80s." While the first trilogy of albums had primarily focused on the local Irish context, this record began a journey into the global conscience, and the world, especially the United States, cheered for more. The result was a mature and seasoned band, poised to create what many critics say became the greatest album of its career and, hence, gave them a bigger platform to champion a set of values and ideals that reached far beyond musical composition.

BECOMING THE BIGGEST BAND ON THE PLANET

The Joshua Tree, the band's fifth studio album, became the quintessential U2 record, representing everything that the quartet had been working toward. It was a combination of thoughtful writing, accomplished musicianship, and cutting-edge production, embracing themes of faith, politics, justice, and philanthropy. Continuing where *Fire* had left off, this 1987 release delved deeper into the mystique of the American West, finding inspiration in the high desert of California. Both the title and the cover art symbolically depict the rugged individualism of the American conscience, simultaneously capturing the perilous isolation and enduring beauty of a lone Joshua tree. While *The Unforgettable Fire* had hinted at U2's fascination with America, *The Joshua Tree* fleshed it out.

With regard to production and composition, the band hit a stride while recording the album. Bono's talent as a lyricist was noticeably improving, combining his lucidity on *War* and his romanticism on *The Unforgettable Fire*. Eno and Lanois continued their roles as producers, but this time with less experimental ambience, appealing to the listener's need for accessibility yet still being intelligent and sophisticated, creating a tangible mixture of pop and art. The band also invited Mark "Flood" Ellis to engineer the recording sessions, asking him to help create a sound that would match the expanse of the desert motif. The work went so well that Flood was called to assist on many successive albums. In postproduction, old friend and producer Steve Lillywhite returned to remix some of the tracks in order to give them stronger commercial appeal, something that had been lacking on *The Unforgettable Fire*. Similar to the recording of its previous album, U2 ditched a professional studio and retreated instead to an eighteenth-century house in the hills of Ireland. The old wooden floors and lofty ceilings of the dwelling provided a perfect, yet unconventional, recording space, as well as a creative and inspiring atmosphere.

Having found the perfect blend of writing and recording, *The Joshua Tree* quickly won the respect of critics and fans, topping charts and breaking records. With a compelling set of musical sketches, U2 had demonstrated something unique: here was a band set on shaping American culture while allowing itself to be influenced by it. The result was not just a collection of songs but a cinematic landscape as big as the country it sought to conquer. This give-and-take, love-hate relationship, however, was not coincidental but rather the product of a series of experiences, events that began two years before U2 released the historic album.

On July 13, 1985, just as it had closed *The Unforgettable Fire* tour, U2 performed at Live Aid. The concert, unlike any other because of its high technical requirements, was a satellite-linked simulcast incorporating major venues in Philadelphia and London, as well as smaller partners around the world, in an effort to raise money for the devastating Ethiopian famine. An earlier yet similar project, the Band Aid recording of "Do They Know It's Christmas?" which was released in December of 1984, had proven that artists and fans wanted to help alleviate suffering in the African nation. At the time, Bono and Adam joined Band Aid and represented U2 with over forty other well-known musicians, including Phil Collins, Boy George, George Michael, Sting, and Bob Geldof, the project's producer. When the much larger Live Aid event developed just six months later, the members of U2 were eager to lend support, demonstrating their unified heartbeat for Africa, a continent they would address again and again through their music and activism.

U2's performance at Wembley Stadium that warm summer day was momentous. Even the band couldn't have predicted how epic the event would end up being. The group's plan to do three songs had to be scrapped midshow due to an extended, unplanned version of "Bad," the second song of the set, as Bono pulled several young girls from the pressing throngs and danced with them. The feat involved some dangerous acrobatics, which had Bono leaping over a barrier and off the edge of a high stage to the cheers of an ecstatic crowd. In that chaotic and serendipitous moment, U2 conveyed one of its primary messages to the seventy thousand people in the London stadium and the nearly two billion watching on TV: this was a band that could flood a stadium with a colossal wave of sound yet still be an intimate member of the audience. The thirteen-minute performance of "Bad" clearly and finally established the group as an incomparable live band—as Jack Nicholson said in his introduction of U2—"whose heart is in Dublin" and "whose spirit is with the world" (U2, "U2—Sunday Bloody Sunday"). Indeed, the band's spirit extended far beyond the United Kingdom, soon reaching across the globe into places it had never considered, ultimately germinating as deeply rooted themes on its next couple of albums.

Specifically, two cross-cultural experiences of Bono's had impacted the development of the album and, thus, the growth of the band. First, as a result of Live Aid, Bono, along with his wife, Ali, accepted an invitation from the international Christian relief agency World Vision to witness the plight and devastation of the ongoing famine in Ethiopia. For nearly a month in 1985, the couple quietly volunteered at a feeding camp in Ajibar, serving refugees and helping at an orphanage. While there, they wrote songs and short plays to help educate children about basic hygiene and eating habits. The sights, sounds, and smells of Ethiopia left an indelible mark on Bono. He remembers,

> In the morning as the mist would lift we would see thousands of people walking in lines toward the camp, people who had been walking for great distances through the night. . . . Some as they got to the camp would collapse. Some would leave their children at the gates and some would leave their dead children at the fences to be buried. (Assayas, *Bono*, 223)

Even so, there was a beauty to the place, a rich culture filled with strong and noble people. Amid the greatest suffering, Bono witnessed an enduring spirit in the laughter and smiles of the Ethiopians. The vast and expansive desert was itself a place of remarkable natural beauty while also a cruel and harsh wilderness, a violent oppressor to those without food and shelter. Bono developed the contrast in one of *The Joshua Tree*'s most popular songs, "Where The Streets Have No Name," singing, "I want to feel sunlight on my face / See the dust cloud disappear without a trace" and "We're beaten and blown by the wind, trampled in dust."

Deeply moved by his visit to Ethiopia, the images became meta-phors for the band's own journey through America, providing connect-ing points between the abject, yet preventable, poverty of a Third World country and the excessiveness of the richest, most powerful na-tion on the planet. But it was a second international excursion, this time to Central America, that angered Bono to the point of openly challeng-ing the US government from the stage.

"Bullet the Blue Sky," the fourth song on *The Joshua Tree*, is univer-sally viewed as one of U2's most political songs, inspired by a trip Bono and Ali took to El Salvador and Nicaragua in 1986. Having just finished a short tour called A Conspiracy of Hope, an effort by U2 and other artists to raise awareness for Amnesty International, the couple set out on an adventure that took them deep into rebel-controlled territory in El Salvador. At the time, people in El Salvador were caught in an extended struggle between a militant government and a leftist guerrilla revolt. There, Bono saw firsthand the effects of America's support for the Salvadoran government, a regime that routinely intimidated rural civilians with violent methods of repression, using death squads and a scorched-earth policy. Here was a people, Bono thought, that had struggled for basic human rights in the same way African Americans had during the civil rights movement. And despite the pleas for the United States to defund El Salvador's government by reformers like Archbishop Oscar Romero, who was later assassinated for his anti-governmental protests, the United States continued to pour aid into the Salvadoran government, ignoring human rights violations.

This was the violent situation Bono stepped into while visiting the small farming project he helped fund. Had he known how intense it was in advance, he might not have gone. One day while walking down a forest path with their guide, he and his small party of travelers encoun-tered a group of government soldiers. In the next terrifying moment, the air came alive with gunfire, bullets whizzing overhead. It was heart-stopping for Bono and his friends, though nothing more than a perverse joke for the soldiers as they discharged warning shots. Once again, on the frontline of violence, poverty, and injustice in a foreign context, Bono's thoughts went beyond El Salvador. "[M]y subject was America," he noted. "I wanted to know what was the on-the-ground effect of American foreign policy, because I was a fan of America" (Assayas, *Bono*, 184). Through this intense experience, Bono penned one of the most biting and cynical songs of U2's career. Recalling the people he had met and the suffering they had endured, he wrote, "See the face of fear, running scared in the valley below . . . Bullet the blue sky." This was also the first U2 song that included a spoken-word segment. Part confession, part rant, the outcome was a blistering, yet somewhat veiled, critique of US involvement in Central America. The song's political commentary has endeared it to both fans and critics as one of their favorite tunes.

Bono's trip to El Salvador also included an excursion to Nicaragua, still another influence on the writing of "Bullet the Blue Sky" and *The Joshua Tree* as a whole. Here, too, the people suffered immensely due to civil war, but in this country, the United States gave its support to the guerillas, a group of violent revolutionaries resolved to overthrow the Communist Sandinista government. Labeling the Nicaraguan president a dictator, President Reagan covertly supplied Contra guerrilla forces with funds and illegal weapons. The resulting armed conflict destabilized the country, confirming what Bono had seen on his Salvadoran trip: America, in its quest to defeat Communism, was guilty of supporting political movements that grossly violated human rights.

> I was angry with what I saw as the bullying of peasant farmers by big aeroplanes supported by American foreign policy and dollars. . . . There was a lot to despise about America back then, there was shameful conduct in the defense of their self-interest. . . . They were bad times. I described what I had been through, what I had seen, some of the stories of people I had met, and I said to Edge: "Could you put that through your amplifier?" (U2 and McCormick, *U2 by U2*, 179)

Indeed, Edge could, and he did, filling out the pounding rhythms of Larry's toms and Adam's bass with layers of compressed distortion, an emotional slide guitar influenced by the Mississippi delta blues and dissonant tones that sounded part siren and part wailing child.

Using experiences gleaned from international contexts, as well as the band's own inherent Irishness, *The Joshua Tree* became a poignant commentary on American culture. On the one hand, U2 was sounding like America's loudest cheerleader, while on the other hand, it came across as the voice of an amped-up Old Testament prophet, calling out the sins of a nation. But there were also moments in the band's performances when fans couldn't quite tell if it was praising or critiquing American culture. The brilliant irony was that U2, through thoughtful artistry, was creatively embedding political and social commentary deep within the vehicle of popular music, taking important subjects like the Ethiopian famine and the civil wars of Central America and translating them into the daily vernacular. The resulting album became a symbol of the 1980s, a pop icon for an entire generation of rock 'n' roll fans.

U2's rise to fame in the 1980s wasn't due solely to its interest in America's foreign policy, though that was a huge part of the project. Some listeners, content to take U2's music at face value, simply heard a good set of new rock tunes on *The Joshua Tree*. For many fans, oblivious to the political and social subtext of the music, U2 was merely a welcome addition to the blandness of the 1980s, providing an alternative to synth-layered new wave and guitar-driven speed metal. For others, the desert expanses of the American Southwest weren't just physical places, they were metaphors for the hopelessness many US citizens felt as they scanned the horizon. Anton Corbijn's album artwork perfectly captured the mediocrity of the times with black-and-white desertscapes featuring a lone Joshua tree and moody photos of a disconsolate band. The bold but pensive cover art grabbed fans' attention and tugged at their hearts even before they had a chance to listen to the music.

For many Americans, the setbacks, disappointments, and tragedies of *The Joshua Tree* era were easily observed, part of everyday life: millions of people watched the explosion of the space shuttle Challenger on live TV; the United States bombed Libya in reaction to terrorism; the Iran-Contra scandal raged on the nightly news; stock markets in America and around the world crashed; nuclear armament reached a peak during the Cold War; Chernobyl became the site of the worst nuclear accident the world had ever seen; acts of terrorism, including airline hijackings and several prominent hostage crises, were becoming more common. It was in this climate that the four members of U2 stepped up to fill the role of the shaman—medicine men of sorts—offering healing through sacred and communal participation, facilitated by an intriguing blend of pop and art.

But contrary to the assumptions of some critics, U2 wasn't exclusively concerned with the dark depths of the American conscience. The band also wanted to experiment with music, bringing a freshness to the industry of rock 'n' roll. While developing ideas for *The Joshua Tree* project, Edge stumbled onto some of his most iconic sounds. Evolving along with the technology, his musical sensibilities, combined with his mathematical wit, provided the foundation for an innovative quality on the album. Using a four-track cassette deck, sequencers, and a drum machine, essential tools for musicians in the midst of a flourishing home studio movement, he tested chord structures, shifting time signatures, and syncopated delays. The efforts culminated in a background demo track for "Where the Streets Have No Name," a tune that he imagined would be as bold live as on a record. Musically, "Streets" proved to be a very complex tune, sounding quite strange at first and requiring hours upon hours of rehearsal time. But the band finally mastered the piece and used it as the opening song for the record and the tour, eventually garnering a peak chart position of thirteen in the United States and four in the United Kingdom.

Edge's imagination and inventive spirit resulted in another signature sound as well. "With or Without You" featured the uncanny and ethereal tones of the prototype "Infinite Guitar," an instrument he had built and experimented with on his 1986 solo album, *Captive*. Layered one on top of another, the heavily compressed and sustained notes became a trademark for Edge. Additionally, as Adam tested a pronounced, driving bass line and Larry blended live and electronic drum parts, the song progressed into something beyond the typical verse-chorus structure of standard pop tunes and became a sophisticated yet understated expression of raw, conflicted emotion. Though it sounded odd compared to the average Top 40 hit, "With or Without You" eventually earned U2 its first number-one spot on the charts in the United States and Canada, turning into a staple of live performances and a fan favorite for decades.

Several videos also accompanied and lent support to *The Joshua Tree*, each of which was nominated for multiple MTV Video Music Awards (VMAs). "With or Without You" presented an artsy and brooding U2, featuring provocative close-ups of Edge's girlfriend interspersed between grainy black-and-white clips of the band performing. Nominated for an astounding seven categories at the VMAs, the song won "Viewer's Choice," signaling its wildly popular reception by U2 fans in 1987. The music video for "I Still Haven't Found What I'm Looking For," a bluesy, gospel-styled spiritual, was filmed on the Strip in Las Vegas. In it, band members wandered through the decadent nightlife of Sin City as Bono sang, "You broke the bonds and you loosed the chains / Carried the cross of my shame." The overt biblical imagery of angels, a devil, and the "kingdom come" sat in stark contrast to the prurient casino culture of Elvis Presley and Frank Sinatra. The quirky formula, however, worked, winning four MTV awards in 1988. "Where the Streets Have No Name" also had a city for its backdrop. Filmed on the roof of a liquor store in downtown Los Angeles, the video was part of an unannounced free concert, a stunt that shut down an area of the civic center and brought police into real-time confrontation with the band, providing footage that ended up as part of the final production. But though fans loved the freshness and spontaneity of the video, it failed to win any of the categories for which it was nominated. Overall, *The Joshua Tree* provided U2 with an opportunity to move boldly into the rapidly expanding and increasingly influential world of music videos, putting the group front and center with MTV's young audience.

The band also made new strides on its tour for *The Joshua Tree*. Starting in arenas and ending in stadiums, venues routinely sold out through three legs across North America and Europe, making it very hard for fans to find tickets. On April 30, 1987, U2 stepped onstage in Detroit as the headlining act in a stadium, a first for the group on a US tour, playing to over fifty thousand people. The show, though successful, also raised a new dilemma for the band and crew, causing them to ask about the place and purpose of video screens in large venues. Would a screen help people at the back of the stadium see and experience the band better? Or would it divide the audience's attention, causing concertgoers to focus on an image rather than the real thing? A difficult challenge, this became a core issue that U2 would revisit on every successive tour, always speculating about the relevance of state-of-the-art technology. The question at hand, however, was answered on September 20 at Robert F. Kennedy Stadium in Washington, DC, when a video screen was installed, the first step in U2's new interest in visual production. And while Willie Williams, the band's longtime stage designer, considered the implications of video projection, he was also responsible for illuminating the stage and the stadium. True to form, U2 wasn't just interested in lighting the show but also wanted to feature and highlight the audience at key moments during the concert. On *The Joshua Tree* tour, Williams and his team installed massive lighting rigs that would periodically flood the entire coliseum. On select nights, U2 would start its show with all of the house lights on as it played the first couple of songs. This practice of lighting the audience was another precedent-setting technique that found a home on all future tours.

U2 also sought to bring a bit of levity to at least three of its stadium shows on the tour. Demonstrating their love for irony, on November 1, 1987, at the Hoosier Dome in Indianapolis, the four members of U2 disguised themselves as a country western band—complete with clothes, wigs, and twangy accents—then took the stage and sang two songs as the Dalton Brothers, essentially becoming an opening act for themselves. (Adding an additional layer of irony, Adam donned a skirt and appeared as a Dalton sister!) Unable to recognize Bono through his thick drawl, a common accent in the southern states of America, fans dismissed the young unknowns as novice and uninteresting, not realizing they were turning their backs on the very band they had come to see. In the end, the harmless prank worked, and U2 discovered the powerful potential of having an alter ego. The Daltons only made two more appearances, in Los Angeles on November 18 and in Hampton, Virginia, on December 12, but this wouldn't be the last time that U2 used misdirection and trickery to intentionally portray something it was not. In the 1990s, U2 employed even greater irony, building shows around multiple alter egos in an effort to convey themes the band really cared about.

In 1987 and 1988, U2 became the hottest ticket on the planet, offering a perfect combination of polished studio production and skillful yet passionate stage shows. Working day and night, the band pursued a relentless schedule of recording and touring, along with media performances and various philanthropic appearances. The hard work eventually paid off, earning *The Joshua Tree* a number-one position in nine countries, selling over ten million albums in the United States, totaling more than twenty-five million worldwide, and winning two Grammy Awards, including Album of the Year and Best Performance by a Duo or Group in 1988. During production, the band continued developing the creative process and deepened its commitment to global justice, simultaneously offering both praise and critique of American culture. U2 learned how to mix playfulness into its sometimes somber set lists and how to nuance its image in the growing eye of the public. No longer merely capable musicians with a moral conscience, the members of U2 were now superstars. But while the band enjoyed its newfound fame and fortune, it showed signs of being unsure of how to deal with the pressures of success.

A MISSTEP IN AMERICA

Never content to stand still, U2's next project continued building on the American experience by offering an album in combination with another video production. *Rattle and Hum*, U2's 1988 follow-up to *The Joshua Tree*, became an experiment for the band in two ways. First, the album featured live versions of its standard hits as well as covers of the Beatles' "Helter Skelter" and Bob Dylan's "All Along the Watchtower," but it also included several new studio recordings. Defying the traditional notion that a rock band should immediately release a live album after a popular record, the group added original content, knowing it had to do more than just capitalize on previous successes. Second, while U2 had earlier dealt with social and political themes from the American context, on *Rattle and Hum* the band set out to be less controversial, choosing the American music scene as its subject of interest. On this record and companion film, U2 sought to venerate the folk, blues, gospel, and early rock 'n' roll of the United States by honoring some of its icons, including Jimi Hendrix, Elvis Presley, Billie Holiday, and B. B. King. But the concept backfired. Critics thought U2 was taking its superstar status a bit too seriously, calling the band pretentious, supposing that the members of U2 were comparing themselves to and aligning themselves with the musical geniuses of America's past. Panned as arrogant and bloated, U2 appeared shallow and superficial to many.

Produced by Jimmy Iovine, the album had intended to capture some of the most symbolic musical expressions of the American experience. The theatrical feature-length documentary, produced by Phil Joanou, showed the band recording at the historic Sun Studio in Memphis, singing with a black gospel choir in a church, strolling down the sidewalks of Harlem, and stopping traffic during an impromptu concert in San Francisco. The ambitious audio/video project featured live performances with Dylan and King and included a prerecorded clip of Hendrix's "Star-Spangled Banner." Using black-and-white footage filmed at a sports arena in Denver, along with color material taken from a stadium in Tempe, Arizona, the documentary added candid shots of the band, including a reverent yet slightly disjointed visit to Elvis Presley's Graceland. A daring musical and cinematic endeavor, *Rattle and Hum* presented a seemingly overconfident and somewhat cheeky U2 in America.

Though some accused U2 of getting lost inside its own celebrity, it did not forget its commitment to the theme of peace and justice. "Silver and Gold," a song featured on both the *Rattle and Hum* record and film, demonstrated U2's ongoing commitment to peacemaking. A commentary on South Africa's system of racial segregation called "apartheid," the song is a perfect intersection of politics, American foreign policy, African culture, and activism.

As U2 was ascending the ladder of superstardom in the 1980s, most countries in Africa were reeling from the effects of World War II colonialism and the Cold War. In the midst of gaining independence from the West, many African nations expressed their anti-imperialist proclivities by accepting Soviet aid, money, and military assistance. In response, the United States looked for its own allies, finding a partner in South Africa, a country considered strategic in the fight against Communism. But as was often the case throughout the Cold War, the US government turned a blind eye to a darker story of human rights abuse.

In South Africa, apartheid was a political system that constrained the civil rights of nonwhite ethnic groups through systematic isolation of the majority black culture. Harsh restrictions imposed by an all-white government forced black people into segregated neighborhoods and stripped them of citizenship and political representation, resulting in inferior education, medical care, and other services. Voices of dissention were not tolerated—those who demonstrated against the South African government were banned or imprisoned. One such antiapartheid leader was Nelson Mandela. As a young visionary in the African National Congress (ANC), Mandela worked as a lawyer, contesting the government-sanctioned system of discrimination. Though committed to nonviolence, he participated in a sabotage campaign against the state in 1961, was arrested, and then sentenced to life in prison. Desmond Tutu, an Anglican bishop of Lesotho in the mid-1970s and later archbishop of Cape Town, also rose to prominence as an outspoken voice of reform. Critical of the United States, Tutu opposed the Reagan administration's passive approach to apartheid and advocated for disinvestment, a strategy meant to financially weaken the South African government via boycotts and reduced trade. Through the activism of Mandela and Tutu, the world began to take notice of South Africa's archaic and unjust system of segregation.

The subsequent call for international sanctions hit the entertainment industry especially hard and had a direct effect on U2. Despite a cultural boycott imposed on the country by the United Nations, many British and American rock groups continued performing at Sun City, a luxurious resort, casino, and concert venue in South Africa. In protest, "Little Steven" Van Zandt, guitar player for Bruce Springsteen, assembled a group of musicians for the 1985 project Artists United against Apartheid. Bono joined the effort, along with other popular performers, to record the album *Sun City* and sang on the title track, "We're rockers and rappers, united and strong / We're here to talk about South Africa, we don't like what's going on . . . I ain't gonna play Sun City." Containing overt criticism of the Reagan administration and implicit condemnation of America's support for the minority government, the album was a success across the globe, heightening awareness of apartheid and raising more than a million dollars for associated projects.

During the recording of *Sun City*, Bono penned another song, one that would eventually find a home on *Rattle and Hum*. "Silver and Gold," a blues-inspired tale about a black prisoner suffering under the boot of the racist government, became an antiapartheid anthem for U2. During the live version that appears on the *Rattle and Hum* film, Bono recalls his inspiration for the song, saying it was the story of a man who was "ready to take up arms against his oppressor, a man who has lost faith in the peace makers of the West while they argue and while they fail to support a man like Bishop Tutu and his request for economic sanctions against South Africa" (*U2: Rattle and Hum*). Restricting the "silver and gold" of the country's lucrative mineral mines and its prosperous economy was meant to be the punch that "hit where it hurts" (*U2: Rattle and Hum*).

Throughout the era of apartheid, U2 often used its expanding platform to inform audiences about the plight of South Africa, the imprisonment of Mandela, and the call for sanctions by Tutu. In 1990, soon after *Rattle and Hum* was issued, an international effort to secure Mandela's release succeeded, and in 1994 the former activist and revolutionary was elected as the country's first black president, marking the end of apartheid. Years later, U2 would honor this antiapartheid visionary, making him the subject of the 2014 Grammy-nominated hit, "Ordinary Love." Throughout their career, the members of U2 have often revisited their two South African heroes, Mandela and Tutu, echoing a commitment to justice and reconciliation while finding new ways to amplify a message of love.

Though the *Rattle and Hum* soundtrack contained important themes and messages, it ultimately left U2 disappointed, selling a little more than half as many copies as *The Joshua Tree*. Accused of becoming the pompous Hollywood personalities they had previously crusaded against, the band bristled at its detractors' claims of grandiose bravado and religious pretentiousness. Still, U2 continued to gain a strong following across the globe, though America—both the place and the idea—was where the band had invested itself most intentionally in the late 1980s. Stung by the criticism, U2 made its way back home to Ireland, unsure of what to do next and certainly unaware of the wild and uninhibited experiment that was coming.

4

IRONY AND THEATRICALITY

In the 1980s, U2 made rapid advancements in musicianship, song writing, and stage presence. Always ready to embrace new ideas and innovative methods, the U2 franchise became a global experience, headed by the best management and production teams of the day, resulting in record-breaking sales. But the growth had not come easy. The band made a risky shift in focus, style, and image with *The Unforgettable Fire*, and increased popularity during *The Joshua Tree* era brought special challenges. By the end of the 1980s, the band members were looking more like sanctimonious celebrities—at least that's the way the critics were imagining them—than artists. And for a group of do-gooders committed to a higher ethic than others in the music industry, the accusations were cutting and discouraging. As the lucrative 1980s came to an end, U2, it seemed, was having a major identity crisis, unsure of the way forward.

Heading into the final decade of the twentieth century, U2 set out to redefine itself, once again charting an unconventional path. In contrast to—but not without regard for—the new winds of global unrest and change, the band members focused inward as they examined the chaos of their own internal demons. Influenced by the fall of Communism in Eastern Europe, the reunification of Germany, and the Bosnian war, U2 used an armory of technology and gimmickry to illustrate and critique the gritty human condition, as well as to explore the depths of the human heart. Concerts supporting the albums *Achtung Baby*, *Zooropa*, and *Pop* became extravagant productions filled with personae that both delighted and baffled fans. Bono put on a mask—in fact, multiple masks—to engage issues by using satire reminiscent of his Lypton Village days. Appearing less committed to global and social activism, the band's cultural influence continued to be compelling, though often veiled in irony. Tackling the taboo subjects of sexual identity, failed relationships, ego, greed, and more, U2 in the 1990s set out to examine its own soul and invited the world to join the epic, larger-than-life journey.

DREAMING IT ALL UP AGAIN

As the calendar turned from one decade to another, the world was an anxious place. U2 was equally unsettled. Still reeling from the harsh reviews of critics, the band took the stage at Dublin's Point Depot at midnight, December 31, 1989, ushering in the 1990s with an inspiring blend of church bells, "Auld Lang Syne," and the introduction to "Where the Streets Have No Name." It was a thrilling yet foreboding moment, as U2 said good-bye not just to the previous decade but to a familiar and comfortable way of doing music. During the New Year's bash, Bono hinted at the band's tenuous state, saying, "Well, it's time to go. . . . It seems there's a lot of people out there, [who] would like to see rock 'n' roll get back in its box. It's only entertainment, man. Is it?" (U2, "U2 Live Lovetown Tour—Point Depot Dublin") And only the night before, at the same venue, Bono told the audience, "This is just the end of something for U2. . . . We're throwing a party for ourselves and you. It's no big deal, we have to go away and . . . and just dream it all up again" (U2, "U2 Live Lovetown Tour—30 December 1989"). Ending its Lovetown tour with four more concerts in Rotterdam, the group quietly slipped away into the new decade, neither fans or band members quite sure how or when it would emerge again.

In many ways, U2's situation seemed to mirror—not coincidentally—the anxieties of a larger culture. Governments across the globe were in transition, sometimes for good, sometimes not. As international economies failed, paralleling the uncertainty and angst of the times, technology developed with unprecedented speed, outpacing the dilemmas it created. More than a few nations faltered. Iraq invaded and attempted to annex neighboring Kuwait, only to face the international community's fierce and swift response as a US-led coalition beat back its forces during Operation Desert Storm. In South Africa, newly elected President F. W. de Klerk began dismantling apartheid amid escalating violence, riots, and acts of terrorism, facing increased pressure from local demonstrations as well as world governments. On the other side of the globe, in China, thousands of students occupied Tiananmen Square, lobbying for democracy and freedom, while the government responded with martial law, killing hundreds of protesters. In the Balkans, civil war raged as Slovenia, Croatia, and Macedonia gained their independence from Yugoslavia. A host of other problems plagued America: the ocean tanker *Exxon Valdez* spilled a catastrophic amount of oil on the Alaskan coastline, the arrest and beating of Rodney King resulted in historic riots in Los Angeles, the United States entered a major recession, and scientists discovered a hole in the ozone layer above the North Pole.

But the greatest global shift happened in the Soviet Union, indirectly impacting the next iteration of U2. For seventy years, the Union of Soviet Socialist Republics (abbreviated USSR or Soviet Union) encompassed over eight million square miles, extending from the Arctic Ocean to Afghanistan and from China to Western Europe. Initially formed during Vladimir Lenin's Bolshevik Revolution, its Communist government was solidified under the harsh rule of Joseph Stalin in the mid-1920s. During this era, the Soviet Union became known for its Marxist government, managed economy of collectivism, rapid industrialization, and suppression of dissent. Through largescale confrontations with Adolf Hitler in World War II, conflicts that resulted in enormous casualties and devastating losses for both sides, the Soviet Union experienced an expansionary period, eventually taking control of a portion of Germany. At the end of the war, negotiations with Western forces led to the partitioning of Berlin into four quadrants, one of which fell under the control of the Soviet Union. Soon after, a flood of immigrants began pouring across the border from East to West Berlin. The Soviet response was swift and harsh as it quickly erected a wall around the American, British, and French quarters of the city, effectively isolating West Berlin from the rest of the free world. This "Iron Curtain" prevented emigration, commerce, and diplomacy. Heavily protected by guard towers, the new Berlin Wall had armed soldiers with orders to shoot anyone attempting to cross over. On the east side of the wall, life was harsh, drab, and repressive, offering few luxuries. With citizens living in a constant state of fear, East Berlin was as austere as West Berlin was friendly, warm, and welcoming.

By the mid-1980s, it was apparent that the Soviet Union's Communist ideal was failing. Echoing unrest around the world, many Soviet republics began to revolt, deeply dissatisfied with their Russian overlord. In response, Mikhail Gorbachev, the last leader of the USSR, attempted to overhaul a bleak economy through a series of reform measures called *glasnost* and *perestroika*. Too little too late, the breakup of the Soviet Union began in 1988, as one by one—starting in Eastern Europe—republics overthrew the Communist Party and seceded. By December 1991, the transformation was complete and the USSR had been completely dismantled.

Effects of the Soviet Union's demise were evident in East Berlin. Increasingly dissatisfied, residents of the Soviet-controlled sector began to escape to the West through newly opened routes in Hungary and Czechoslovakia, leaving others in the city to openly protest East Germany's Communist government. By the fall of 1989, demonstrations were common in East Berlin, and in early November as many as half a million people rallied together in protest. On November 9, all crossings were opened, paving the way for unobstructed travel from east to west. Immediately, East Berliners streamed out of the Communist quadrant into the welcoming arms of West Berliners, who offered them flowers and champagne. As both sides danced together on the wall, some people began to chip away at the concrete symbol of repression, eventually demolishing large segments. Broadcast live around the globe, the world looked on in amazement, celebrating vicariously as the wall came down. The reunification of Berlin signaled a new day.

By the time U2 took the stage at Dublin's Point Depot on New Year's Eve of 1989, East and West Germans were being allowed visa-free travel back and forth across the once-impermeable border. On a figurative level, it seemed that the band also needed to cross over into new territory, transcending the boundaries of its iconic image. Whereas most megagroups of the 1980s had trouble reproducing their success, Bono, Edge, Adam, and Larry were tired of parading their hits around in front of audiences and were ready for something new. In search of a creative space, a place that would kindle imagination, U2 rushed to be part of the action in Berlin in October of 1990. Arriving on the same day that German reunification was finalized, the group and its production team set up camp in the renowned Hansa Studios in West Berlin, where they were able to see the infamous wall through a window. Within sight of the Berlin Wall, Hansa is where the trendsetting glam rocker David Bowie found solace from drug addiction and inspiration for his own trilogy of albums, including *Low*, *"Heroes,"* and *Lodger*, all collaborations with Brian Eno and all reflecting the tenuousness of the Cold War and the gloominess of a divided Berlin. Eno persuaded U2 to expect that something similar could happen for them at Hansa and that a spark from the studio would ignite their own creative fire.

For its seventh studio album, titled *Achtung Baby* (a cheeky nod to the German culture in which it was birthed), the band invited some familiar folks back to lend a hand. Along with Eno came Daniel Lanois and Mark "Flood" Ellis for engineering and mixing. Lanois and Eno had produced the innovative *Unforgettable Fire*, and Flood had joined them on *The Joshua Tree*. While Lanois would stay in the studio on a day-to-day basis, Eno came in and out, trying to listen to each new recording with fresh ears, pushing the band beyond its previous work. Eager to move past the pop and Americana feel of *Rattle and Hum*, U2 looked to the cutting-edge methods of this progressive and talented team in search of a new and relevant sound for the 1990s.

Though the move to Hansa was well intended, U2 encountered a number of obstacles as it began production of the new album. The studio itself, a ballroom used by Hitler's forces, was in disrepair, requiring some significant work and a fresh supply of up-to-date equipment and resources. In addition, the winter was brutally cold, a harsh landscape as bleak as East Berlin, a sterile city of monotonous streets and featureless buildings. From Adam's perspective, "[I]t was depressing and intense and dark and gloomy" (U2 and McCormick, *U2 by U2*, 221). But worse still, the malaise of their physical environment seemed to affect the morale of the band members themselves.

Confused and irritated, they struggled to find a common purpose, often arguing and fighting about ideas and musical direction. Edge preferred to move toward a more progressive sound and experimented for the first time with electronic dance beats and hip-hop influences, while Bono worked on lyrics that seemed dark, nebulous, and morose. Larry, however, opted for a more conservative approach, suspicious of and threatened by Edge's experiments with drum machines. He favored, along with Adam, a refinement and adaptation of *The Joshua Tree* sound. Years later, Larry recalled, "It was particularly depressing because of the separation within the band. It felt confrontational. It seemed like I was out of the loop." The atmosphere was so intense that the very existence of U2 appeared to be in jeopardy. Larry continued,

> I thought this might be the end. We had been through tough circumstances before and found our way out, but it was always outside influences that we were fighting against. For the first time ever it felt like the cracks were within. And that was a much more difficult situation to negotiate. (U2 and McCormick, *U2 by U2*, 221)

Expecting to be inspired, the band's move to Hansa Studios in a reunited Berlin had been counterproductive, stressing the members almost to the point of dissolution. Conflicted and exasperated, U2 was nearly out of time, money, and patience, feeling as if there was no way forward. It was the band that needed reunification now.

Fortunately, a moment of inspiration came in a particularly significant jam session. As the band bickered about the style of a song it was working on, Edge began improvising with a completely different chord progression. After a few suggestions from Lanois, Edge quickly shaped a series of phrases that caught the attention of the other three members, and soon Adam and Larry were laying down a rhythm while Bono tested a lyric idea he had been developing. The result was "One," a simple yet evocative ballad about the pain of separation and the hope of reconciliation, themes that the band members were working out in their own lives at the moment of the song's creation. Bono's subdued vocals sounded both tender and tortured as he sang, "We're one, but we're not the same." Not a hippie anthem or a sappy love song as some fans have supposed, the song is the tortured story of a gay son seeking the acceptance of a father. Written in an intentionally ambiguous way, it could also be interpreted as the story of two irreconcilable lovers, of a parishioner ostracized from church, or of the sad history of East and West Berlin. But "One" is not completely tragic. In the last refrain, the listener is reminded, "We get to carry each other," emphasizing that bearing with one another through difficult times is not a burden but a privilege. "One" eventually became a hit, recognized by many critics as the best song U2 ever recorded and by some as one of the all-time greatest compositions of rock 'n' roll, earning the band multiple awards and chart-topping recognition. With "One," U2 had recovered the spirit and fire of its early years, finding the new beginning it so desperately needed.

The writing and recording of "One" demonstrates another key element of the artistic process for U2: the best work doesn't come just when sessions are smooth and harmonious but often through volatile times of discord. Contrary to popular assumptions, conflict itself, when dealt with and addressed, can be a vital component to creativity. Though he himself has often been at odds with fellow band members, Bono is quick to acknowledge the power of disagreement: "[T]he friction of different points of view makes you better. And the thing that'll make you less and less able to realize your potential is a room that's empty of argument. And I would be terrified to be on my own as a solo singer, not to have a band to argue with" (Assayas, *Bono*, 152). Anger and emotion served U2 well as its members debated musical ideas and fought about direction safely within the boundaries of a committed friendship. Bono, Edge, Adam, and Larry, four hot-tempered Irishmen, learned to use disagreement as a useful tool in the creative process.

Moving to Hansa Studios in search of a new sound was, in Larry's words, "the start of the chopping down of *The Joshua Tree*" as well as "the dismantling of U2 as we had known it" (U2 and McCormick, *U2 by U2*, 221). As the band and producers pushed ahead on the project, there was no way of knowing if fans would receive the new, odd-sounding material as well as they had the previous album. Though it's now considered essential to U2's sound, several innovative production techniques debuted on *Achtung Baby*. Gone was the simplicity of Edge's trademark chimes and delays. "Zoo Station," the album's first track, opens with a heavily distorted, nearly atonal effect as Edge slides down the neck of his guitar, grinding away and hinting at the industrial and electronic influences to come throughout the rest of the record. Adam's bass, mixed to take full advantage of innovative and popular subwoofer technology, is less plucky yet provides a fuller tone than had been heard before, and Larry supplemented a live set with the techno beats of drum machines and sequencers, forsaking the reverb-laden toms of the 1980s. Bono's opening lyric, heavily processed with distortion and other electronics, also signaled a new direction: "I'm ready, ready for the laughing gas / I'm ready, I'm ready for what's next." Together with other sound effects and production innovations from Flood, Eno, and Lanois, "Zoo Station" set new industry standards for rock 'n' roll.

Achtung Baby demonstrated other new sounds as well. Bono's vocals are often doubled, with the melody being sung in two separate octaves. Throaty, airy, and passionate, Bono also began to feature his softer falsetto, singing the whole chorus of "The Fly" in his upper range. Edge continued to experiment with the guitar, building on the grittiness of "Bullet the Blue Sky" by incorporating more distortion, dissonance, and feedback. In "Love Is Blindness," he channeled the pain and emotion of a failing marriage into an extended riff, tapping out notes with a pained and mournful-like quality, paying little attention to the meter and structure of the song. Lyrically, the album is less concerned with political conflicts, focusing more precisely on broken relationships, personal struggles, hypocrisy, infidelity, and primal desires. Once again, the song "One" serves as an example. For the cover of the single's release, the band chose a photograph by David Wojnarowicz, a gay artist who had died of AIDS. Wojnarowicz's image displayed a herd of buffalo plummeting off a cliff, symbolizing the hidden forces that push humanity into unpredictable places of despair. The serious nature of the content matches well the darkness of the production. Whether applied to two cities, a pair of lovers, or the dueling sides of a conflicted self, this less pretentious version of U2 whispered right into the souls of its fans rather than shouting at them through a bullhorn.

The packaging of *Achtung Baby* also represented a significant departure from U2's previous image. Conceived and designed by longtime collaborator Steve Averill, the artwork and related material were set in stark contrast to prior albums. Whereas *The Joshua Tree* featured Anton Corbijn's black-and-white photographs of a serious and subdued band, the new album cover featured sixteen brightly colored vignettes of the band members and related scenes in a carnivalesque fashion, laid out in a four-by-four grid. With the feel of an eccentric family photo album, the pictures included symbols of Communism, fashion, and sexuality, as well as the silhouette of a nude Adam Clayton. Though some were more abstract than others, the photos scattered throughout the album represented a study in contrasts, seen most clearly in a picture of a Trabant, the unostentatious, commonly derided, and mass-produced East German automobile, which was painted in a flamboyant patchwork of colors for *Achtung Baby*. The album was also trendsetting because it was one of the first to use the cardboard Digipak, an environmentally friendly packaging that eliminated much of the plastic jewel case. As a whole, whether purchased on a cassette, CD, or vinyl record, the visual design of *Achtung Baby* was groundbreaking.

The entire *Achtung Baby* project was wildly successful due to rich collaborations, creative production, and a fresh spirit reminiscent of a more playfully adolescent U2. Peaking at number one in the United States and number two in the United Kingdom, the album produced multiple hits. "Mysterious Ways," "Even Better than the Real Thing," and "Who's Gonna Ride Your Wild Horses" all broke into the Top 40 in Britain and America. And although "The Fly" hit number one in Ireland, Australia, and the UK, it only advanced to sixty-one in the United States. One more release, "Until the End of the World," failed to chart but became a fan favorite. Including "One," U2 released six singles from *Achtung Baby*, receiving more international acclamation than it had for *The Joshua Tree*.

Adding to the success of the album was a compilation of music videos featuring the work of famous directors such as Corbijn, Kevin Godley, Stéphane Sednaoui, Mark Pellington, and Phil Joanou. Especially notable was Godley's video for "Even Better than the Real Thing," winning MTV's Best Group and Best Special Effects awards in 1992. Eventually selling twelve million copies worldwide, with eight million alone in the United States, *Achtung Baby* received broad critical acclaim and continues to represent one of U2's finest and most creative records. The grand gamble for a new direction, it seems, had worked.

THE DREAM COMES ALIVE

As U2 painted rich and colorful pictures of a fresh Europe through the music and art of its new album, the franchise also set out to revolutionize the touring industry. In support of *Achtung Baby*, in 1992 the band embarked on a worldwide tour that redefined the live concert experience. Emulating the innovation and irony of its hit record, U2 constructed a colossal production, combining state-of-the-art staging, multiple personae, and choreographed theatrics of a scale never seen before at a rock concert. At the core of the show was an elaborate multimedia presentation, designed around massive screens that simulated an oversaturated TV and media experience. Shirking the religious and political zeal of *The Joshua Tree* tour, Zoo TV, as the tour came to be known, was more satire than rant. As fans were never quite sure if U2 was serious—either about its content or about its own self-deprecation—they cheered for the sensational video clips, satellite linkups, prank calls, and general sensory overload. With dozens of large screens filling the stage, it felt like all the pictures on the *Achtung Baby* album cover came alive at once, creating a hyperexaggerated and heavily satirical event.

Blurring the lines between news, entertainment, sports, religious programming, and the home shopping phenomenon, U2 used a barrage of live and prerecorded video to illustrate and anticipate the complexities of broadcast technology in a decade that witnessed an explosion of media outlets and resources. At the time, hundreds of television channels were offered through multiple companies via a four-to-six-foot-wide satellite dish, an increasingly common sight in residential yards by the early 1990s. The Internet also became popular as modems improved, bandwidth increased, and high-speed options were made available. Services like America Online and CompuServe became popular for accessing e-mail, news, forum discussion groups, and other Internet features. During the Persian Gulf War, satellites linked news agencies with their reporters for real-time coverage of the first heavily televised war. As cell phones, computers, and other digital devices became more prevalent, it felt as though the globe was shrinking, and U2 was there to chart out the ironies, instructing its audience in satire-laden messages such as "Watch More TV."

Though U2's focus on media at once conveyed both the band's fascination with and apprehension of the new technologies, Zoo TV featured three specific characters that further illustrated the precarious state of an oversaturated media culture. First, Bono created an alter ego called "the Fly" while writing the song of the same name. Accused of being ostentatious and egocentric by critics, the lead singer crafted a character that accentuated the allegations to the point of absurdity. Peering through oversized sunglasses, clad in leather pants and jacket, the Fly spewed aphorisms as ambitious as the show itself. Bono's inspiration for the character, at least in part, came from C. S. Lewis's *The Screwtape Letters*, in which a head demon, Screwtape, mentors a younger disciple, Wormwood. The senior demon's task was to teach his fledgling apprentice how to distort the truth in slight, almost imperceptible ways, allowing for the greatest chance of success against the enemy (in this case, God). Screwtape instructed, "Everything has to be twisted before it's any use to us" (Lewis, *Screwtape Letters*, 118). Picking up on Lewis's brilliant satire, Bono sang as if he were placing a phone call from hell, during which he would spin the secrets of his malevolent trade. Interspersed with half-truths and partial lies, the Fly quipped, "They say a secret is something you tell one other person, so I'm telling you, child," as gigantic screens flashed a hypnotic stream of messages, including, "Everything you know is wrong" and "Reject your weakness." In one case, the quickly streaming message that read "It's your world you can change it" morphed into one a bit more cynical of a consumerist culture: "It's your world you can charge it." During "Mysterious Ways," the pompous and eccentric lead singer serenaded a belly dancer, ebbing and flowing with the rhythm of the dance, reaching out and then retreating but never quite able to touch the object of his desire. Maniacal and deceptive, the Fly wore the clothes and the attitude of an overbearing rock star, a guilty pleasure that fans wanted to believe but knew they shouldn't.

Bono's second persona, Mirror Ball Man, was a flamboyant character dressed in a shining silver suit with sparkling shoes and a hat to match. A combination of car salesman and greedy televangelist, this slick showman with a heavy southern drawl trumpeted a type of prosperity gospel. A parody of self-made success, Mirror Ball Man loved to gaze at his own reflection as much as he loved to be the object of other people's affections. Consumed with a sense of self-importance, he would prank call the White House, asking for the president, often bemused and confounded as to why his call wouldn't be received. It was great fun for the audience but also felt a bit tragic, as if Mirror Ball Man was unaware of being both the setup and the punch line of a joke he had never heard.

Bono's third character was MacPhisto. This character came into existence after the release of *Zooropa* in 1993, an album that was recorded mid-tour and was itself inspired by the hypermedia culture of Zoo TV. MacPhisto was a greasy-haired, red-horned, decrepit, has-been rock star, representing the logical result of living too long as the Fly and Mirror Ball Man. Dressed in a gold suit with matching platform shoes and dripping with irony and sarcasm, this persona would offer audiences all they ever wanted, nightly showering concertgoers with fake money during the satirical "Daddy's Gonna Pay for Your Crashed Car" then espousing the "virtues" of self-gratification, media saturation, and overindulgence. Though clearly suffering the effects of his devilish alter ego run amok, MacPhisto taunted his naive followers with quasimotivational messages such as, "People of the former Soviet Union, I've given you capitalism, so now you can all dream of being as wealthy and glamorous as me" (U2: Zoo TV Live). The not-so-subtle subtext of all of this was be careful of what you wish for, because it may be your undoing. The washed-up and washed-out demon, obviously reeling from many regrets, ended the concert singing "Love Is Blindness," a haunting tune that was both love song and lament. As MacPhisto exited the stage, the fantastic, media-saturated experience came to a full-circle completion. Just two hours earlier, near the opening of the show, the Fly had sweet-talked the audience, snuggling up to each concertgoer and whispering into every ear, "They say a secret is something you tell one other person, so I'm telling you, child." But the disingenuous MacPhisto concluded the show with far less confidence, conviction, and intimacy, confessing the depths of his failed ideology, singing, "Love is drowning in a deep well, all the secrets and no one to tell."

In many ways, Bono's interest in alter egos was an extension of the theatrics he had explored in the mid-1970s. Along with his friends—Gavin Friday, Guggi, Strongman, Guck Pants Delany, Dave-iD, Dik, and others—Lypton Village became a private universe for a set of adolescent boys who longed to escape the banality and violence of Dublin's failed efforts in population relocation and social management. A sanctuary for misfits and outsiders, the Village was a surreal, secretive world, that formed around the use of art, music, and literature as a way of coping with the general bleakness of the day. It was there that Bono and his mates rechristened each other with new names, developed their own language, and began experimenting with acting, improvisation, performance art, and the integration of audio and visual modalities. The boys used irony and humor to defeat the crisis of apathy so prevalent in Dublin's conservative status quo. Theater, along with music performance, allowed for creative expression and gave a voice to the otherwise silent malcontents. As a consequence, Lypton Village gave birth to an incredible cadre of creative artists, including U2 and the slightly lesser known Virgin Prunes, an avant-garde band that staged mad, chaotic costumed musical performances. Later on, during *The Joshua Tree* tour, U2 would experiment again with disguises and alter egos by dressing as a country western family act and actually opening incognito for its own concert. These experiences germinated and gave birth to a full-scale integration of satirical theater in the 1990s but also laid the foundation for other characters Bono would play in concerts throughout the coming decades.

While Bono was acting out the vices of celebrity in grand theatrical fashion from the stage, one of U2's members seemed precariously close to being overcome by his own real-life demons. As the most eccentric person in the group, Adam had always seemed to enjoy the playboy lifestyle of a rock star. In 1989, he was busted in Dublin for possessing a small amount of marijuana but resolved the minor offense and kept the arrest off of his permanent record by making a charitable contribution, a provision allowed for by the court. Though it's the only time any member of U2 has ever been arrested, Adam's troubles with substance abuse did not end there. On November 26, 1993, his flamboyant lifestyle caught up with him—Adam was so hungover from an alcoholic binge that he couldn't play the concert in Sydney that night. The situation was exacerbated because this show was supposed to be a dress rehearsal for a live global broadcast of Zoo TV the next night. Fortunately, bass guitar technician Stuart Morgan was there to capably step in at the last minute. Adam was back onstage for the broadcast, but soon after realized the depth of his problem: "It was a moment where I had to face a lot of things I hadn't really been facing and realize if I was going to be able to go on and be a useful member of this band—and indeed a husband—I had to beat alcohol. . . . So I'm kind of glad I finally had to confront it" (Flanagan, *U2: At the End of the World*, 443). Having survived a debilitating personal vice, Adam—in true U2 fashion—turned the defeat on its head and emerged stronger, with greater confidence and personal conviction, as a new man.

The Zoo TV tour, like *Achtung Baby*, was a calculated risk. Unsure of whether fans would grasp the dual layers of entertainment and irony, U2 nonetheless committed vast amounts of money and resources to the project. The creative team responsible for the new concert format included artists, technicians, and longtime collaborators with the band. Brian Eno had suggested that a stage full of chaotic, simultaneous videos would be the perfect concept for the new album. Willie

Williams, who had helped with cutting-edge projection on David Bowie's Sound+Vision tour in 1990 and had been U2's lighting designer since the *War* tour, brought considerable expertise and ingenuity to the team. For other input, U2 turned to Catherine Owens, an Irish artist with extensive work in sculpture, paint, video, sound, and photography, and Mark Fisher, a stage architect who had previously worked with Pink Floyd and the Rolling Stones. Along with the band and manager Paul McGuinness, the team began dreaming up the ostentatious stage show nine months before the first concert. It was a bold and formidable task.

Part of Zoo TV's uniqueness lay in the extravagant technical setup it used. Owens was responsible for turning eleven Trabants—the nondescript, mass-produced car of East Germany—into works of art, painting them with colors and designs that countered the bleakness of Communism. Suspended above the stage, the cars served multiple purposes as props, pop art, and moveable lighting trusses. The amount of technology used was staggering, including a million-watt sound system, nearly a thousand speakers, more than thirty TVs, four video walls, eighteen projectors, and multiple handheld cameras. For the stadium version of the show (the tour started in arenas and then moved outdoors on the third leg in North America), the crew would build a television control studio, employing thirty technicians whose sole responsibility was to run the camera systems, laser disc players, satellite dish, and mixing stations.

Perhaps the most remarkable accomplishment of technology-meets-stagecraft came when U2 conspired to highlight the devastating consequences of the Bosnian War, which raged in Eastern Europe between 1992 and 1995. At the insistence of Bill Carter, an American aid worker and journalist living in Sarajevo, U2 accomplished two things by satellite linking with the bombed-out city during concerts in 1993. First, the band helped bring a sense of urgency to the plight of Sarajevans, calling attention to a prolonged conflict that remained hidden to much of the world. The linkups were extremely costly and difficult, requiring Carter to transport multiple women to a television studio on a nightly basis, risking their lives while driving through "Sniper Alley," a particularly volatile area of the city. Second, highlighting victims of war during a concert that emphasized the extravagance of entertainment media created an absurd moment, brutally jarring the audience with a juxtaposition of contradictory images. An ethical debate ensued as fans and critics discussed the appropriateness of forcing unsolicited scenes of violence and chaos on an unassuming crowd of music enthusiasts, prompting some to accuse U2 of gratuitous sensationalism. The point was valid, illustrated and punctuated by a group of Sarajevan women who chastised one concert audience via satellite, saying, "We don't know what we're doing here. This guy dragged us in. You're all having a good time. We're not having a good time. What are you going to do for us?" When Bono tried to console them, they continued, "We know you're not going to do anything for us. You're going to go back to a rock show. You're going to forget that we even exist. And we're all going to die" (U2 and McCormick, *U2 by U2*, 253). It was an intense and awkward incident, leading Larry to believe that the band might be guilty of exploiting Sarajevans for the sake of entertainment. Many people outside the U2 franchise felt the same.

Though U2's antics on the stage helped to support the music and the message of *Achtung Baby*, it was the band's retreat to Berlin amid the political upheaval of Eastern Europe that inspired its own reunification and renewal. In the end, the determination of Edge, Adam, Larry, and Bono resulted in far-reaching innovations in music production, technology, staging, and concert theatrics. U2 also learned that collaboration with other creative artists and technicians was essential to the creative process, enhancing the ability to be imaginative and pioneering. Surrounded by a team of resourceful people, the band accomplished what it had set out to do, dreaming it all up again.

DREAMING OUT LOUD AGAIN, AND THEN AGAIN

While *Achtung Baby* became the means for U2's rebirth, two other albums also helped further refine the group's image in the 1990s. *Zooropa*, an unconventional, futuristic romp in experimental music, was released during the middle of the Zoo TV tour, and *Pop*, a brazen exploration of consumerism and materialism, rounded out the decade. Each project presented the band with new challenges, but each also brought fresh rewards.

Released in 1993, *Zooropa*, U2's eighth studio album, has a unique origin, actually born out of the Zoo TV tour. A further experimentation with electronic, dance, and rock music, the album expanded *Achtung Baby*'s use of techno beats and sound effects, creating a postapocalyptic musical landscape—a kind of dystopian projection of media's future. Once again nuanced with irony and satire, *Zooropa* presented a serious investigation of technology and modernity set to industrial beats and party music. Through *Zooropa*, U2 seemed to be echoing the messages of two prominent mid-twentieth-century philosophers. First, Marshall McLuhan, an influential communication theorist in the 1960s and 1970s, had popularized the expression "the medium is the message" and accurately predicted a "global village" that would one day be linked by electronic and visual media. In this sense, U2, through its Zoo TV tour, appeared to be crafting a quintessential McLuhanesque experience, mixing live video feeds from across the globe with other forms of media-driven art and using the medium to critique the medium, fully aware that it was also being consumed by the medium.

Sociologist Jacques Ellul, a second influential author of the post–World War II period, published *The Technological Society*, in which he argued that technology has become the new god, replacing process, risk, and ambiguity with technique and efficiency. The song "Zooropa" laments a world that no longer values mystery and doubt, as Bono counsels the song's female protagonist, "Don't worry, baby / It's gonna be alright / Uncertainty can be a guiding light." Another important book by Ellul, *Propaganda*, addressed how popular media can be a powerful tool for controlling individuals through larger social forces. Either by intention or chance, U2's official fan club magazine from 1986 to 2000 was called *Propaganda*, as both an obvious parody of the band's perception of its own influence on fandom and as an attempt to literally distribute information to its fans. Both McLuhan and Ellul boldly prophesied that extensive use of mass media technologies would quietly and unwittingly change the users of technology. In U2, the presentation and performance of the music became a commentary on the delivery of the music itself, an ironic admission that the very medium of rock 'n' roll could both reflect culture and shape it.

Not inconsequentially, many similar themes show up elsewhere on *Zooropa*. Through a cacophony of sampled background voices, the first words on the album ask, "What do you want?" The answer comes in a series of advertising slogans, such as "Be a winner, eat to get slimmer" and "Fly the friendly skies." Bono finishes "Zooropa," the first song on the record, offering an antidote to cultural banality by giving advice to the tune's female protagonist, singing, "She's gonna dream up the world she wants to live in / She's gonna dream out loud." Self-referencing its own ability to successfully reimagine and shape its destiny, U2 challenged the listener to do the same. In "Numb," an atypical song composed and sung by Edge, the narrator offers a bleak, monotone commentary on the modern condition, concluding in the chorus, "I feel numb, too much is not enough." Continuing the exploration of an industrial apocalypse, "Lemon" contrasts a man who "dreams of leaving" a mechanical wasteland with a woman who personifies ingenuity and creativity. Bono sings of the heroine, "She is the dreamer, she's imagination." On the album's final track, "The Wanderer," Johnny Cash sings on top of heavily synthesized backing tracks as a lonely drifter "under an atomic sky" in a "city without a soul." Dark and foreboding, *Zooropa* uses a wealth of technological gadgetry to offer a commentary on technology itself, ending with two possible outcomes—the quiet acquiescence of the wanderer or the stubborn resilience of a hope-filled dreamer.

As with *Achtung Baby*, the message of *Zooropa* struck a chord with fans, whether they fully grasped the layered meanings or not. Charting at number one in more than a dozen countries, including America, the album sold seven million copies and was an international success. Though it was well received by fans and critics, earning it a Grammy Award in 1994 for Best Alternative Music Album, the decidedly European feel, heavily influenced by Eno and Flood, didn't carry as well as previous albums in the United States, where none of its four singles entered the Top 40. While some in the U2 organization thought the album was rushed, and thus flawed, it was still, in Bono's words, "A wonderful, wild, fling of an album" and "grand madness" (Bono, "*Rolling Stone* Interview").

With *Pop*, U2's ninth studio album, the band continued its image of eccentricity. Winding out a set of three records in the 1990s, producers Flood and Howie B led the recording project, extending the use of techno, dance, and electronic music and incorporating new sampling, looping, and sequencing technologies. *Pop*'s investigation of pop culture and consumerism represents a culmination of the thematic inquiry U2 undertook through the 1990s, starting with a brooding look at personal demons on *Achtung Baby* and being refined on *Zooropa* into an

examination of the effects of technology and media on the human condition. Using the medium of satire, each album critiques Western culture while asking how to be fully human in a fragmented world. Continuing to distance themselves from their do-gooder image of the 1980s,
the members of U2 completely embraced celebrity, exaggerating their
own rock star status through extravagant personae and lavish displays of
pop art.

The *Pop* recording sessions included multiple collaborators for production, engineering, and mixing, as U2 tried to broaden its own knowl-
edge of a somewhat new genre. Heavily influenced by Howie B's expertise in electronica music, the band spent time hanging out in dance
clubs, experiencing the music firsthand. To its detriment, U2 and crew
faced an unnerving set of pressures in the studio, causing them to
struggle with the album's production. First, Larry had to have surgery
on a debilitating back injury, forcing him to miss a significant amount of
recording time while recovering. A second issue arose when Larry re-
joined the band in the studio and had to spend an extensive amount of
time rerecording drum parts that had been written and sampled in his
absence. In a similar way, the whole band labored to reproduce Howie
B and Flood's complex samples and loops. The third and most significant problem emerged when Paul McGuinness booked the supporting
tour without the album being completed. Initially, the band gave its
approval and didn't consider it an issue. But as the team struggled with
complicated production and engineering tasks, deadlines were missed
and the album's release was delayed by months, putting the band precariously close to the start of the new tour. In the end, production had
to be rushed, resulting in what the band, as well as many critics, believed was an unfinished product.

In spite of the group's missteps in the studio, U2's PopMart tour,
launched in the spring of 1997, rivaled Zoo TV's expansive production
and complex stage. Extravagant and excessive, the tour included a 165-
foot-wide state-of-the-art LED screen, a 100-foot-tall golden arch that
parodied the famous McDonald's logo, and a huge, gaudy mirror-coat-
ed lemon, big enough to hold the entire band, a prop that looked more
like a space ship than a piece of fruit. Driven by designers Willie
Williams, Catherine Owens, and Mark Fisher, the show featured the
largest video screen ever to have been built at that time. The 150,000-
pixel screen became the backdrop for a stage that took its inspiration

from a supermarket. Reinforcing the theme of decadent consumerism were images of the evolution of a monkey transitioning to an upright human, who then walked as a shopper pushing a cart. The screen was also used to display colorful and kitschy pictures of the band members in a style reminiscent of pop art created by Roy Lichtenstein and Andy Warhol. Mimicking the art-imitates-life quality of pop culture, U2 even announced its tour, appropriately, at a news conference from the lingerie department in a New York City Kmart. And though some would again accuse the band of selling out, U2 considered its embrace of pop culture as the best defense against it.

One of the tour's most significant moments involved a promise that Bono had impulsively made during a Zoo TV concert in 1993. Holding to its word, in 1997 U2 took its entire production to Sarajevo, the Bosnian capital that had been held captive for nearly four years by Serbian forces. A highly anticipated event that came at great financial loss to the franchise, U2 was the first major act to perform in the devastated city. Broadcast live throughout Bosnia and around the world, emotions were high as forty-five thousand people, many of whom had been on opposite sides of the war, filled the stadium. At the last minute, ten thousand more were allowed in even though they hadn't purchased tickets, while thousands of soldiers and peacekeeping forces looked on for any sign of trouble. A spectacular success, the evening transcended all expectations of a normal concert, becoming a de facto celebration of the end of the siege of Sarajevo. Though it took four years to do so, the band and crew had kept its promise. As they headed out of the area, humbled and changed, they realized it was one of the most moving and meaningful events of their career.

Though the PopMart tour was immensely popular, even setting a record for the most attended concert ever, *Pop* itself was one of the least commercially successful albums in U2's catalog. Initially well received by fans and critics, it reached the number one position in the United States but lacked the staying power of previous records, only selling a million copies. Despite its relative obscurity, many hardcore fans revere *Pop* as a U2 classic, an innovative and imaginative convergence of pop culture and art.

The members of U2 engaged in several other lesser known projects in the 1990s as well—specifically, they made a foray into movie soundtracks. Earlier, in 1986, Edge released *Captive*, a solo album written for a film by the same name. Notable for Edge's use of the infinite guitar—the instrument that two years later gave the hit single "With or Without You" its signature sound—and for being the only solo project from any member of U2, *Captive* also included one track featuring Larry on drums and vocals by a young, up-and-coming Irish artist named Sinead O'Connor. In 1995, however, the entire band contributed to the soundtrack for the movie *Batman Forever* with "Hold Me, Thrill Me, Kiss Me, Kill Me." The tune was played regularly on the PopMart tour, received strong airplay on the radio, and was accompanied by an animated music video that featured both the Fly and MacPhisto. With a story line about a pretentious star in a rock band, "Hold Me" not only served as a dark and foreboding interpretation of the enigmatic Batman character, it also provided a summative commentary on U2's entire Zoo TV experiment.

That same year, Bono and Edge collaborated to create the theme for the latest James Bond movie, *GoldenEye*. Written specifically for Tina Turner, the song was a hit internationally and helped introduce Pierce Brosnan as the new Bond, as well as reenergize the aging series. In a similar way, Larry and Adam teamed up to write and perform the title track for the 1996 blockbuster film *Mission: Impossible*. Inspired by the theme from the original TV series, this updated electronic version gained global attention, became a Top 10 hit, and set a contemporary, youthful tone for the Tom Cruise movie reboot. Whether as a band or individuals on separate ventures, U2 continued to engage and shape pop culture in the 1990s through work with film soundtracks and also laid a foundation for related projects in the new millennium.

Fleeing its pious image of *The Joshua Tree* era, U2 had reinvented itself at the tail end of the twentieth century. Both the content and the musical style of *Achtung Baby*, *Zooropa*, and *Pop*, along with the accompanying tours, exhibited an artsy and introspective band that delivered its message through satire and theatrics. While U2 in the 1980s had been consumed with global justice and conflicts in distant places such as El Salvador and South Africa, the U2 of the 1990s focused on the inner demons of greed, lust, addiction, and hypocrisy. Bono's lyrics became self-deprecating and confessional, giving voice to his own internal struggles in the first person as he donned several alter egos reminiscent of his much earlier experience in Lypton Village. Edge's guitar parts changed, too, moving from his trademark chiming rhythms to impassioned lead lines processed through heavily distorted effects. In-fluenced by European electronica, Larry and Adam laid down driving beats that were built from sequenced patterns, pushing the band into places in which it wasn't always comfortable. In the end, the trilogy of albums demonstrated U2's fascination with pop culture and marked a visionary—and expansionary—period in rock 'n' roll history.

5

RAGE CAN ONLY TAKE YOU SO FAR

The first decade of the twenty-first century revealed, yet again, a redefined U2. Forsaking the artsy introspection of previous albums, the band stripped music and stage performances down to the basics. Now as mature and seasoned artists, U2 attempted to reengage its fan base with intimacy and authenticity. Concerts became community gatherings as U2 focused primarily on smaller arenas (compared to the huge outdoor stadiums of the previous tours), redesigned the stage for maximum contact with fans, and used new technologies to give audiences a global view. In a post-9/11 world, fans would often say that going to a concert was like entering a sanctuary, and U2 was their priest.

Aware of missteps in the 1990s, the U2 franchise applied what it had learned, even as it faced new challenges. Though it had abandoned the high-tech experimental sounds of the previous decade, production efforts in the studio, as well as supporting album tours, continued to be innovative yet not excessive. The band's flirtation with new media grew through a partnership with Apple, resulting in pioneering ways to market music and advance both the Apple and U2 brands. The outcome was a triumphantly successful duo of albums, *All That You Can't Leave Behind* and *How to Dismantle an Atomic Bomb*. Apart from recording, however, U2 faced a growing conflict as Bono's avid interest in philanthropy often interrupted productivity and delayed the release of albums, leaving the other bandmates concerned about the front man's perceived lack of commitment to the group. Still, as U2 stepped into the new millennium, its members appeared confident and content in their roles as both middle-aged family men and veteran rock stars, championing a message of love and grace instead of the rage and moody self-reflection of years past.

LEAVING IT BEHIND

The final track on 1997's *Pop*, a dark and sullen lament called "Wake Up Dead Man," was a parting shot to a decade of experimentation. Hinting at what the 2000s might bring, Bono whispered to fans in the song's bridge, "Listen to the words, they'll tell you what to do / Listen over the rhythm that's confusing you." "Listen . . . Listen . . . Listen," the singer repeated in a litany of phrases, even questioning Jesus, "Are you working on something new?" At the end of PopMart, the fanciful art project that made use of a lavish display of pop culture to critique consumerism, U2 once again retreated to the studio in search of a new sound, a fresh spirit, and a replenished soul. Remarkably reminiscent of its departure from the 1980s at Point Depot ("We have to go away and . . . and just dream it all up again"), the band left the 1990s—in Bono's oft-quoted words—with a desire for "going back to scratch, re-applying for the job [of] best band in the world" ("43rd Grammy Awards Highlights").

The very first lyric of *All That You Can't Leave Behind* (2000), U2's tenth studio album, christened the new millennium with a spirit of optimism: "The heart is a bloom, shoots up from the stony ground." The opening instrumentation, including a chiming set of arpeggios cascading from a seemingly forgotten place within Edge's arsenal of guitars, also conveyed a bright and hopeful restart. Even the name of the tune, "Beautiful Day," signaled, yet again, a new beginning for the group. Fans eagerly and joyfully embraced the sentiment, and for many it felt like the old band was back. But U2's new project wasn't just fluff and superficial sentiment. "Beautiful Day" also contrasts the song's initial optimism with the harsh reality of daily life, as Bono sings "there's no room," "you're out of luck," and "you're not moving anywhere." Beautiful lives, U2 counseled, are not trouble-free lives. The whole album, in fact, presents a study in contrasts, simultaneously acknowledging despair ("Stuck in a Moment You Can't Get Out Of"), inspiring joy ("Elevation"), and encouraging endurance ("Walk On").

But it's on "Beautiful Day" that all of these themes converge as an overture to the rest of the album, reinforcing a thesis of love and uniting those who suffer with those who have overcome. The hopeful message of the song clearly resonated with fans around the world, propelling it forward as one of U2's biggest hits ever and earning the group three Grammy Awards in 2001. Adding to its impact and appeal in concert, Bono would shout repeatedly during the song's final instrumental break, "The goal is soul!" To be sure, imagining such a beautiful day in the midst of adversity was a lofty goal worthy of U2's effort and time, a perfect message of grace for the new millennium. As one of the band's most endearing (and enduring) songs, "Beautiful Day" has become a kind of anthem for the twenty-first century and to date has never been omitted from a U2 concert.

The success of "Beautiful Day" didn't happen in isolation but was a response to the larger cultural milieu. As U2 headed into the studio for production of its new album, the world was an increasingly unsettled and unfamiliar place, surpassing a population of six billion. On the international scene, Serbs continued a campaign of ethnic cleansing in Kosovo, Boris Yeltsin resigned as president of a highly destabilized and economically depressed Russia, Pakistan was at war with India, and Osama bin Laden had set up his al-Qaeda base camp in Afghanistan. Acts of terrorism were on the rise, and the bombings of US embassies in Tanzania and Kenya, as well as the USS *Cole* in Yemen, heightened people's awareness of hostile anti-American sentiments. With 150 million people using the Internet across the globe (half of whom lived in the United States), the Y2K bug had people fearing that computers and other electronic devices would fail at midnight on December 31, 1999, potentially plunging the planet back into the Dark Ages. At the same time, religious fundamentalists believed the advent of 2000 would bring an apocalyptic end of the world.

Always aware of and in tune with its global surroundings, U2 teamed up once again with producers Brian Eno and Daniel Lanois—an intentional effort to rekindle the essence and style of earlier albums such as *The Unforgettable Fire* and *The Joshua Tree*, along with a reinvigorated spirit of optimism. Choosing to stay close to home this time, the band retreated in late 1998 to Hanover Quay Studios in Dublin. For this project, the seasoned foursome wasn't interested in far-off exotic production facilities as when recording *Achtung Baby*, nor was it attracted to the progressive sounds of hip European dance clubs like it had been during the *Zooropa* and *Pop* sessions. This iteration of U2 exuded confidence, security, and contentment in midlife and seemed to find the inspiration it needed in the very place it called home. While in the studio, the band combined the best of its classic sound—less ambiguous vocals, straightforward rhythms, ringing guitars, and singable melodies—with techniques gleaned from experimental work in the 1990s, using electronic effects, ethereal keyboards, and digital drums in a way that nuanced, rather than dominated, the new material. Surrounded by close family and friends, U2 recaptured its core values and produced an album that represented its very soul. Bono reiterated this in an interview, summing up the production saying,

> The idea was, "What is the essence of our band? What do we have to contribute?" For ten years previous, we'd been doing exactly the opposite. We'd been thinking, "What is it we don't have?" and going after it. [On this album] in order to keep it fresh, we say, "What is it we do have?" (Bono, "*Rolling Stone* Interview")

What the members of U2 did have was a generous spirit—not the righteous anger of the 1980s or the biting cynicism of the 1990s, but a graciousness that was more a natural outcome of well-lived lives than a strategy for selling albums. Concerned with casting away nonessential things, *Leave Behind* was like journal entries about the most important things in life—the stuff of family and friends. "Stuck in a Moment You Can't Get Out Of," was written about Bono's good friend Michael Hutchence, the lead singer of the rock band INXS who had committed suicide in 1997. The song functioned as a difficult but necessary conversation between two intimate souls. "Kite," originally composed with his own children in mind, eventually became a statement about Bono's relationship with his cancer-stricken father, who passed away less than a year after the album's release and just a few days before U2's historic concert at Slane Castle in 2001. The closing track on *Leave Behind*, "Grace," was written as a bookend to "Beautiful Day," personifying the essence of life as both a "name for a girl" and a "thought that could change the world."

But the notion of grace really came to the forefront in "Walk On," one of the album's strongest and most popular songs, as U2 championed the plight of Aung San Suu Kyi, a Burmese political dissident.

Sentenced to house arrest in 1989, Suu Kyi was the rightful president of Myanmar, the country known as Burma prior to its takeover by a military junta in 1962. Having received a majority of the vote in a general election, she was never allowed to take office. Despite the hostile and oppressive efforts of Myanmar's corrupt regime, the civil rights leader remained committed to a posture of love and nonviolent resistance, inspiring her own party, the National League of Democracy, to do the same. In 1991, she was awarded the Nobel Peace Prize for her efforts but rejected an offer by the regime to leave and claim her prize in Oslo, knowing she would never be allowed to reenter the country. Likewise, upon the death of her husband in London in 1999, she again rejected an opportunity to leave the country, choosing imprisonment as she stood in solidarity with the Burmese people. U2 learned about Suu Kyi's heroic story while recording the *Leave Behind* album and was so moved that it wrote "Walk On" as a tribute to her spirit of patient compassion. Though specifically about Suu Kyi's courageous and noble opposition to a corrupt junta, fans facing a range of hardships also heard the chorus of "Walk on, walk on" and interpreted it as a call to endure. The song's strong emotional appeal quickly transformed it into a classic, ultimately earning the band another Grammy Award for Record of the Year in 2002, making U2 the first artist ever to win the award two years in a row for two different songs on the same album.

Though "Walk On" told the story of a political dissident suffering under the repressive efforts of a corrupt regime, it also came to play a significant role in American culture at large as the country faced the worst terrorist attack in history. On September 11, 2001, Islamic extremists coordinated a series of four attacks using hijacked commercial airliners. Under the control of nineteen al-Qaeda terrorists, four planes filled with hundreds of people were deliberately crashed into separate targets. Two of the suicide missions targeted the pair of World Trade Center buildings in New York City, resulting in devastating explosions massive enough to bring both of the 110-story towers down. The damage was catastrophic, plunging the borough of Manhattan into chaos and killing 2,606 people. Combined with a third attack on the Pentagon in Virginia and a failed fourth attempt that crashed in a field in Pennsylvania, nearly three thousand lives were lost, resulting in the deadliest attack on American soil since the Japanese bombing of Pearl Harbor in 1941. In New York, life came to an abrupt and shocking halt as residents waited for news of the missing and dead, many of which were never found or identified. In the weeks and months to come, a disfigured skyline reminded people of their loss on a daily basis and prolonged a sense of fatigued disorientation and despair. Through it all, the soul of America had been gravely wounded, and 9/11 became a pivotal moment in global history, ushering in a new age of fear, anxiety, and insecurity.

This was the global stage when U2 took the literal stage at Madison Square Garden, just three miles from the World Trade Center site and six weeks after the attack, as the first major artist to perform in New York City after the tragedy. Though some people felt concerts and other public festivities were inappropriate so soon after the catastrophe, and others thought it might be unsafe for the band, U2 used the occasion to nurture the soul of the city. On the first of three nights in the Garden, images of the Twin Towers appeared on enormous screens during the song "New York," and names of victims, including police and fire personnel, scrolled across while Bono sang a tearful and impassioned version of "One." On the third and final night, fire and emergency workers were brought onstage during a highly charged version of "Walk On," and then stayed to give tributes after the band exited. As the firefighters spoke of their fallen colleagues, the arena wept, traversing a chasm between overwhelming sorrow and celebration of life. After the Manhattan concerts, fans spoke of U2 with great affection, referring to the performances as "healing," "comforting," and "cathartic," a unifying force amid the pain and grief of a city. If, as Bono repeatedly said on the Elevation tour, the "goal is soul," then New York had experienced the full effect of the message, and "Walk On" (released as a single just three weeks after the Madison Square Garden shows) had become a soothing hymn for America. Just a few months later, in February of 2002, U2 reproduced its moving tribute to the victims of 9/11 in front of eighty-six million people at the Super Bowl, delivering its reverent, spiritual, and highly charged memorial to an entire nation. The *San Francisco Chronicle* reported, "U2's live breath of fresh air and dramatic, emotional spectacle that paid homage to the victims of Sept. 11 was both daringly bombastic and also pretty damn cool" ("North American Media Comment"). Both *Rolling Stone* and *Sports Illustrated* eventually called it the best halftime show ever. U2 had once again filled the role of America's priest.

U2's visit to New York City was only one stop on the third leg of a much larger tour that crisscrossed the Atlantic in 2001. Supporting *Leave Behind*, the Elevation tour abandoned the flashy overindulgence of Zoo TV and PopMart, opting instead for a minimalist experience. The tour's intimate staging mirrored the starkness and simplicity of the album, working with neutral color schemes, clean lines, and flowing draperies. Once again, designers Willie Williams, Catherine Owens, and Mark Fisher took the lead, using images, lighting, and scrims to convey warmth and intimacy in arenas across North America and Europe. At one point, graphics were even superimposed on the audience, drawing fans into an all-encompassing artistic experience. During "Walk On," often the concert's closing song, a projection of a suitcase with a heart would scroll up arena walls, filling the dark spaces between stage and ceiling and highlighting the theme of love's eternal and transcendent nature.

One of the tour's most poignant and striking innovations, however, was in the design of the stage. After pioneering the concept of a smaller, separate "B-stage" on the Zoo TV tour (an idea that was first experimented with way back at a Yale University gig in 1983), U2's members continued efforts to find new ways to physically place themselves in the audience, removing as many barriers as possible. On the PopMart tour, U2 had transported itself right into the crowd using a huge lemon-shaped mirror ball, an intentionally gimmicky stunt that brought audience and band closer to one another. For the Elevation tour, Fisher discarded the actual B-stage but took the concept one step further by creating a catwalk that looped from one end of the stage, out into the audience, and then back to the stage again. The shape of this walkway, though not immediately obvious from the floor, could be seen from the upper decks for what it was—a huge heart. It was a beautiful expression, a symbolic representation of U2's own soul being offered in the midst of the arena. With fans on both sides of the ramp—inside and outside the heart—audiences were given unprecedented access to the band, especially while standing on the floor in general admission. Underneath the stage, another "first" was taking place. The band began to include a fifth musician, keyboardist Terry Lawless, giving him the task of filling in the musically subtle spaces so that tunes would sound like they did on the albums while still keeping the freshness and spontaneity of a live performance. Lawless continued to play from the "Under-world" on all subsequent tours.

The opening moment of each Elevation concert set the tone for the evening. As U2 walked out onto the stage to perform the opening song, "Elevation," they did so under the naked, white light of the arena, as if saying to the crowd, "We've come to expose ourselves tonight. No pretense, no persona. We're just here to bear our souls." Continuing on with a theme of love and grace throughout the show, Larry, Edge, Adam, and Bono paraded their own hearts out in front of audiences in an act of solidarity and authenticity.

Though U2's cultural impact in this period rivaled that of *The Joshua Tree*, it didn't come without controversy, especially with regard to the new album's distribution. In the 1990s, the US radio industry saw a dramatic evolution as business models changed. Taking advantage of reduced government regulation, radio stations began to amalgamate services, making it possible for large corporations to own and control multiple elements, including radio stations, concert venues, and tour companies. As a result, artists were encouraged to make deals with promoters in order to have their music played, but these deals included stipulations about where artists could perform, how their music would be distributed, and how much airtime they would receive. The effect was that musicians essentially had to buy their way into a station's rotation. Though completely lawful, the complex negotiations felt more like "payola," the illegal practice of paying or in any way bribing a radio station for airplay, an activity especially common in the 1950s and 1960s in the United States. The consequences were similar, and artists in the new millennium were often forced into stringent deals that seemed both unethical and unfavorable to them.

With the release of *Leave Behind*, U2 faced a critical dilemma: should the franchise play the game and enter into negotiations that would limit rights to its own music in return for radio play? Or would it be better to venture out alone, taking its chances with independent promotion and distribution? It turns out that the band's manager, Paul McGuinness, did a little of both. For "Beautiful Day," U2 capitulated to the industry and paid for promotion—by some accounts paying twice as much as other artists—gaining it considerable radio play and earning it the number–twenty-one spot on *Billboard*'s Top 100. The song also charted in several other US markets and became one of U2's most appealing hits ever. The outcome, however, was entirely different for the band's next single, "Electrical Storm," released in 2002 on *The Best of 1990–2000*. Thinking the momentum of U2's previous success with "Beautiful Day" would carry it forward, McGuinness decided not to "pay for play" during the promotion of the new single. The varying degree of success between the two songs was striking. While "Electrical Storm" reached the number-one spot in Canada and other European countries, it languished in the States, only reaching number seventy-seven on *Billboard*'s Hot 100. In contrast, the *1990–2000* album was itself successful, peaking at number three in the United States, offering further proof that the failure of "Electrical Storm," at least in part, could be traced back to U2's decision against engaging in the practice of paying for airplay on radio stations in America. Trying to take the ethical high ground, its anti-music-industry posture left the band flat and disheartened.

Several other complications delayed the production of *Leave Behind*, as the band members' schedules conflicted with recording. Specifically, Bono's philanthropic work frustrated some of the crew, causing them to wonder if he was more committed to the band or to his humanitarian efforts. It was a busy season for the lead singer, as he increasingly became known as "the Front Man," not just for a rock band but also for multiple campaigns focused on alleviating suffering in sub-Saharan Africa. Deeply committed to the work, Bono endeavored to engage critical global issues of Third World debt relief, preventable disease, and AIDS eradication by studying with influential economists, activists, and investors such as Jeffrey Sachs, Bobby Shriver, and Bill Gates. Not content with the role of a typical celebrity activist—someone with a mild interest in a cause who benefits from charitable tax deductions and an increased public profile—Bono became proficient in foreign policy, international humanitarian efforts, and global fiscal models. Several related projects took him out of the studio. The Jubilee 2000 effort was an international coalition of over forty countries that agreed to cancel Third World debt by the year 2000. That project was also related to and eventually evolved into the British Drop the Debt campaign. Both organizations believed that debt forgiveness of the world's poorest countries is essential to the work of justice and the alleviation of poverty, a motif that became more and more common in U2's music and concerts. Another project involved the Millennium Development Goals, an initiative of the United Nations to eradicate extreme poverty and promote human rights. Bono worked diligently and tirelessly with each of these organizations, exhibiting a passion that a few years later would nearly turn into a second full-time occupation.

An additional recording project also took U2 away from the production of *Leave Behind* and led the band to some unusual artistic connections. *The Million Dollar Hotel*, released in 2000, was a film based on life in a skid-row hotel in downtown Los Angeles and was cowritten by Bono, directed by Wim Wenders, and produced by Mel Gibson. The writing and filming of the movie took considerable effort and time on Bono's part, but it also included the other members of U2, as they contributed several songs to the movie's soundtrack. Most notably, "The Ground beneath Her Feet," an emotive lament about the loss of a lover, was based on a Salman Rushdie novel of the same name. Rushdie and Bono formed a friendship in the Zoo TV days, about the same time the author became a highly controversial figure in the Islamic world for his novel *The Satanic Verses*. The book prompted Iran's Ayatollah Khomeini to issue a death threat against Rushdie, irreversibly altering his life and driving him into seclusion. Later in the 1990s, Rushdie gave Bono a copy of a new story he was working on, which eventually became the inspiration for "The Ground beneath Her Feet." Recorded with Daniel Lanois playing pedal steel guitar, U2 credited Rushdie with the lyrics on the soundtrack for the film, illustrating a unique partnership of author and musicians. The artistic collaborations with Wenders, Gibson, and Rushdie spurred U2 on in its own creativity but, at the same time, also contributed to the delayed release of *Leave Behind*.

To capture the essence of the new album for its cover and packaging, U2 reunited with another innovative artist, Anton Corbijn, the band's longtime photographer. Along with Steve Averill, U2's reliable friend and graphic designer, the team of musicians and artists decided to contrast the garish and colorful schemes of U2's previous three album layouts, with pictures of a subdued, mature-looking band. Shot in the Charles de Gaulle Airport in Paris, the cover of *Leave Behind* shows a single monochrome photograph of the band members standing in a nearly empty terminal, small luggage in hand, waiting. What precisely U2 is lingering for is open to the viewer's interpretation. Is the quartet waiting for the next flight? For a ride? For family members? Whatever the perspective, Corbijn's artwork and Averill's design conveyed a sense of expectation, if not a complete departure from the previous decade. In one understated image, U2 announced to the world it was "packing a suitcase for a place none of us has been" ("Walk On").

As 1999 turned into 2000, U2 was again at the top of its game with a soul-filled album that netted seven Grammy Awards, four hit singles, and several ancillary projects. Now as seasoned artists, Adam, Edge, Larry, and Bono entered their forties strong and confident, the successful contenders of a twenty-plus-year career. Having experienced both the fortune of fame and the stinging disparagement of their critics, these veterans of rock 'n' roll had survived without imploding, neither succumbing to internal conflicts nor buckling to the pressures of the music industry. U2 dared, yet again, to imagine the world not as it was but as it should be, believing that a simple musical idea—grace—could shape and influence culture and appealing to listeners as a type of spiritual guide amid the fear and anxiety of a post-9/11 context. In response, fans wholeheartedly accepted this new iteration of U2, seeing the musicians as both rock 'n' roll royalty and intimate soul mates on the journey of life.

BOMBS AND MONSTERS

While the first twenty years of U2's career produced three easily defined sets of trilogies—*Boy*, *War*, and *October*; then *The Unforgettable Fire*, *The Joshua Tree*, and *Rattle and Hum*; and finally *Achtung Baby*, *Zooropa*, and *Pop*—the first album of the new millennium, *All That You Can't Leave Behind*, was nicely paired with the band's eleventh studio album, *How to Dismantle an Atomic Bomb*. Continuing the themes of essence and love (and despite its explosive name), *Atomic Bomb*, like its predecessor, stood in contrast to the flagrant excessiveness of the Zoo TV era, favoring a more relatable and accessible style. With the new record, U2 looked back to its past for musical inspiration as it addressed existential issues of life, death, and faith and implemented innovative production and promotional strategies. Along the way, Bono continued to develop his philanthropic interests, raising more than a small amount of concern with the other band members. Nonetheless, *Atomic Bomb* marks one of the most successful and energetic periods as the band battled the global monsters of poverty and terrorism, and the franchise grew to a colossal size through new business deals.

In its quest for a big rock 'n' roll album, U2 invited Steve Lillywhite to return as head producer for the new record but also included Flood, Jacknife Lee, Daniel Lanois, and Brian Eno, all previous collaborators with the group. For this project, Lillywhite and company were charged with reshaping and updating the band's original aggressive sound, resulting in the most mainstream rock album of U2's career. "Vertigo," the opening track of the 2004 album, anchored *Atomic Bomb* with a punk-influenced guitar riff and a driving rhythm section reminiscent of the band's early club days. Filled with angst and spirit, the song's aggressive music complemented the lyrical theme of hope amid a dizzying new culture of fear and anxiety and quickly become an international hit. But the success of "Vertigo" was due to something more than just good music and polished lyrics, receiving a huge push from an extraordinary and innovative partnership.

In 2004, U2 surprised the music industry and fans alike by partnering with Apple, creating a first-of-its-kind cross-branding campaign. In collaboration with the legendary computer maker, the band promoted its new album and blurred the lines between music and marketing, culminating in several iconic projects. First, prior to the release of *Atomic Bomb*, Apple used "Vertigo" in a commercial for its relatively new line of iPods. Introduced along with iTunes in 2001, the iPod had revolutionized the music industry by offering new modes of music storage and distribution at precisely the same time the file-sharing giant Napster was being forced to shut down due to legal challenges of copyright violations. In advance of *Atomic Bomb*'s release, Apple created an iPod commercial in the style of its "silhouette" campaign that featured U2 performing "Vertigo," ostensibly cross-promoting both its media player and the band's new single in one breakthrough moment. Looking more like a music video than an advertisement, the commercial was broadcast widely on television, creating an unprecedented level of publicity for a yet-to-be-released album. In a second trendsetting move, in the United States "Vertigo" was offered exclusively through the iTunes Music Store ahead of the full album's release, giving fans a chance to download the single directly to their own computers and music players. A third collaboration resulted in the production of a special edition iPod, featuring a red-and-black color scheme (similar to *Atomic Bomb*'s own album artwork), as well as custom engraving of the band members' signatures. Finally, the band offered a first-ever digital box set, *The Complete U2*, containing all of its albums, as well as a significant number of rare and previously unreleased songs. Unparalleled in the music industry, the run-up to the release of *Atomic Bomb* initiated a long and productive relationship between U2 and Apple.

Not everyone, however, was pleased with the new alliance between the supergroup and a monstrous corporation. Critics immediately accused U2 of selling out to one of the commercial monoliths it had been making fun of in the 1990s. Both Apple's CEO Steve Jobs and the band's members were quick to defend the partnership, citing the innovative convergence of music, art, pop culture, and technology. Jobs said the collaboration provided a chance to make innovative products together. Jimmy Iovine, the head of U2's record label (and one of U2's former producers) supported the relationship as a way to "redefine the music business," while Edge predicted, "iPod and iTunes look like the future to me and it's good for everybody involved in music" ("Apple Introduces the U2 iPod"). Reacting to the band's critics, Larry responded,

> [Apple makes] products that we like, also they have single-handedly saved the music industry, they have developed the technology to download the music and for it to be paid for. Record companies couldn't do that—they were faffing around suing people. We are big fans of Apple, we're happy to stand up and say that, "yes, these guys design the best stuff." (Boyd, "Meet the Bomb Squad")

Though U2 endorsed Apple along with its iTunes and iPod products, the band was quick to point out that it never received any money for its commercial, believing that the television airplay of "Vertigo" was comparable to radio play but using a different medium. Not seen in any way as a compromise, the band gladly partnered with the computer company, welcoming the corporation as an innovative point of distribution in an age of new media. With the release of *Atomic Bomb*, U2, it seemed, was everywhere, an unstoppable force of resilience on the shifting landscape of an outmoded music industry. To its critics, it had become a voracious commercial marketing giant.

In support of the *Atomic Bomb* album, U2 crafted a technologically innovative and emotionally provocative tour, called Vertigo, that traveled to arenas and stadiums around the globe in 2005 and 2006. Featuring both indoor and outdoor configurations, the tour spread across five legs, selling out all 110 shows. Continuing a stage element that was implemented on the Elevation tour, U2 again featured a long ramp that extended out into arena audiences, this time in the shape of an ellipse. At many points in the show, either individual members or the entire band would perform in the midst of the audience, making everyone in the arena feel as if they had the best seat in the house. For many fans, their goal was to get inside the ellipse, something only achieved through a random selection process when entering the venue. Primarily used in North American indoor concerts, outdoor shows in other countries reconfigured the stage, replacing the ellipse with two catwalks that led to smaller B-stages in the middle of the stadium.

Again under the direction of Willie Williams, Mark Fisher, and Catherine Owens, the show's design implemented another piece of state-of-the-art technology. Using tennis-ball-sized LED lights, the designers constructed curtains of lighted beads that hung from floor to ceiling, displaying abstract patterns, colors, maps, symbols, and flags at highly choreographed moments in the concert. When not in use, the curtains were retracted into the rafters, essentially creating two completely different stage sets. The effect was thrilling, artistic, and provocative, as images accented the themes of the songs being played, resulting in a show that blended the minimalism of Elevation and the imagery of PopMart. When U2 played outdoors in stadiums, the curtains were replaced with a massive wall of LED panels, which functioned as a nonmoveable backdrop to the stage. Once again making innovative leaps in staging and lighting design, U2's production team helped create a dynamic yet intimate concert environment for fans.

While the Vertigo tour set new trends in stage design, it also highlighted some important and controversial themes of the day, specifically focusing on conflict in the Middle East. After the terrorist attacks of 9/11 (which happened during the Elevation tour), President George W. Bush organized a coalition of forces and led an invasion of Iraq. The purpose of the military action was to topple the regime of Saddam Hussein and to disarm the country of weapons of mass destruction. The incursion led to a protracted war, beginning in 2003 and ending in 2011, with an estimated death toll of over 500,000 Iraqis—a stark contrast to the multinational coalition's loss of 4,491 lives. The "shock and awe" campaign against Iraq was swift and hard-hitting, largely viewed by the public as an act of retribution for the terrorist attacks. Critics accused the Bush administration of rushing to blame Hussein without proper proof and verification, warning that the incursion would destabilize the Middle East by provoking further sectarianism and extremism in the area. As U2 toured in support of its *Atomic Bomb* album—and perhaps not coincidentally—Middle Eastern countries were exploding amid the chaos and violence of fiendish forces both within and without.

U2 highlighted the conflict during an especially poignant set of politically charged songs. With an appeal for dialogue between the Abrahamic faiths in particular, Bono sang, "Lay down your guns / All you daughters of Zion, all you Abraham sons" in "Love and Peace or Else," a haunting call to Middle Eastern reconciliation. "Lay your love on the track / We're gonna break the monster's back" was the plea from U2. Through an effective and seamless transition between tunes, the band ripped into another call to peace with "Sunday Bloody Sunday," appropriately reinterpreted, this time, as a response to the war in Iraq. During the song, Bono would explain the symbols on a headband he wore: the word *coexist* incorporated the Muslim Crescent in the letter *c*, the Jewish Star of David in the *x* and the Christian cross in the *t*. With a third song to drive home U2's critique of warfare as a senseless attempt to resolve conflicts, "Bullet the Blue Sky" also found new and emotive meaning as the LED curtains displayed modern jetfighters, and Edge mimicked the sounds of war with his guitar. In the song's instrumental bridge, Bono would fall to his knees, blindfolded, with hands crossed over his head, in a startling and provocative demonstration, evoking images of a terrorist execution. Playing the part of a prisoner of war, he then moved to the microphone and sang, "These are the hands that built America," with a final chorus of "When Johnny Comes Marching Home Again," often adding the tag, "No matter what he see, no matter what he hear, just as long as Johnny comes home safely here." When performing at outdoor venues, the massive LED backdrop displayed a conspicuous "Coexist," and Bono would strike a fire, simulating an explosion on one of the smaller B-stages. An obvious and pointed commentary on the American-led coalition's invasion of Iraq, U2 had reinvented its original call to peace and justice through a series of new and old songs alike.

One other moment on the Vertigo tour was quite notable and innovative. Immediately preceding "Pride (in the Name of Love)," the show featured a partial reading of the Universal Declaration of Human Rights. Ending with the fifth article, "No one shall be subjected to torture or to cruel, inhuman or degrading treatment or punishment," and then the sixth, "Everyone has the right to recognition everywhere as a person before the law," it was a moving reminder of America's own recent and controversial use of waterboarding during the interrogation of terrorist suspects in Iran. As U2 concluded "Pride," flags of African nations streamed down the screens, while the band transitioned into "Where the Streets Have No Name," and Bono reminded audiences that Dr. Martin Luther King, Jr's dream was not just an American dream but was also an African dream. With an extended and impassioned plea to consider the AIDS epidemic in Africa, Bono urged concertgoers to join the ONE advocacy campaign by texting a message to the organization as the band sang "One." It was a remarkable and pioneering use of mobile technology, with some concerts even projecting new ONE members' names on the screens in real time.

U2's inclination toward activism wasn't limited just to the Vertigo tour. The mid-2000s found the band members busy at work calling attention to injustice and poverty. Specifically, Bono continued developing his interest in Africa, speaking on behalf of its people, and furthering his own education about the ongoing plight of sub-Saharan countries. In particular, he began to meet regularly with highly influential political leaders in North America and Europe. Working tirelessly, Bono straddled the aisle of the US Congress, moving between conservatives and liberals, networking with political rivals, making presentations, and promoting an African agenda. Ironically, just a decade earlier, while pedaling the satire of Zoo TV, he often prank called the White House—and was promptly disconnected. But during the Vertigo era, heads of state such as President George W. Bush, US treasury secretary Paul O'Neill, and Senator Jesse Helms, all arch conservatives, eagerly embraced Bono and any positive media attention an encounter with the rock star would bring. For all his effort, Bono was extremely effective in creating alliances, advising policy, and speaking on behalf of those in Africa who had no voice.

While his indefatigable devotion ultimately resulted in increased attention on the situation of sub-Saharan Africa and impacted economic policies in those countries, it also brought criticism in a couple of ways. First, Bono's critics again cried "Sellout," interpreting the lead singer's political activities as akin to sleeping with the enemy. The people Bono was now courting were the very ones he had chastised from the stage in his earlier days. The accusation of "compromise" would follow Bono for many years to come. A second conflict came from within the band itself—Edge, Adam, and Larry's patience was being tested as Bono ran around the planet on a mission to save Africa while at the same time neglecting the band. The consequences of what many would call Bono's new "day job" meant less time in the studio, postponed albums, and delayed concert appearances. Though given numerous awards and honors during this period, Bono had jeopardized his relationship with his bandmates and with the most ideological of fans in the process.

Controversies aside, *Atomic Bomb* and the Vertigo tour were massive triumphs for U2. Apart from the song "Vertigo," the album found success in three other singles as well, especially on the international front. "All Because of You," "Sometimes You Can't Make It on Your Own," and "City of Blinding Lights" all broke into the Top 10 in the United Kingdom, Canada, and Ireland and charted in the Top 100 around the world. The tour also produced three concert films, of which one was notably innovative. *U2 3D*, the band's second theatrical concert release, was the first-ever live-action three-dimensional (3-D) film and was distributed exclusively in IMAX 3-D and other 3-D capable digital theaters. Directed by Catherine Owens and Mark Pellington, the film made use of state-of-the-art technology to give viewers a surprisingly realistic concert experience without being gimmicky. And while *U2 3D* depicts the main flow of a typical concert on the Vertigo tour, including the political and social themes, it is especially impressive in its presentation of "The Fly." Picking up where Zoo TV left off, the film displays the song's cacophony of messages as 3-D images that cascade down the screen in front of the band, emphasizing the words themselves, confronting viewers with the power of text. Beautiful, stimulating, and pioneering, *U2 3D* again showed the band's enthusiasm for using the latest technology to deliver its message. Rounding out a prominent list of successes in this period, U2 was inducted into the Rock and Roll Hall of Fame in 2005, a sign of the band's nearly unprecedented accomplishments.

On the Vertigo tour, Bono was fond of using the phrase "Don't become a monster in order to defeat a monster," an idea found in Friedrich Nietzsche's *Beyond Good and Evil*, aphorism 146: "He who fights with monsters should be careful lest he thereby become a monster." A key theme of both the album and the supporting tour, U2 delivered its worldwide countermessage of love and peace as an antidote for a post-9/11 culture of anxiety, suspicion, and terror. Now a global presence, Bono became a tenacious activist, negotiating legislation on behalf of Africa and calling national leaders to accountability, defying behemoth systems and institutions alike. In the process, he and the band were often criticized for collaborating and compromising with the enemy, accused of filling their own monstrous appetites for fame, success, and wealth at any cost.

Bono has said that he and the band don't write the songs as much as the songs write them, often unaware of the significance a lyric will come to have. The period of *Leave Behind* and *Atomic Bomb* provides good examples of this. When writing "Walk On," U2 could not have known that its song would eventually function as an anthem for a city, and a country, devastated by the worst act of terrorism the world had ever witnessed. Nor could the band foresee that its classic hits from an earlier era, "Sunday Bloody Sunday" and "Bullet the Blue Sky," would find new meaning against a backdrop of violence as forces invaded a volatile Middle East. Now in midlife, Larry, Edge, Adam, and Bono were able to look back in awe at the way their music, their career, and their colossal organization had developed, both proud of and pensive about the journey. Edge's reflections during his acceptance speech at the Rock and Roll Hall of Fame exemplify the wisdom he and his friends had gleaned over the years:

> Above all else what U2 have tried to avoid over the last twenty years is not being completely crap. But next on the list down from that was to avoid being typical and predictable and ordinary. . . . And as far as U2 goes, I've stopped trying to figure out how, or more importantly when our best moments are going to come along. But I think that's why we're still awake. And that's why we're still paying attention. We know in the end that it is magic. And so we end up waiting. (U2, "Transcript")

Indeed, waiting had helped the band produce some of its best material, and waiting was something that both U2 and its fans would have to do again as the band entered another long period of indecision, struggling for a fresh sound and a pertinent message. And though U2's view of the horizon looked promising as it packed away the LED curtains of the Vertigo tour, the way forward ended up being far more murky and unsure than the band could have anticipated.

6

NEW HORIZONS

Dissatisfied with the lackluster career track of other bands its age, and unwilling to become a "top hits" novelty act, U2 redoubled its commitment to produce artistic and meaningful music after *How to Dismantle an Atomic Bomb* but with mixed results. *No Line on the Horizon* was released in 2009, just a month after the band stood on the steps of the Lincoln Memorial in Washington, DC, with a thrilling performance of "Pride (in the Name of Love)" and "City of Blinding Lights" for the presidential inauguration of Barack Obama. The new album was a complex and imaginative project that fused North African cultural influences, timeless questions about the meaning of life, and a range of fictional stories but received only mediocre commercial success. In support of *No Line*, the band embarked on the grandest, costliest, and most technically challenging tour audiences had ever seen, shattering stadium attendance records around the world. In doing so, U2—which now included a substantial roster of artistic, technical, and financial advisors and partners—gathered the global tribe through a state-of-the-art concert experience. However, in spite of a record-setting tour, the band members began to doubt their relevancy. Was it possible that Bono, Edge, Adam, and Larry, like so many older artists before them, had become victims of their own fame, fortune, and success?

Unsure of its ability to influence culture, the group searched painstakingly for purpose and place in a world of new media, taking more than five years to release *Songs of Innocence* in 2014. Both the album and the supporting tour transported fans back to the Ireland of U2's childhood for an introspective look at the group's roots while also presenting a critical commentary on current issues. In the process, the band once again inflamed its critics, primarily due to an innovative yet misguided method of record distribution. Nonetheless, U2 emerged older and wiser, unequaled in its accomplishments as a band, with no signs of slowing down as it concluded the fourth decade of its career.

CHARTING A NEW COURSE (AGAIN)

U2's twelfth album, *No Line on the Horizon*, continued fostering a spirit of authenticity and intimacy with fans while also showcasing U2's ability to create sophisticated rock. *No Line*, however, generated a bit of a paradox for the band. Though its 360° tour attracted record-breaking audiences with the biggest stadium production in the history of rock, the album's complex music and thoughtful lyrics failed to resonate with the masses.

Coming off of two extremely successful albums, *All That You Can't Leave Behind* and *How to Dismantle an Atomic Bomb*, U2 approached its next record with a bit of ambivalence, once again seeking to adapt and revise its sound. The rhythm of rebirth certainly must have felt familiar to the band. It had already labored to reinvent itself numerous times: in 1984 with *The Unforgettable Fire*; again in 1991 with *Achtung Baby*; and once more with *All That You Can't Leave Behind* in 2000. And though the band continued writing and recording new music in the interim following *No Line*, it wrestled to find a unifying direction. Nowhere was this struggle seen more clearly than in its vacillation between producers. In 2006, two years after *Atomic Bomb*, U2 set out to revamp its sound with the help of Rick Rubin, the well-known and highly regarded producer of artists such as LL Cool J, Run-DMC, Aerosmith, Johnny Cash, Mick Jagger, Tom Petty, and the Red Hot Chili Peppers. The collaboration with Rubin was extremely productive, but it also created a problem. The band wasn't happy with the overall artistic direction he was taking them in and decided to end the relationship, discarding the sessions' material with the hope that it could be used on a future project.

Choosing instead to restart the creative process, U2 turned yet again to Brian Eno and Daniel Lanois for production assistance. Though work resumed in numerous locations, primary inspiration for *No Line* came from the team's trip to Morocco, where it camped out in a *riad* it had converted to a makeshift studio. For two weeks in 2007, U2, along with Eno and Lanois, enjoyed the exotic sounds of Hindu, Sufi, Joujouka, and Jewish music at the World Sacred Music Festival in the historic city of Fez, prompting them to experiment with North African and Arabic elements. The visit was dynamic and inspiring, resulting in some outstanding recording sessions. Eno described the time as the best studio experience he had ever had. Even Larry, who is usually reserved and prone to more traditional approaches, referred to the weeks in Fez as "the most joyous and liberating part of the whole album process" (O'Hagan, "From Fez to Dublin"). In Morocco, U2 looked to the ancient desert wilderness and moved beyond its own preconceived notions of what it meant to be a modern band.

While the album's new sound could be traced back, at least in part, to a unique North African culture, *No Line*'s cover art was also unlike any that U2 had used before. Previous records had typically portrayed either images of the band or photographs and artwork created specifically for each project, relying often on the talents of Anton Corbijn. For *No Line*, however, the band turned to Hiroshi Sugimoto, a Japanese professional photographer who specialized in abstract seascapes. *Boden Sea*, the image selected by U2 for its new cover, merged an endless waterscape with an equally boundless skyline and served as an inspiration for the album's title track. Sugimoto agreed to let U2 use his image but with one stipulation: he would not allow any text to be printed on top of his image. In a creative concession, Steve Averill and AMP Visual, the band's graphic design agency, included an equal sign superimposed over Sugimoto's photo on the CD's cellophane wrapper, further highlighting a balance between earth and sky. For good or for bad, the cerebral nature of the image paralleled the aloof aesthetic of the music, contributing to the artsy impression fans and critics had of the album.

In addition to a unique recording process and sophisticated album artwork, *No Line* took U2 into new territory in several other ways as well. Breaking with tradition, the band included Eno and Lanois as writing partners, giving them credit for music and lyrics on a majority of the album's tracks. Bono also modified his songwriting process in an uncharacteristic way, opting to use the perspectives of fictional characters rather than singing about his own life and experiences. The result was a multifaceted group of narratives including a traffic cop, a junkie, and a soldier in Afghanistan, each of whom told stories of life's joys and heartaches. Compositionally, the structure of the album was as complex as its characters, with instrumentation including a cello, violin, and French horn, as well as African-themed percussion and ambient samples, loops, and synthesizers, many of which were performed by the band's touring keyboardist Terry Lawless. In addition, rapper and hip-hop artist will.i.am contributed keyboard, vocal, and production skills on one song. Richly layered and densely packed, the tight harmonies, unusual chord progressions, and nontraditional instrumentation all led to what the band considered another experimental album, though not as extreme as those in the 1990s. In the end, *No Line* suffered from its lack of accessibility, selling little more than a million copies in the United States, with global sales reaching only five million. It was a disappointing outcome for the band.

Though the production of *No Line* was very distinct from the previous two albums, it did retain a number of thematic similarities. Along with *Leave Behind* and *Atomic Bomb*, *No Line* was a deeply personal album for U2, again asking questions about the purpose and meaning of life. Specifically, the idea of "grace" runs through the three records from 2000 to 2009, uniting a myriad of ideas. "Beautiful Day," the first track on *Leave Behind*, references a friend who can "lend a hand in return for grace," while the last song on the record is an understated lullaby-like blessing, simply and appropriately titled "Grace." *Atomic Bomb* picked up the theme in "All Because of You," with Bono singing, "I was born a child of grace," and when "City of Blinding Lights" was performed in concert, he often added a tag to the final lyric of the song, shouting, "Grace abounds, grace abounds!" On *No Line*, the topic comes to the forefront yet again, especially in concert. Opening its shows with "Breathe," U2 sang, "I've found grace inside a sound / I've found grace, it's all that I've found" as a type of invocation for record-breaking audiences across the globe. While on the 360° tour, during an introduction for "Where the Streets Have No Name," Bono would sing from the most famous of all hymns, "Amazing grace, how sweet the sound, that saved a wretch like me," and in the concert's final song, the band concluded an impassioned and stirring arrangement of "Moment of Surrender," with Bono rapping about grace. As late middle-aged musicians, Adam, Larry, Edge, and Bono conveyed a simple peacefulness about life—even as their music became more complex—exuding graciousness and compassion through both recorded and live performances.

Mirroring the complexity of *No Line*, U2, guided again by the creative design team of Willie Williams, Catherine Owens, and Mark Fisher, crafted an equally complicated and multifaceted outdoor tour in support of the album. Called the 360° tour, its revolutionary stage design allowed audiences to view the band from all sides and included a number of state-of-the-art technologies. The primary focal point of each show was an enormous circular screen composed of nearly half a million pixels, which could move up and down as well as expand like an accordion fold. Complementing the screen was a groundbreaking sound system that projected the band's music in 360 degrees to every corner of the stadium. Above the stage, 200 tons of audio and video gear was suspended from a massive 250-ton structure nicknamed "the Claw," a four-legged girder that looked part spaceship and part gothic cathedral. On the ground, a ramp encircled the entire stage, allowing U2's members closer contact with the audience, especially with those fans who stood on both sides of the catwalk. Due to its unprecedented size, tech crews needed days to both set up and tear down the structure. In order to keep the tour moving quickly, three separate Claws were used, allowing U2's crew to simultaneously assemble or disassemble the stage in different venues while the band played in another. The reconfigured seating, which allowed fans to occupy the field and nearly all of the seats of a stadium, helped the 360° tour break attendance records in a majority of the venues to which it traveled and shattered ticket receipt records, selling out at every stop.

But as U2 toured, it faced a new kind of controversy unrelated to its musical style or thematic content. With 360° in high gear, environmentalists criticized U2 for the massive carbon footprint it was leaving on the planet. They asserted that the band's mission to end AIDS, fight poverty, and care for the earth was at odds with the carbon dioxide emissions generated by the unparalleled transportation needs of the tour, requiring 120 trucks for each of the Claws, a private jet for the band, and travel accommodations for nearly 200 crew members. In response, U2 began purchasing carbon offsets and facilitating carpools for fans in some cities. Still, protests in its home town of Dublin, as well as a stinging critique from Talking Heads' David Byrne, left U2 scrambling to defend itself in a culture increasingly concerned about the impact of global warming.

The 360° tour carried *No Line*'s message of grace to North America, Europe, Oceania, Africa, and South America but also focused specifically on a number of global themes. Making use of the stage's science fiction–like appearance, U2 used the metaphor of a spaceship throughout its show, walking onto the stage while David Bowie's "Space Oddity" was playing and exiting each stadium to Elton John's "Rocket Man." In the middle, concerts featured one of several prerecorded segments in which astronauts delivered messages from the International Space Station (ISS)—either the ISS crew holding up signs reading "The future needs a big kiss," astronaut Frank De Winne reciting a verse from "In a Little While," or astronaut Mark Kelly introducing "Beautiful Day." The Kelly video was especially poignant as he greeted his wife, Gabrielle Giffords, a US congressional representative who was recovering from a gunshot wound to the head, a consequence of a failed assassination attempt. In a second prerecorded video sequence, a jubilant Archbishop Desmond Tutu promoted the ONE campaign by both congratulating fans for their role in reducing the amount of AIDS cases in Africa and encouraging them to continue the global fight to eliminate poverty and preventable disease. A third meaningful moment came when U2 performed "Walk On" and featured images of the jailed Burmese political dissident Aung San Suu Kyi. In an unexpected twist, midway through the 360° tour, Suu Kyi was released from nearly fifteen years of house arrest, transforming the song from a plea for her freedom into a celebration of life.

But perhaps the greatest contribution to a global conversation came during U2's performance of "Sunday Bloody Sunday." Using a blend of music, lyrics, lighting, and imagery, the song took on new meaning, challenging fans around the world to remember the plight of Iranian activists recently jailed or killed by their government. As a Middle Eastern chant wailed through the sound system and Persian text scrolled across the screen, the words of Rumi, a thirteenth-century Sufi mystic, descended on audiences with the full weight of the 450-ton stage. "Listen!" cried the ancient poet in a lament for his native Persia—modern-day Afghanistan and Iran. Then, as the screen displayed men, women, and children protesting the corrupt Iranian election of 2009, floodlights drenched the stage and audience in green, honoring the peaceful demonstrations of nonviolent protesters, an uprising that became known worldwide as the Green Movement. U2's message of love and solidarity was inescapable as the band stood squarely with imprisoned, disenfranchised, and oppressed people living under the hand of a brutal dictator. "Tonight, we can be as one," sang Bono at the Rose Bowl in Los Angeles, uniting Americans, Iranians, and the world.

A tour the size and scope of the 360° tour required massive support, including a couple of new commercial affiliations that set precedents for the band. Prior to the tour, U2 signed a twelve-year contract with Live Nation, giving the promoter command of its concert scheduling, sponsoring, merchandising, and web management. It was the first time the franchise had released control of such essential operations to an outside agency. A second deal brought a sponsorship by BlackBerry to the tour, reversing a lucrative relationship with Apple and giving the appearance that U2 and the computer giant were at odds with one another. For some fans and onlookers, the tour sponsorship was a further indication that the band had sold out. Undeniably, concertgoers couldn't miss a broad range of promotional material bearing the caption "U2 360° Presented by BlackBerry," as well as giant banners displaying the corporate sponsor's name at venues. In addition, the accompanying "Blackberry Loves U2" advertising campaign offered a "U2 Mobile Album" that would revolutionize the listening experience for a digital age, a promise that never fully developed (and an album that many BlackBerry users clamored to have removed from their devices). Nonetheless, already a substantial brand, U2 continued to expand its image through business sponsorships.

Aside from innovative business partnerships, the U2 organization also developed an unprecedented network of professional relationships and personal friendships over three decades, resulting in a franchise that felt more like a family than a corporate monolith. Some of the most creative and talented people in the music industry had been with the team from the beginning, contributing to the group's formation and eventual success. Paul McGuinness, U2's manager, has been considered by many as the fifth member of the band. Arguably, he was the seminal influence on the adolescent musicians, serving as a pioneering visionary, a caring guide, and a protective guardian. His company, Principle Management, flourished alongside the ever-growing franchise, operating as the band's only management agency until 2013 when

McGuinness retired. Though he kept a low profile, his fatherly concern, efficient leadership, and intuitive business sense transformed an unknown quartet from Dublin into international superstars. Savvy and wise, McGuinness scrutinized contracts, negotiated record deals, and defended the band's right to intellectual property, always looking out for the best interests of his four clients, a rare posture in the music industry of the 1970s and 1980s. His influence cannot be understated. It's hard to imagine what U2 would be like today without McGuinness's thirty-five years of consistent and passionate supervision.

Other influential members of the U2 organization can also be traced to the early days. Back in 1978, still in its infancy and barely able to play instruments, U2 hired another longtime associate. Joe O'Herlihy built and ran the band's sound systems for gigs in bars and clubs throughout Ireland and the United Kingdom, eventually signing on as one of the first permanent crew members in 1980 for the *Boy* tour. He has mixed sound on every tour since. Another pioneering member of the U2 community was Dennis Sheehan. Beginning in 1982, Sheehan worked as the tour manager for the band's stage shows, often intervening when Bono placed himself in some precarious situation. It was Sheehan who rescued the front man when he plunged into the audience or climbed perilously up towering scaffolds. Tragically, the well-loved tour manager died unexpectedly of a heart attack in his hotel room while traveling with the band in 2015. During a concert the following day, Bono gave an emotional tribute to Sheehan and noted the closeness of the band and crew, saying, "U2 is a kind of family. U2 is a brotherhood. Although there are a lot of sisters in it now that I think about it. The extended family are everything to us, we look after each other. Last night we lost a member of our family. Dennis Sheehan was his name" ("A Kind of Family"). By all accounts, the band had lost one of its most capable and influential crew.

Other members of the U2 team also helped launch the organization. Willie Williams first saw U2 perform in 1981 at Greenbelt, a Christian music festival in England. He began working full time with the band during *The Joshua Tree* tour in 1987, and has continued to function as its stage, lighting, and multimedia director, contributing groundbreaking technology as well as spiritually charged imagery to U2's live performances. Bob Koch became the band's business manager in 1984 and has influenced the organization's financial practices, especially when the band is touring. A number of technical staff have helped shape the sound of individual U2 members as well: Sam O'Sullivan began as Larry's drum technician in 1986, Dallas Schoo joined as Edge's guitar assistant in 1987, and Stuart Morgan became Adam's bass technician in 1992. Rocko Reedy filled the role of stage manager beginning in 1990, providing oversight for details of safety and production. Steve Averill, though not an official staff member, worked repeatedly with the band as a consulting graphic designer, helping with the cover art for every U2 studio album to date. Martin Wroe, a figure who has played multiple roles including journalist, editor for *Propaganda* (the fan club publication), U2.com editor, poet, Greenbelt contributor, and most recently, spiritual advisor, continues with the band as another longtime influence. Jack Heaslip, one of U2's most inspirational partners, met the band members when they were teenagers. There from the beginning, Heaslip was both a teacher and a counselor at Mount Temple and an especially important confidant for Bono after he lost his mother. Later, Heaslip served as a mentor to the band and officiated at Bono's wedding, eventually becoming the group's "traveling pastor," providing spiritual care for hundreds of crew members while on tour. His death in 2015 was another unexpected blow to those who had come to love and revere him. U2's hiring practices reflected its mission to be an organization that stood in contrast to the rest of the industry and included people who functioned both as family members and specialists. Many have spent decades, if not entire careers, in the studio or on the road with the band. But as unique as U2's employment priorities have been, there was another area of staffing that set the franchise apart from all others.

WOMEN HOLD THE BIG REVELATIONS

While U2 was setting industry standards through album production and concert tours, it also broke ground in an unlikely area: the hiring of women in important and influential positions. At the band's induction into the Rock and Roll Hall of Fame in 2005, Bono summed up the importance of females in the organization, specifically honoring them for their influence and expertise. He reflected,

> I see around friends and people that we've worked with for a very
> long time. . . . It's too many people in the room to thank, but I'd like
> to thank the really gorgeous women that work for us. Because they're
> fun to thank. Beautiful, gorgeous women of Principle Management.
> Ellen Darst, thank you very much. Sheila Roche, thank you very
> much. Anne Louise Kelly, thank you very much. Keryn Kaplan,
> thank you very much. Beautiful, sexy, sometimes Irish, sometimes
> American women, thank you. (U2, "Transcript")

The comments about the women Bono mentioned weren't offered as
sexist or patronizing remarks but as deeply personal acknowledgments
of jobs well done. Indeed, these and other women had worked hard in
key roles throughout most of U2's career.

At just nineteen years old, Suzanne Doyle was hired by Principle
Management to work on *The Joshua Tree* tour. The subsequent nine
years she spent with U2 were exciting and formative, giving her multiple opportunities to develop leadership skills that would later be used in
other careers. Doyle recalls her time as a management assistant with
fondness, saying, "Bono and Paul McGuinness are two of the finest
mentors you could have" (Byrne, "Rock 'n' Roll Graduates"). Well
known for his efficiency and exacting standards, it was McGuinness's
attention to detail that particularly shaped Doyle's own administrative
prowess. She eventually moved up in the organization and spent another three years as Bono and Ali's personal assistant, handling confi-
dential correspondence, organizing special gatherings, coordinating
Bono's speeches, and arranging charity events. Starting as a young and
impressionable teen, Doyle progressed through the ranks, was allowed
to cultivate her own interests and abilities, and ultimately started her
own consultant agency.

In the mid-1980s, soon after founding Principle Management, Paul
McGuinness hired another powerful young female who helped shape
U2's destiny. Working through several different roles, Sheila Roche was
promoted in 1997 to managing director, a prominent position that left
her in charge of the band's day-to-day management. Working closely
with U2, it was her job to represent the concerns of the band to Principle Management and vice versa. After eighteen years of functioning as a
trusted advisor and confidant, Roche resigned and began a new venture
helping Bono and Bobby Shriver launch the (RED) AIDS organization
in 2005. Since then, she has directed all of (RED)'s major campaigns,

organized collaborations of electronic musicians for the DANCE (RED) SAVES LIVES project, curated a groundbreaking auction that raised $44 million for the Global Fund to Fight AIDS, and led many other humanitarian efforts, serving most recently as the head of global communications for (RED). Innovative and pioneering, Roche recognizes the importance of new media and technology for relaying vital messages about global poverty, saying,

> Social media has given us the ability to broadcast to an audience of up to 350 million when you combine (RED)'s social networks with those of our partners. . . . We can get to a lot of eyeballs when we create smart content and compelling ways for people to get involved, spread the word, and raise money. ("Advocate of the Week")

A person of remarkable influence and authority, Roche continues to reflect the values and spirit of the band and management company that gave her a job and launched her into a career of activism.

Another influential woman, Regine Moylett, was there at the beginning and can be credited for U2's image in both direct and indirect ways. In the late 1970s, she operated the only punk shop in Ireland, a place where Bono and his friends would buy trendy clothing. She also had her own punk band (the New Versions) and gigged in the same circles as the upcoming U2. More importantly, however, Moylett was instrumental in organizing outdoor concerts behind Dublin's Dandelion Market. It was there that U2 honed its stage performances in front of packed Saturday afternoon crowds—mostly other teenagers who were not old enough to hear U2 play in bars—in the summer of 1979. Little did she know that this series of free concerts would help the young band gain a loyal fan base, increased media attention, and a recording contract for its first mini-album, *U2-3*. Soon after, Moylett's love for music and aptitude for administration landed her a job with Island Records, where she refined her skills and developed strong ties in the music industry. In 1986, encouraged by Bono, the twenty-eight-year-old began to look after U2's tour publicity. When *The Joshua Tree* tour launched a year later, she became its full-time press liaison. Always exhibiting "a quality of kindness, thoughtfulness and consideration rare in [the] business," according to journalist Neil McCormick, Moylett advanced quickly, earning a reputation for being committed and tenacious, as well as warm and humorous (McCormick, *Killing Bono*, 358).

Today, her company, RMP, handles all of U2's publicity needs, directly shaping the band's image on a global scale.

The Dandelion Market was home to yet another longtime U2 associate. Catherine Owens, the bassist for the Boy Scoutz, an all-female punk band managed by Steve Averill, became friends with Adam Clayton, as her group played often at the outdoor summer venue. When her musical career fizzled out, Owens went to art school in Belfast but remained in touch with the members of U2. Sharing a love for art, music, politics, and activism, she began collaborating with the band while it recorded *The Unforgettable Fire*, painting a series of inspiring backdrops for the rehearsal hall. But it was in 1992 that Owens really took the lead as artistic director, creating complex screen graphics, painting Trabants, and influencing the whole look of the Zoo TV set. The first of many projects, she continued to contribute animation, film, video, and other key graphic content for the PopMart, Elevation, Vertigo, and 360° tours, as well as codirecting *U2 3D*, the groundbreaking three-dimensional cinematic release of the Vertigo tour, blending music and art at every step. Since 2010, Owens has gone on to work with other musicians and film projects, becoming a widely respected and internationally known visual content creator and artist.

In many ways, the Owens-U2 relationship is emblematic of professional partnerships in the franchise, often starting with a friendship in the band's formative years, then nurturing the development of a skill, and culminating in a trusted and thoughtful collaboration that lasts for decades. Owens sums it up by saying,

> Even as kids, we had a sophisticated agenda. Everyone knew they wanted to work in areas where no compromise was the order of the day. That's [U2's] great strength. That driving force is the same with all of us. It's taken us this long to trust that all of our talents can develop separately, but still work comfortably together. (Clarke, "How Did U2 That?")

In similar ways, other notable women have also played key roles in U2's inner circle. Cecilia Coffey—Larry's older sister—has worked with Principle Management since the beginning, often opening and responding personally to the band's mail in the early years. Ellen Darst and Keryn Kaplan headed the agency's New York office, while Anne

Louise Kelly ran the headquarters in Dublin, all longtime associates who had foundational roles.

In "Get on Your Boots," a song from *No Line*, Bono sings, "Women of the future hold the big revelations," a lyric affirming and acknowledging the need for feminine leadership and perspective. U2's inclusion of women in long-standing, high-level management and artistic positions is yet another indication of the band's commitment to operate outside the music industry's status quo. Early on, band members realized they could be advocates for women's rights, even headlining a benefit show in 1978 called Rock against Sexism. Gender equality continued to permeate and shape the band, becoming a unifying theme across its long career. In 2005, while working on the Vertigo tour, Catherine Owens reflected on why partnerships with females are paramount to U2: "As a woman, one of the things I bring is some feminine perspective. As Willie Williams, the show director says, I am constantly reminding everybody that there needs to be some arcs and circles" (Mulrooney, "Vertigo Vision"). As Bono closed a concert at Slane Castle on the Elevation tour, he echoed a similar sentiment, saying, "I want to thank Paul McGuinness our manager. I want to thank Principle Management, all the women and men—mostly women—who wrote the show for us" (*U2 Go Home*). Without a doubt, in the broad network of the ever-expanding U2 family, professional partnerships and personal relationships converged to create a completely new business model, due in part to a forward-thinking manager and the talented cadre of women he and U2 employed.

FROM INNOCENCE TO EXPERIENCE

As U2 wrapped up the most elaborate and complex concert tour the world had ever seen, it had much to be proud of. But it also faced a dilemma. On the one hand, it had become a monolith unlike any band in the history of rock, with unprecedented financial earnings, a massive corporate staff, and seemingly unlimited production resources. On the other hand, the band struggled, once again, to find a way forward, stymied by its own popularity and success. Bono even joked during the long, silent gap after *No Line* that the band's new album would be titled, "Ten Reasons to Exist," a facetious admission that U2 was wandering without direction or purpose. To look at U2 from the outside, the casual fan would see only what every band dreamed of achieving: a massive discography, record-breaking ticket sales, an international fan base, corporate partnerships, and a lavishly successful investment portfolio. But when asked about the challenge of sustaining a thirty-plus-year career, Bono confessed, "We were trying to figure out, 'Why would anyone want another U2 album?' And then we said, 'Well, why would we want one?' . . . We felt like we were on the verge of irrelevance." (Newman, "9 Biggest Revelations"). Ironically, as the band searched for a new and progressive sound, it ultimately found inspiration in its roots.

U2 explored a number of options as it navigated the biggest identity crisis of its career before it finally released *Songs of Innocence*. Even while stumbling through artistic limbo, however, the band was productive, working on at least four recording projects after it packed up the 360° tour. One involved a collection of meditative and reflective modern-day psalms. Tentatively labeled *Songs of Ascent*, it was intended to be a companion piece to *No Line*, potentially including some abandoned material from the *Atomic Bomb* sessions with Rick Rubin. The band, however, felt the concept might be a bit artsy for the general public and shelved it indefinitely, still aching from the underwhelming sales of *No Line*. A second endeavor was a record of straight up rock 'n' roll, but the band thought it too was irrelevant and left it unfinished. Described as a "club-sounding album" by Bono, a potential third project featured dance mixes, but again it didn't feel like the right fit for a new release. A possible fourth album involved rerecording an original Broadway soundtrack—a wildly creative and remarkably ambitious score by half of U2.

Never content to sit still, Bono and Edge had earlier forged a unique but controversial artistic venture on Broadway, partnering with Julie Taymor to create *Spider-Man: Turn Off the Dark*. Taymor, the celebrated director of the stage musical *The Lion King* and the first woman to win a Tony Award for directing, was responsible for *Spider-Man's* story development, while Bono and Edge wrote the music and lyrics. Initially a productive and creative collaboration, the relationship soured as the show suffered from continual delays, poor reviews, high costs, and numerous technical difficulties, resulting in Taymor's dismissal and a residual court battle. The strained relationship was just one of many problems that plagued *Spider-Man*. An extravagant mixture of music, drama, technical stunts, and aerial acrobatics, the show was infamous for having the longest preview period and being the most expensive production in Broadway theater history. And though its visual effects were often praised, critics had little good to say about the story line and musical score. *Spider-Man* also kept Bono and Edge busy before and throughout the 360° tour, often requiring their urgent input during its troubled production phase, which included rewrites, crew injuries, and cast replacements. Despite its many failings, the show had popular appeal and ticket sales were strong, breaking box office records in the first week. The momentum, however, was not enough to offset the excessive expenses, and the extravagant show closed less than four years after its opening in 2011. With relatively limited success, *Spider-Man* was a grand and risky experiment in theater arts for Bono and Edge but ultimately may have contributed to U2's overall sense of insecurity and irrelevance.

Though plagued equally by distractions and doubt, the band finally found its focus by turning to its past. *Songs of Innocence*, U2's thirteenth studio album, was released in 2015, five and a half years after *No Line*, marking the longest period between albums. A combination of multiple producers including Danger Mouse, Paul Epworth, Ryan Tedder, Declan Gaffney, and Flood, *Innocence* went through numerous iterations before U2 was satisfied and felt it was good enough to release. The title of the album was inspired by a pair of William Blake's eighteenth-century masterpieces, *Songs of Innocence* and *Songs of Experience*, a collection of poetry and etchings contrasting the simplicity of childhood (innocence) with the harsh reality of adulthood (experience). Blake is no stranger to U2. Author Tassoula Kokkoris notes, "The band's history with this collection of poems goes all the way back to the late '80s, when they recorded the song 'Beautiful Ghost/Introduction to Songs of Experience,' taking the lyrics directly from Blake's Introduction to *Songs of Experience*" (Kokkoris, "William Blake"). As a fan of literature, Bono has cited other influences on U2's music, including W. B. Yeats, Oscar Wilde, John Donne, Emily Dickinson, T. S. Elliot, C. S. Lewis, and Salman Rushdie.

U2's *Innocence* became an exploration of its own beginning, reflecting on early musical heroes such as the Ramones and the Clash, as well as band members' families and other youthful events. Several of the songs portray a wide-eyed and excitable adolescent band discovering its purpose, as it was fueled equally by idealism and adrenaline. More specifically, Bono recalls the pain of losing his mother, as well as the fear that came from growing up on North Dublin's Cedarwood Road. Closer to a concept album than any other of U2's productions, its theme of youthful innocence harkened back to the band's very first record, even echoing *Boy*'s cover art, this time with Larry hugging the waist of his own shirtless son.

While the theme of childhood was plainly and beautifully portrayed on *Innocence*, it was made even clearer in concert. The Innocence + Experience tour, launched in 2015, used cutting-edge technology to tell the story of U2's earliest years, blending music, choreography, graphics, and lighting in a spectacular presentation that felt more like a Broadway musical than a rock concert. Designed exclusively for arenas, the main stage sat at one end of the floor, connected to a circular "e-stage" ("e" for "experience") at the other end by a long ramp. Hanging above the walkway was a first-of-its-kind dual-sided LED screen—a type of long video cage the band could enter and which would allow them to interact with coordinated video images. Willie Williams, the show's creative director, referred to it as the "screen-stage-bridge-lighting object," saying it was the centerpiece of the concert. Set designer Es Devlin noted the formidable presence of the screen, as well as her hope that it would still evolve as an important artistic medium, commenting, "The rock show is an art form. . . . [W]e have created this powerful sculpture in the arena and are barely using forty-nine percent of its forces" (O'Hagan, "Imaginary Spaces"). The two stages, ramp, and screen created four separate areas where U2 could perform, each accenting a different theme of the concert. The innovative screen and stage were supported by a revolutionary sound system that hung from the ceiling at the middle of the arena, distributing sound equally to all sides. Williams summed up the plot of the tour as "the story of four teenagers growing up in '70s Dublin looking out of their bedroom windows and trying to figure out how they fit into the often violent and disrupted world outside" (Sandberg, "Willie Williams"). And though the Troubles were never mentioned during the show, it was clear that the three-decade period of violence was deeply intertwined in the story. The band also incorporated brand-new live streaming technology in its shows, inviting an audience member up onto the e-stage to broadcast the performance of a song, such as "Elevation," to the world via the Meerkat smartphone app. In a similar way, some fans used the popular Periscope platform to stream whole concerts, while others watched on devices and computers from home.

As the show progressed from the "innocence" of U2's childhood to the "experience" of its seasoned years, the band also addressed some urgent contemporary issues. In North America, the focus of "Bullet the Blue Sky" shifted from military conflict in El Salvador to ongoing violence against African Americans in the United States. In 2013, social movements such as Black Lives Matter began to protest and call attention to a long string of high-profile cases involving police brutality against the African American population. U2 addressed this injustice as part of a larger overarching theme of "surrender" in the concert. Prompted by the suspicious deaths of a number of unarmed black men—Trayvon Martin in Miami Gardens, Florida; Michael Brown in Ferguson, Missouri; Walter Scott in North Charleston, South Carolina; and Freddie Gray in Baltimore, Maryland—Bono concluded "Bullet" by shouting, "I got my hands up . . . Don't shoot . . . I can't breathe!" The last phrase was an obvious reference to the choking death and the final words of Eric Garner in New York City at the hands of police. Visuals on the massive screen overhead complemented the chaos of the musical score by displaying scenes of civil unrest and racially charged protests.

When the tour moved to Europe, the uniquely American segment was replaced with a series of songs focusing on the mass migration of refugees fleeing North Africa and the Middle East. In 2015, more than half a million Syrians, Afghans, and Iraqis crossed the Mediterranean Sea into Southeastern Europe in an attempt to escape war in their home countries, creating the largest refugee crisis since World War II. While some traveled across land, most took the more direct route across the treacherous sea, a voyage that often ended in death. In one high-profile instance, the lifeless body of three-year-old Alan (Aylan) Kurdi washed up on a beach in Turkey. He, his five-year-old brother, and his mother drowned when their small dingy capsized. Ironically, they were from Kobani, the bombed-out village captured in drone video and displayed on the screen during U2's chilling rendition of "October." The image of little Aylan was broadcast around the world, heightening media attention and even prompting Bono to change a lyric in "Pride (in the Name of Love)" from "one man" to "one *boy* washed up on an empty beach." During the "Bullet" sequence, Bono challenged the prevailing fear of Syrian refugees—many Europeans worried that an influx of Syrians would increase the likelihood of terrorist activities in their countries—by taking on the character of a refugee himself, pleading from the stage: "I'm a boy. I'm not dangerous. I'm in danger." The segment was a poignant call for action to welcome the refugees. Bono continued by asking audiences, "What do you want? A Europe with its heart and borders closed to mercy? Or a Europe with its heart open?" ("U2 Use Concert"). As the Twitter hashtag #RefugeesWelcome filled the screen, U2 demonstrated once again the same passion for justice it had started with nearly forty years earlier. Coming full circle, the band that had been shaped by the violence of the Troubles was now shouting a message of peace through a bullhorn to hundreds of thousands of Europeans, both reflecting and affecting the culture it inhabited.

Sold out at every stop, Innocence + Experience became another in a long series of successful record-breaking and innovative U2 tours. But it didn't come without problems. Undoubtedly, one of the greatest missteps of the band's career happened during the distribution of *Songs of Innocence*. In a lavishly staged media event, U2 joined Apple's CEO Tim Cook for a press conference, surprising and delighting fans with a live performance of "The Miracle (of Joey Ramone)." In the spectacle that followed, Bono and Cook touched index fingers together, simulating the push of a virtual button and actually releasing the new album to over five hundred million iTunes users around the globe. But while fans were elated at the gift, not everyone was happy. Critics immediately responded with unexpected animosity, citing the oft-heard charge of "sell out," but this time adding a much stronger condemnation related to the mode of distribution. Charging the Apple/U2 collaboration with invasion of privacy, the automatically downloaded album was equated with spam, junk mail, and corporate hacking. The problem was so widely reported in the media that Apple had to create a dedicated webpage instructing users on how to remove the record from their devices, and U2 issued sheepish apologies, blaming the blunder on its own overenthusiasm for the new album. Despite the criticism, the record was generally received well by music critics, with some giving it their highest praise for the band's ability to reflect on and tell the story of its own birth with creativity and emotion.

In another unusual step, "Song for Someone," a quintessential U2 song distributed as one of the three singles from *Innocence*, was also released as four different videos. The first was from a compilation called *Films of Innocence* and featured the artist Mode 2 painting a mural filled with hopeful scenes on a city wall in Omagh, Northern Ireland. A second video was a short film directed by Vincent Haycock starring Woody Harrelson as a convict on the day of his release from the penitentiary. As the soon-to-be ex-con takes his final walk across the grounds and through the prison gates to freedom, he appears to be filled with fear and anxiety, not joy, as he prepares to meet his daughter in the parking lot. A third video for the song featured scenes of Bono falling to earth, floating through water, and drifting across the stars, in a symbolic exploration of good and evil by director Matt Mahurin. A fourth video for "Song for Someone" used cutting-edge technology in collaboration with Apple and the revolutionary Vrse app to create a 360-degree, three-dimensional interactive experience. Viewed through Google Cardboard headsets, viewers are immersed in a combination of scenes that begin on the e-stage of U2's tour staging and then progress to different sites around the world, resulting in a stunning, immersive encounter unlike any rock music video before.

In 2015, while preparing for and launching the unique Innocence + Experience tour, the band experienced a number of personal setbacks. The death of Jack Heaslip, U2's spiritual advisor, in February left an emotional hole for many in the organization. Then in May, Larry's father died, taking Larry away from eleventh-hour rehearsals in Vancouver to attend the funeral in Dublin just a day before the start of the tour. And Dennis Sheehan, U2's longtime and beloved stage manager, died of a heart attack in Los Angeles, only seven shows into the tour, leaving the crew grief stricken. The physical well-being of a couple of band members was further threatened in 2015, as Bono had a serious bike accident requiring extensive surgery and several months of recuperation before the tour's start, and Edge narrowly escaped injury when he fell off the stage on the tour's opening night. Innocence + Experience also faced a couple of serious security incidents on its European leg. One of the Stockholm shows was postponed due to a breach that forced police to evacuate the arena—a first in U2's history. More significantly, the two final concerts in Paris—the first of which was scheduled to be broadcast live on HBO on November 14, 2015—were postponed due to the tragic terrorist attacks in that city on November 13, which left more than a hundred people dead and several hundred injured. As U2 played its Ireland shows just days later, fans organized a "white out" in support of Paris, holding white signs and tweeting with the hashtag #strongerthanfear, a reference to "Raised by Wolves," a central song on the tour that told Dublin's own story of a terror-filled past. As "Wolves" concluded, dates and places filled the screen, reminding fans and band alike of the violence during the Troubles that originated on both sides of the Irish border.

U2 finished 2015 by returning to Paris and playing the two rescheduled concerts, one of which was broadcast live on HBO as originally intended. It was a powerful and emotional set of shows for both the audience and U2. Reminiscent of the band's role in New York City after 9/11, the names of victims scrolled across the giant LED screen at the end of "City of Blinding Lights." And on the final night in Paris—and the last show of the tour leg—Bono, Edge, Larry, and Adam exited the stage, surrendering the arena to the Eagles of Death Metal, the musical group that had been performing in a crowded theater where most of the deaths had occurred just three weeks earlier. It was a tremendous moment of gracious humility on the part of U2.

In returning to the city of its childhood innocence, U2 brought with it the experience—both through joy and pain—of a lifelong career. In concert, Bono had often asked a rhetorical question, "What do you want?" and then, playing the part of a desperate refugee, would answer, "I want a place called home!" In a sense, U2's wanderings for nearly four decades had taken them back to the one thing they had committed to from the beginning: the city of Dublin was still their home, and it was there that they intended to compile *Songs of Experience*, the seasoned complement to *Innocence* and the continuing tale of four late middle-aged artists reflecting on a well-lived musical journey.

Deeply shaken by the relative failure of its *No Line* project, U2 emerged from the record-breaking 360° tour confused and ambivalent about its future. Bono summarized, "We'll find out if we're irrelevant. I'm perfectly prepared for people to try and blow us off the stage. We're just not going to make it easy" (Newman, "9 Biggest Revelations"). In an attempt to stay relevant, the band produced its most personal album, *Songs of Innocence*, by revisiting the story of its younger days. With the supporting tour's focus on smaller-arena audiences, an intimate story line, and engaging technology, the band felt as close as it ever had been to its fans. Well into their midfifties, the members of U2 appeared to be a long way from retirement, still ready to engage and shape the world in which they lived. Edge made this especially clear, saying, "We don't want to ever be a heritage act. It might happen, but we'll go kicking and screaming into that mode. We feel the place for us to be is part of the conversation of contemporary culture and music and film and everything else" (Espen, "U2 Interview"). Not ready to rest on the success of a massive discography, a dazzling array of hit singles, groundbreaking tours, and countless awards, as well as an impressive history of activist engagement in local and global causes, U2 seemed to think that some of its best work was still to come.

7

FAITH AND ART

U2 has delivered a consistent message blending spiritual faith and social activism since its 1980 debut album. The band members, heavily influenced in their early years by living in war-torn Ireland—and three of them having belonged for a time to a Christian community called Shalom—fill their music with rich biblical imagery, both overt and implied, resulting in a spirituality that is inseparable from their art. Commenting on the role of imagery in religion, Bono said, "The only way we can approach God is—if we're honest—through metaphor, through symbol. So art becomes essential, not decorative" (Bono and Peterson, "Bono & Eugene Peterson"). For U2, music is not something to be added as an accessory to the practice of faith. Rather it is a primary way to access God directly. Art functions as a core component for the spiritual life lived out in the daily context of work, school, family, and relationships.

Not comfortable in institutional Christian churches, the group members found themselves outside organized religion and, in fact, often critiquing it through their craft. Somewhere between orthodoxy and idealism, U2 has developed a unique integration of faith and culture that transcends traditional approaches to popular religious music by engaging the world, not by remaining isolated from it. Throughout its extensive catalog, the band has repeatedly embraced important themes from the Bible, integrating faith and art in ways that both acknowledge and reflect the spiritual hunger of a restless culture. Widely accepted by fans who search out the biblical themes in U2's music, this posture has troubled many other conservative Christians, creating a dilemma for a church that is skeptical of the band's unorthodox spirituality. In "The Miracle (of Joey Ramone)," Bono sings on behalf of his bandmates and reflects on their simple beginnings, "We were pilgrims on our way." Indeed, U2's journey into spiritual and artistic formation is one that has been navigated in a highly public context and continues to be lived out in the company of a host of faithful traveling partners.

SHALOM THEN AND NOW

U2 formed in a religiously turbulent culture. The context of the Troubles impacted the young musicians in ways they may or may not have been aware of, but it certainly left its mark as they searched for identity. Ireland's history could be viewed as a long religious argument, starting in the fifth century with St. Patrick's apocryphal arrival on the island as an ambassador for the Catholic Church, then escalating when England's King Henry VIII broke with the pope and created the Protestant Church of Ireland in the 1500s. The schism culminated four hundred years later in the Troubles—a dark period of sectarianism that began in the early 1960s and was formally ended by the Good Friday Agreement in 1998. U2's members were born and raised in a conflicted Ireland that was often split along religious lines: the northern portion of the island favoring Protestantism and the south supporting Catholicism. Growing up in a religiously divided culture, Bono, Adam, Larry, and Edge experienced firsthand the outcomes of rigid dogma and narrow-minded sectarianism.

There was, however, a bright light in the midst of Ireland's banal and religiously intolerant culture. Dublin's Mount Temple Comprehensive, the secondary school the boys attended, was a progressive, "experimental" institution that offered an alternative to the sectarianism of the day. Though the school had Protestant origins, the members of U2 found it to be an open and accepting environment, inclusive of those from other religious traditions as well as those who had no allegiance to a faith tradition. It was also at Mount Temple that the quartet met teachers and mentors who inspired them to think broadly and holistically about education, encouraging an integration of faith and life. History teacher Donald Moxham was one of U2's first advocates, encouraging the boys' creativity and providing a classroom for their unorthodox rehearsals. Albert Bradshaw, the school's choir director, inspired the teens to actively engage music and make it a part of their daily lives rather than merely listen to it or treat it as an abstract subject. Sophie Shirley taught Mount Temple's religious education class but did so in a way that fostered creativity, not denominational dogmatism, specifically helping Bono to see "God's fingerprints everywhere" (McCormick, "Boy to Man," 12).

But more than any other, it was Jack Heaslip who influenced the boys' spiritual formation through a decades-long friendship of pastoral care. There from the beginning, his highly relational and creative approach made him a popular teacher and counselor at Mount Temple. Versatile enough to oversee the sex education class and read from Leonard Cohen, he could also teach English and lead Bible studies. When Bono's mother died unexpectedly, Heaslip was instrumental in helping the enraged fourteen-year-old cope with the loss, always attending to the teen's needs with patience and empathy. Though Heaslip eventually left Mount Temple to become an Anglican clergyman, he maintained a nurturing relationship with U2, ministering to hundreds of staff and crew members as their "traveling pastor" while on tour, as well as officiating at Bono and Ali's wedding, baptizing their children, and burying Bono's father.

The impact of Heaslip's integrative approach to life and faith runs deep through U2's music and activism. Shunning a duality between the sacred and the secular, he quietly counseled the group to engage its art as an expression of spirituality, emphasizing that U2's job was simply to join God in the ordinariness of everyday life. Two examples of how Heaslip's holistic theology has affected U2 can be found in an album title and a Bible verse. First, the title *No Line on the Horizon* assumes a unified creation, in which heaven and earth balance and interact with one another. On the CD's packaging, the addition of an equal sign superimposed over Hiroshi Sugimoto's photograph of a boundless sea meeting a never-ending skyline accentuated the seamless interface of heaven and earth, giving equal significance to both. A second example is from one of Bono's favorite scriptures, found in the Lord's Prayer from Matthew 6:9–13: "Thy kingdom come, Thy will be done, *on earth as it is in heaven*" (emphasis added). Taken at face value, Jesus was highlighting the parity of both the physical and spiritual realms, refuting a common belief that the natural world is somehow less divine than the supernatural. This theology of an integrated creation is central to U2's understanding of its mission.

The rejection of such a dualism—earth is evil and heaven is holy—was a consistent theme for Heaslip and can be heard in his prayer before the start of the Elevation tour in 2001. While offering a blessing during the final rehearsal, the Anglican priest gathered the crew and asked God for "an anointing on everything to do with this tour—every body, every thing." He continued praying,

> We think of the band, but we think of every piece of equipment and everyone who works that piece of equipment, everyone who packs up, everyone who drives a car, everyone who does the catering, everyone who is responsible for technology, every joint of wire, every plug, every soffit, every light. (U2, "Jack Heaslip/Bono")

For Heaslip, the intersection of the spiritual and the physical meant that both crew and equipment equally could be conduits of the divine.

Heaslip also helped U2 understand that Christianity should not merely be relegated to a Sunday morning church gathering and that God is to be found in the most commonplace activities—including rock concerts! Faith is something to be thought about and acted on, not just in a traditional religious environment but in every experience of daily living. Commenting on Heaslip's holistic approach and its influence on the band, Neil McCormick notes, "[I]t is [Heaslip's] openness that is reflected in Bono's own faith and its practical interactions with the corporeal world" (McCormick, "Boy to Man," 12). Together with the others at Mount Temple, Heaslip both taught and demonstrated an integrative approach that became foundational for U2's own understating of faith and life.

The band, however, didn't always have such a holistic and open philosophy. Early on, as Bono, Edge, and Larry participated in the Shalom community, Christianity looked very different. While the idealistic punk and hippie movements of the 1970s raged on throughout Europe and North America, three of U2's four members were attracted to the "born-again" Bible studies and squeaky-clean living of a conservative commune. It was there, in this countercultural enclave, that they found a higher purpose and grounded themselves against the pitfalls of drugs, alcohol, promiscuity, and the other vices that typically brought young bands down. Steve Stockman summarizes the experience:

> The idea of it being radical attracted U2. In any other city in the Western world, this kind of Christian behavior would have been seen as old-fashioned and almost nerdish. In any other city, Bono would have laughed at such middle-class, respectable, religious behavior. But in Dublin, this was radical stuff. . . . In some ways, Shalom was an out-there kind of gang on parallel lines with the Lypton Village gang. It wasn't as if one of them was dangerous and the other one safe. (Stockman, *Walk On*, 17)

In a sense, the three members of U2 were rebelling against the rebellion commonly found in the world of rock 'n' roll, instead favoring the zealous Shalom community.

Eventually, Shalom's appeal of communal living was overshadowed by its separatist dogma. As leaders required greater loyalty from Bono, Edge, and Larry, the young musicians were forced to choose between a career in secular music and commitment to the religious community. Additionally, the common trajectory of other Christian musicians in the 1970s and 1980s was to join the contemporary Christian music industry—a phenomenon that allowed pioneering artists such as Larry Norman, Randy Stonehill, Phil Keaggy, Amy Grant, and Michael W. Smith to build careers performing for church audiences. This self-sustaining profession, complete with recording companies, distributors, and publications, existed solely for the benefit of other Christians and didn't appeal to nor resonate with U2's worldview. The dilemma resulted in a personal crisis as each of the three members had to examine his own understanding of music and faith. In the end, all three opted to leave Shalom, rejecting what they saw as a false dichotomy, choosing instead a more holistic and integrated approach to faith and art. Taking the best of what they had learned from their participation in the Christian commune and the years spent at Mount Temple, U2 began to fashion its growing franchise, not merely as a business but also as an open, welcoming, and spiritually nurturing family.

As Bono, Edge, and Larry exited Shalom, they did so with a fresh understanding of their own Christian witness. They emerged knowing they didn't want people to follow the band just because it had Christian members. Rather than holding up a banner announcing U2's spirituality, they wanted the music to speak for itself. At twenty years old, Bono was clear about the group's purpose: "We didn't want to be involved in Christian subculture, which was a lot of Christians coming on to the gigs. We're not interested in preaching to the converted" (*U2's Vision*). When one magazine actually published the news that U2 was a "Christian band" (an error, since Adam did not profess any kind of faith), Bono bemoaned the damage done, responding, "We weren't going to tell anybody, we were going to witness by our lives" (*U2's Vision*). The sad irony was that as their faith became more public, he feared "the witness had ended" (*U2's Vision*). Such a unique integration of faith, art, and a mainstream career was a direct contrast to the Christian subculture of the day. In comparison to other religious musicians, U2 was looking more like a band with Christian members than a Christian band.

Later in their career, U2 experienced a different kind of shalom. Whereas the commune had been narrow and dogmatic, the band's rediscovery of an Old Testament concept brought new meaning and life. Often translated as "peace," the ancient Hebrew word *shalom* actually reflects a broad, holistic engagement with culture in the pursuit of justice. Motivated by biblical texts as well as global activists including Martin Luther King, Jr., Mohandas Gandhi, and Nelson Mandela, U2 embraced the idea of shalom as an active and effectual presence in the world. Far from being weak and passive, this scriptural notion of peace challenged U2 to boldly oppose crippling systems of injustice and to champion the cause of the poor and disenfranchised. The songs "Sunday Bloody Sunday" and "Bullet the Blue Sky" did this indirectly, while "Peace on Earth," "Love and Peace or Else," and "Staring at the Sun" were much more overt. But whether waving a white flag on the *War* tour in 1983 or unabashedly endorsing global peacemakers during the Innocence + Experience tour in 2015, U2 has used every means within its vast pool of resources to personally combat poverty, inequity, and injustice while calling its audiences to do the same.

As a young band, several members of U2 began their journeys of faith shaped and influenced by Mount Temple Comprehensive and a Christian commune. The band emerged from these experiences rejecting the religious/secular dualism so predominant in their native Ireland and forged ahead to super-rock-star status with a unique and integrative view of music and faith. Over time, the band contextualized their Christian faith in ways that led to greater public engagement, demonstrated both in concerts and in their offstage lives. Shalom itself was much more than the name of a commune—it also became a deeply guiding ethic for engaging an imperfect world. Bono summarized the band's integrative approach by referencing one of his musical idols:

> Bob Marley is one of the great, great heroes of mine. He did whatever he wanted with his music. He had his faith, his belief in God, or Jah as he called it. He had no problem combining that with his sexuality and the sensuality of some of his love songs. He was tender and open and politically a hard-ass. He had those three dimensions and it's everything I want from U2. (Takiff, "From 'Good Voice'")

This inclination toward a holistic understanding of faith, politics, sexuality, justice, art, and activism provided rich experiences for U2's members. It also allowed for a vast and deep pool of biblical imagery in its music.

BIBLICAL IMAGERY

U2 has used biblical imagery as a foundational poetic device throughout its career. At times, scripture is referenced in subtly nuanced lyrics—such as the New Testament's Greek idea of unconditional *agape* love in "I Will Follow"—while at others, the Bible is directly referenced—as in the quote, "I was a stranger, you took me in," from Matthew 25:35 and used in the song "Miracle Drug." But most often, U2's considerable use of biblical material is so tightly woven into the text of its songs that the casual listener might never know scripture is being referenced. In this sense, U2's lyrics are "polyvalent." That is, they take on multiple layers of meaning, but interpretation of a song is dependent on which layer(s) the listener is hearing.

"Song for Someone," from *Songs of Innocence*, is a perfect example. On a popular level, the song has a singable tune, is musically accessible for the average fan, and is easy to relate to, especially for those who have had a close friend endure with them through difficult times. Bono has often said it is a love song for his wife. But on a deeper level, the song speaks to serious ontological questions about the conflict of good and evil. In one of several music videos featuring "Song for Someone," director Matt Mahurin works at this level, portraying Bono as a lost soul trapped between earth and heaven, struggling through the darkness to reach a distant light. Similarly, Vincent Haycock's short film set to "Song for Someone" focuses on a convict being released from prison and addresses themes of fear and liberation. Both of these video interpretations lead listeners to thoughtfully consider underlying meanings, opening the way for a more artistic experience with the song. There is, however, yet another level, a deeper spiritual plane, that also permeates the tune. The entire song could be sung as a prayer directly to God, the divine "Someone." Using metaphysical language, "seeing," "healing," and "searching" all become metaphors for a spiritual journey. Bono closes the song with "I'm a long way from your hill of Calvary," a traditional reference to the cross of Christ. And the lyric "the kiss I stole from your mouth" is a strong allusion to Judas's betrayal of Jesus in the Garden of Gethsemane (which is also a narrative found in "Until the End of the World"). For those aware of the scriptural implications, "Song for Someone" becomes an intimate spiritual experience. In the same way, many of U2's songs function on multiple levels, first tapping into universally popular themes, then moving into weightier questions, and finally hinting at a spiritual realm. Assuming from the start that its fans were smart and inquisitive, U2 has always tried to layer its music in ways that appeal to those who want to look deeper.

Another way U2 has incorporated scripture into its music is through the use of biblical genre—types of ancient literature that include poetry, historical narrative, letters, prophecy, apocalypse, parables, and more. In particular, U2 has always been fond of the book of Psalms. Primarily ascribed to King David, this anthology of songs and poems was used in Jewish religious rituals and served as a worship hymnal for the ancient Hebrew people. Filled with honest words to God, individual psalms contain expressions of joy, celebration, and praise, as well as grief, lament, and even doubt. Bono discussed his love of this genre when he penned the introduction for a new translation of Psalms in 1999, writing,

> Abandonment and displacement are the stuff of my favourite psalms. The Psalter may be a font of gospel music, but for me it's despair that the psalmist really reveals and the nature of his special relationship with God. Honesty, even to the point of anger. (Bono, "Psalm Like It Hot")

Psalms have been part of U2's spiritual and musical journey from the earliest days. In a 2016 interview, Bono recalled, "In the dressing room before a show, we would read the psalms as a band and then walk out into arenas and stadiums—the words igniting us, inspiring us" (Bono and Peterson, "Bono & Eugene Peterson"). Long before the invention of electric guitars, tube amplifiers, and LED screens, the poetry of an ancient people was filled with raw and powerful emotion. For U2, the psalms have both inspired and infused its entire catalog.

A specific phrase found repeatedly in Psalms has also been used frequently in U2's lyrics. The simple question "How long?" can be traced back to multiple scriptural texts. In Psalm 13, the poet interrogates God using the phrase four times in two verses. Psalm 62 is even more incriminating, accusing God with, "How long will you assault me?" In Psalm 89, the psalmist doubts God, asking, "How long, Lord? Will you hide yourself forever?" and in 119 he begs for relief from his enemy's relentless pursuit, pleading, "How long must your servant wait?" Bono has borrowed this theme for lyrics in several of U2's songs. In "Sunday Bloody Sunday," he responds to violence and injustice with the cry, "How long must we sing this song?" In a similar way, U2 has often closed concerts with (Psalm) "40," echoing a three-thousand-year-old lament, "How long, to sing this song?" And Bono has been singing "how long" in "Out of Control" since *U2-3*, the band's very first recording project, as well as more recently in a U2/Green Day collaboration covering the Skids' 1979 hit, "The Saints Are Coming."

The book of Psalms has influenced U2 in many other ways as well. Psalm 23 became an anchoring theme on the Innocence + Experience tour of 2015. As the band paid tribute to the forgotten victims of the 1974 bombings in Dublin, Bono ended "Raised by Wolves" with a dramatic recitation, repeating the well-known verse, "Yea, though I walk through the valley of the shadow of death, I will fear no evil: for thou art with me; thy rod and thy staff they comfort me." And while Edge's wailing guitar transitioned to the frenzied intro of "Until the End of the World," Bono embodied the pain and doubt of the original psalmist, screaming, "Comfort me! Comfort me! COMFORT ME!" The chilling effect was made even more poignant after the band's longtime tour manager and friend Dennis Sheehan unexpectedly passed away soon after the tour started. During the conclusion of "End of the World," leaflets containing text from *Alice in Wonderland*, Dante's *Inferno*, and a variety of psalms fell from the ceiling in a final simulation of the Dublin explosions. Altogether, each concert on the first leg of the Innocence + Experience tour typically referenced more than thirty-five different psalms in both obvious and obscure ways.

There are many different translations of the Bible, but U2 has consistently turned to Eugene Peterson's contemporary paraphrase called *The Message*. Peterson intentionally crafted his version of scripture for those who don't have a church background and aren't familiar with the formal language of traditional translations, hoping that it would resonate with a new generation of readers. Favoring this version, Bono used it during the Elevation tour in 2001 as he moved from the somber message of "Bad" to the ecstatic "Where the Streets Have No Name." It was a redemptive moment, both festive and jubilant, punctuated by the lead singer's loose quotation of Psalm 116: "What can I give back to God for the blessings you poured out on me? I lift high the cup of salvation—a toast to our Father. I'll follow through on a promise I made to you. Hear my heart." This time, rather than mourning a loss, U2 used a psalm to rejoice, bringing the audience into a communal celebration. Peterson has joyfully affirmed the band's use of his paraphrase, commenting, "Bono is singing to the very people I did this work for. I feel that we are allies in this. He is helping get me and the Message to the very people Jesus spent much of his time with" (Bono and Peterson, "Bono & Eugene Peterson").

In a less obvious way, but still reflective of ancient Hebrew poetry, U2 has also crafted its own modern-day psalms. "Wake Up Dead Man" is a heavy lament that could have been written by King David if he lived in the twenty-first century. In it, Bono pleads, "Jesus, Jesus help me / I'm alone in this world / And a fucked up world it is too." Bare and stripped down, it's a gut-wrenchingly honest prayer that demonstrates U2's careful yet authentic blend of faith and doubt in a culturally relevant way. Mimicking a psalm of thanksgiving, "Magnificent" is a grand and upbeat expression of exuberant praise. As the band plays the joy-filled anthem, Bono sings, "Justified till we die / You and I will magnify the magnificent."

The poetry of the psalms isn't the only biblical genre used by U2. Wisdom literature in the Bible often questions accepted notions of the way life works and is brilliantly demonstrated in U2's collaboration with Johnny Cash on "The Wanderer." Mirroring the biblical book of Ecclesiastes—which literally means "the teacher"—the song paints the portrait of a wandering soul consumed by cynicism. "Chasing after the wind," the Teacher and the Wanderer each go on a desperate search for meaning in life. Robert Vagacs notes that the protagonist of U2's song is roaming aimlessly through the dystopian landscape of "Zooropa," a "journey into the emptiness of Babylon" (Vagacs 52, *Religious Nuts*). Cash sings, "Yeah, I left with nothing, nothing but the thought of you / I went wandering," reflecting the restless spirit of all who search for purpose in life. In doing so, both the Teacher and the Wanderer remind the listener of the bleakness of a world without God and thus point to God himself as the antidote to cynicism and hopelessness.

The parables of Jesus have also influenced U2's catalog. In the biblical sense, a parable is a story that uses the element of surprise to teach a truth about the kingdom of God. "The First Time," another song on *Zooropa*, is a perfect adaptation of this type of scripture. Taking inspiration from Luke 15:11–32, Bono says, "It's the story of the prodigal son but in it the prodigal son decides he doesn't want to return" (U2 and McCormick, *U2 by U2*, 249). Having gone out and squandered his inheritance, the boy comes home expecting to face his father's wrath. Instead, the patriarch opens his arms and lavishes the lost child with gifts. But in U2's telling of the story, the son ends up leaving through the back door, throwing away the key and turning away from love. Even so, and in spite of the rejection, the father's steadfast commitment remains. The unexpected ending gives the story the punch that parables originally would have had in Jesus's day.

The prophetic style of literature in the Bible has also shaped U2's recordings and concert performances. The prophets of the Hebrew scriptures are not, as is often thought, simply fortune tellers or predictors of the future. Speaking on behalf of Yahweh, the prophets brought messages that had spiritual, social, political, and cultural implications, including the firm and consistent reprimand to love the widow, the orphan, and the alien (three groups that were routinely marginalized). Often stern and cautionary, the prophets identified injustice and called God's people to make corrections. Many U2 songs blend political and spiritual themes in the same way. In "Love and Peace or Else," the band highlights instability in the Middle East and challenges, "Lay down your guns / All you daughters of Zion / All you Abraham sons." In concert, Bono wore a headband that read "coexist" and chanted, "Jesus, the Jew, Muhammed, all true—all sons of Abraham." The phrase was not meant to say all of these faiths can be blended into one but to remind Christians, Jews, and Muslims of their common lineage. "Bullet the Blue Sky" has also been consistently used in a prophetic way, calling all people, but particularly Americans, to examine foreign policies related to global military aggression. Originally a commentary on the Reagan administration's controversial activity in Central America, "Bullet" has been updated numerous times to address the conflicts in the Middle East, as on the Vertigo tour of 2005, and the 2015 refugee crisis in Europe on the Innocence + Experience tour.

But it is "Sunday Bloody Sunday" that has been one of U2's most prophetic and versatile pieces, being reinterpreted and adapted to many different contexts over its thirty-plus year history. Written in 1983 for the *War* album, the song was originally conceived as an impassioned and peaceful response to the violence of the Troubles. In concert, Bono symbolized the call to unity by waving a white flag of peace. "Sunday Blood Sunday" found new life on the PopMart tour as Edge moved to the spotlight to perform the song as a solo. Soft and gentle, the moving ballad was a stark contrast to the decadence and excess of the tour's theme of commercialism. In 2005, the song was reinterpreted yet again on the Vertigo tour. This time Bono's cries of "No more!" during the bridge served as a jarring reminder that terrorism had changed the world in dark and irreversible ways. On the 360° tour, U2 continued calling attention to global concerns by championing the cause of peaceful Iranian dissidents. Known as the Green Movement, "Sunday Bloody Sunday" became a statement of solidarity with the men, women, and children who had been unjustly killed and imprisoned by Iran's oppressive regime. In 2015, on the Innocence + Experience tour, the band reinvented the song once more as a dramatic re-creation of the 1974 Dublin bombings. Slow and dirge-like, in this iteration of "Sunday Bloody Sunday," Bono dropped the climactic final line, leaving out the lyric, "The real battle just begun / To claim the victory Jesus won / On Sunday, Bloody Sunday." Void of this key theological statement, the song functioned as a corporate lament, offering a confession for the atrocities of Ireland's past. Through more than three decades of usage, U2 has demonstrated its appreciation of the prophetic tradition by adapting and contextualizing one of its greatest hits.

Along with poetry, wisdom, and prophetic genre, U2 has also been
influenced by apocalyptic literature. In the Bible, an apocalypse uses
imagery—sometimes bizarre and eccentric—to speak of judgment and
the collapse of systems and structures, which give way to a new (or
renewed) future. The book of Revelation, the most well-known example
of an apocalyptic text, is filled with images of angels, demons, earth-
quakes, dragons, and flames. But contrary to popular belief, its main
theme is a positive one—it is a message of hope for those who suffer
under the daily hardships of a fallen world and a promise that evil in all
forms will one day be vanquished. In the 1970s, an ardent wave of
apocalyptic fervor was sweeping across North America and Europe.
Promoting the imminent return of Christ and the consummation of all
history, this "end times" theology was nearly inescapable, especially for
communities like Shalom and the three young, zealous Christians of
U2. The influence is seen in "Fire" on *October* (arguably the most
religious-themed album of U2's catalog), with lyrics including, "The sun
is burning black," "The moon is running red," and "The stars are falling
down," all direct references to Revelation 6:12–13. Similarly, in "Tomorrow," a mournful song about the loss of his mother, Bono sings,
"He's coming back . . . Jesus is coming / I'm gonna be there, mother."
The apocalyptic style of scripture can also be seen in some of U2's later
works. From *Achtung Baby*, "The Fly" alludes to the destructive forces
of evil in an unbalanced cosmos, as Bono's alter ego sings about stars
falling from the sky, a world in darkness, and the universe exploding
"'cause of one man's lie." "Until the End of the World," as the title
suggests, also has elements of apocalypse. In recent years, "Where the
Streets Have No Name" and "City of Blinding Lights" have been used
in concert to present the vision of a restored creation while alluding to a
future age when evil is banished and the kingdom of God comes in its
fullness. Each song hints at the heavenly city of perfection described in
Revelation.

U2 has always assumed that its fans want deeper content than what
the average rock band could provide. From the beginning, the band and
its management set out to engage audiences on multiple levels by creating polyvalent experiences through studio recordings and concert performances. While the surface layer is immediately the most popular,
deeper subtexts can include social-cultural and spiritual themes. The
Joshua tree itself—perhaps the most iconic symbol of U2's career—is a

subtle allusion to Jesus (the Hebrew word *Yeshua* means "salvation" and can be translated to English as both Joshua and Jesus) and to the cross (which is referred as a tree in the book of Acts). Other more overt uses of scripture are plentiful as well. During the Innocence + Experience tour, "City of Blinding Lights" was accentuated with lighted crosses hanging from the ceiling and featured a stage in the shape of a cross. Despite the abundance of biblical imagery in U2's work, the group has always believed that its message would be strongest outside of a Christian subculture, opting instead to incorporate faith and art in the mainstream music industry. Summing up the band's spirituality, Larry reflected, "We don't want to appear to be flaunting our beliefs. It's a very personal thing and you don't want it to look like some sort of lecture or gimmick. The music, the lyrics say everything the band has to say about their feelings" (Mann, "U2"). Bono's attitude is similar: "This is how we worship God, even though we don't write religious songs, because we didn't feel God needs the advertising" (Assayas, *Bono*, 147). U2 remains confident that fans wanting a deeper experience will understand the messages underlying its songs. As the band has forged ahead with innovative production and creative artistic efforts, it also has fashioned a deeply spiritual culture unlike any other. And though its unique brand of Christianity has attracted others who also value community, activism, and scriptural reflection, its unorthodox spirituality hasn't always been well received by the institutional Christian Church.

THE CHURCH OF U2

The Dublin of U2's childhood provided many opportunities to experience religious discord firsthand. Edge's parents sang in a Protestant church choir and Larry served as a Catholic altar boy. Bono's mother would take him and his brother to a local Protestant congregation, while their father, a member of the Catholic Church, waited outside or went to Mass at a different time. Their interdenominational marriage was considered scandalous and was not even valid in some areas of Ireland. Schools in Dublin were segregated—they were either Catholic, reflecting the vast majority of people in the Republic of Ireland, or Protestant, representing the official Church of Ireland. It wasn't until each of the four teens started attending Mount Temple that they had the chance to experience a nonsectarian education that valued both denominational perspectives. The culture in Dublin, heavily impacted by a conservative Catholic presence, was repressive and restrictive. Topics including sexuality, contraception, divorce, and abortion were taboo. Movies were censored, homosexuality was criminalized, and rock 'n' roll could only be heard on the stolen waves that drifted across the sea from England. Driven by religious authoritarianism, the typical institutional church in Dublin during U2's formation was inhibiting, heavy-handed, and provincial.

Despite the restrictive nature of the church, the band did have some positive experiences. Many of its earliest gigs were actually in chapels or parish social halls. Following a 1981 concert at a Grand Rapids church, the local newspaper linked the band's spirituality to its sacred venue, reporting,

> U2 hardly fits the choirboy image, but the Irish rock band found a perfect Saturday night sanctuary in Fountain Street Church. The Dublin boys had some 1,100 fans on their feet for a spirited one-hour set that baptized the locals in the joyous, mystical gospel of U2. Its sermon of rock tunes with religious overtones won over new followers. ("U2 May Be the Band")

Whenever they performed in a church, the guys seemed comfortable and at home. And for the three born-again Christians, the drugs and alcohol so readily available at wild after-parties common to the rock scene were replaced, very naturally, with Bible study and prayer. On Sunday mornings, the trio would often break from rehearsal to quietly attend a church in whatever town they were currently touring.

Looking back again at the Shalom experience also provides some insight into U2's understanding of church. Though Bono, Edge, and Larry initially had good interactions with Shalom, in the end the community drove the young men away because of its own controlling practices, as it sought to compel them to give up their career in secular rock music. Larry was the first to leave, frustrated by the coercive environment. Years later he reflected on his time with the movement:

> The idea was to create a Christian community, where people would live and work under strict Christian standards. When you're young and impressionable it all sounds ideal. But there was something ter-

ribly wrong with the concept. It was a bit like the bigger the commitment you made, the closer you were to heaven. It was a really
screwed-up view of the world and nothing to do with what I now
understand a Christian faith to be. . . . I learned a lot though and I
also gained a faith I didn't have before, and that's still with me. (U2
and McCormick, *U2 by U2*, 117)

For Bono, the split was especially painful. The guys had come to love
and admire some of Shalom's leaders, but these same leaders, as well as
some of their close friends, were pressuring them to conform to the
conservative commune, causing them to be torn in two between their
music and their mentors. A twenty-nine-year-old Bono eventually confessed, "In the end, I realized it was bullshit, that what these people
were getting close to with this idea was denial, rather than willful surrender. It was denial, which is the next-door neighbor to self-flagella-
tion" (Block, "Bono Bites Back"). For U2, Shalom's rejection of culture
was merely a form of legalism and self-asceticism, just another version
of the repressive religious structures they grew up in.

In part, the internal conflict U2's members experienced in their
separation from Shalom was later reflected on in *Achtung Baby*. Aban-
doning its explicit presentation of social and political themes, the band
turned instead to look inward at its own personal demons. As Bono
sang, "Let me be your lover tonight" on "Even Better Than the Real
Thing" and painted a sultry portrait of Salome as she stood in contrast
to an ascetic John the Baptist in "Mysterious Ways" (complete with a
belly dancer in concert!), the new emphasis on human sexuality—especially as U2 mixed in themes of spirituality—left some pious fans questioning the band's own faith. If that wasn't enough to cause concern,
"Acrobat" seemed to be a direct assault on the institutional church, as
Bono confessed, "I'd join the movement, if there was one I could believe in / Yeah, I'd break bread and wine, if there was a church I could
receive in." *Achtung Baby* represented a radical shift not only in musical style but also in U2's interpretation of faith and art. Preferring the
straightforward agenda of the 1980s era, with its emphasis on love and
activism, many Christians were confused by the dark direction the band
seemed to be pursuing. The overstimulating themes, decadent images,
and taboo subjects of sexual identity, failed relationships, ego, greed,
and consumerism raised the suspicions of those in the established
church. U2's ironic approach during the last decade of the millennium

was lost on many of its fans—especially the conservative and religious ones—and could partially explain why sales were down for *Zooropa* and *Pop*, specifically in America.

But that wasn't the end of U2's journey with the church. Later in his career, Bono found a renewed passion for faith and institutional Christianity. Having just returned from a tour, he went to a Christmas Eve service at St. Patrick's Cathedral in Dublin. Tired and somewhat bored, he picked up the Bible and began to read the story of Jesus's birth. But on this night, the story took on new life, leaving the middle-aged lead singer stunned and transformed. Reading the narrative as if for the first time, he noticed,

> The idea that God, if there is a force of Love and Logic in the universe, that it would seek to explain itself is amazing enough. That it would seek to explain itself and describe itself by becoming a child born in straw poverty, in shit and straw . . . a child . . . I just thought: "Wow!" Just the poetry. . . . Unknowable love, unknowable power, describes itself as the most vulnerable. There it was. I was sitting there, and it's not that it hadn't struck me before, but tears came streaming down my face, and I saw the genius of this, utter genius of picking a particular point in time and deciding to turn on this. . . . Love needs to find form, intimacy needs to be whispered. To me, it makes sense. It's actually logical. It's pure logic. Essence has to manifest itself. It's inevitable. Love has to become an action or something concrete. It would have to happen. There must be an incarnation. Love must be made flesh. (Assayas, *Bono*, 125)

Bono further stunned both the rock and religious communities in 2006 when he brought the two worlds together in a collision of pop culture, social justice, and personal faith. Speaking via a taped interview with Bill Hybels, the pastor of one of America's largest megachurches, Bono used the opportunity to chastise Christian leaders from around the world, saying, "The church has historically always been behind the curve. It's amazing to me—on civil rights, fighting against the racism in the '60s and the '50s in the South in United States, and apartheid in Africa." He continued, "[And] the church had been very judgmental about the AIDS virus in particular" (Lawrence, "Preaching to the Converted"). But Bono didn't just criticize the group of religious leaders gathered that day at Willow Creek Community Church in Chicago. He also commended them. On behalf of the ONE campaign, he confessed that Hybels had helped change his own view of organized Christianity, acknowledging "the importance of the church in creating the moral as well as the practical infrastructure to deal with some of the biggest problems facing the world" (Lawrence, "Preaching to the Converted"). On a return visit to Hybels's church three years later, Bono again admitted, "I can honestly say that as a person who's really enjoyed giving off about the church, you have completely ruined it for me because the church has done incredible things" (Lawrence, "Bono Returns"). With the Hybels interviews, Bono seemed to be redoubling his effort to engage the same religious structures that he and the band had been so critical of in the past. And having just released *How to Dismantle an Atomic Bomb* in 2004—an album that contained a significant amount of unambiguous faith language, including "Yahweh," a modern hymn of commitment and consecration—Christians were again ready to claim the band for themselves. Bono's pursuit of contemporary Christian musicians, including Michael W. Smith, Switchfoot, and Jars of Clay, as well as other evangelical leaders, such as Pastor Rick Warren of Saddleback Community Church in Southern California, demonstrated a gradual yet consistent embrace of conservative Christianity. As a result, some music critics returned to their old accusations that Bono and the band had once again compromised their artistic integrity.

Bono has never claimed to be a theologian, nor has he been trained in the academic discipline of theology. He has, however, taken a very active interest in the study of God, as well as the interpretation and application of scripture, through avid reading and wise counsel. While Larry and Edge have, from the Shalom days, assented to their faith in quieter ways, they, too, have played important roles in shaping the band. Adam is the least explicit about spirituality and perhaps the most honest. Not opposed to discussing faith, he uses less definitive terms about the spirit of a U2 concert: "I don't quite know what it is . . . but I definitely know when it's there. It doesn't happen every night, but some nights there's a sense of community and fellowship. And people have said there's a spiritual aspect to what's happening in the house" (LePage, "Bass Notes").

Consumed by a unique desire, and with few models to imitate, U2 set out to mix faith and art in unconventional ways on a scale that was unprecedented. Committed to an open, nonsectarian understanding of

Christianity, U2 infused its music with biblical imagery and opened its growing family of associates and fans to those of other faith practices, political persuasions, and sexual identities, taking a path that led them far away from the Christian subculture. Author Beth Maynard concludes,

> U2 is anything but a "Christian rock group." They are simply artists who find it natural to draw on biblical imagery and raise religious issues in their work. . . . They wrestle with spiritual themes and set nuggets of scripture in the midst of their work, but they compete in the marketplace rather than preach to the choir. (Whiteley and Maynard, *Get Up Off Your Knees*)

Eschewing the judgmental experiences of childhood and adolescence, the band embraced love, grace, and tolerance. More than a nice sentiment or an idealistic experiment, the tangible outcome of U2's mission has always found embodiment in cultural engagement and activism rather than Sunday morning worship services. Both suspicious and supportive of the mainstream church but deeply concerned that Christianity must be integrated into daily living, Bono summed up his thoughts, advising, "Whenever you see religious people, where their faith is more important than love, they've got it the wrong way round in my view" (Robinson, "'I Nearly Quit'").

U2 has created a quandary for the church, especially for evangelicals in America. On the one hand, the band has resisted the perennial trappings of the standard "sex, drugs, and rock 'n' roll" culture, loaded its lyrics with biblical imagery, and called fans to action against the evil and unjust systems of this world. On the other hand, U2 has not fit preconceived notions of the institutional church as it has critiqued organized religion, enjoyed wealth and fame, and celebrated the human condition with a transparency uncharacteristic of musicians in the Christian subculture. Bono is quick to recognize the dilemma in a conversation with Eugene Peterson:

> The Psalmist is brutally honest about the explosive joy that he's feeling, and the deep sorrow or confusion. . . . And I often think, "Why isn't church music more like that?" . . . I find in Christian art a lot of dishonesty. . . . I would love if this conversation would inspire people who are writing these beautiful voices, these beautiful gospel songs,

[to] write a song about their bad marriage; write a song about how they're pissed off at the government. Because, that's what God wants. (Bono and Peterson, "Bono & Eugene Peterson")

The church can easily love Bono when he claims it as his own, but it's quick to turn away when he drops the "f-bomb" at an awards show.

A true enigma, the U2 organization has continued to expand, growing closer as a community and reenvisioning corporate spirituality. Ironically, this has made the band accessible, even attractive, to those of other faiths, as well as those who don't profess any faith. Christian or not, many irreligious fans have alluded to a spiritual presence at a concert, often referring to the experience as "the church of U2." And though he attributes the work more precisely to a movement of the divine, Bono is quick to acknowledge what fans also sense:

It feels like there's a blessing on the band right now. People say they're feeling shivers—well, the band is as well. And I don't know what it is, but it feels like God walking through the room, and it feels like a blessing, and in the end, music is a kind of sacrament; it's not just about airplay or chart position. (Tanner, "Courageous Crooners")

U2 believes that music is a sacrament—an activity that mediates and ushers in the divine presence of God. On the Innocence + Experience tour, Bono would often improvise during the bridge of "I Will Follow," singing, "We come here to surrender, surrender to your love / We come here to surrender, to the spirit of the holy dove." The simple yet profound statement works as a theological tenant for those who believe ("I will follow the God of unconditional love and submit to the presence of his Spirit"), or as a supreme ethic for those with no religious affiliation ("I will follow and give my life to others even when unconditional love is not reciprocated"). Either way, fans can't miss the call during a U2 concert to turn the music's message of love into practical and tangible action. If faith and spirituality are one side of a proverbial coin, then the other would be a sustained demonstration of that faith through activism and social engagement. For U2, these two foundational values are inseparable.

8

SOCIAL ENGAGEMENT

U2 would like to believe it is a band that can change the world. The faith of its members won't allow for anything less. Inspired by the ancient Hebrew prophets, they are committed to a form of social engagement that challenges unjust systems and works toward peace and fairness for all. Bono defines the band's activist roll, saying, "Charity is OK, I'm interested in charity. Of course, we should all be, especially those of us who are privileged. But I'm much more interested in justice. . . . These things are rooted in my study of the Scriptures" (Assayas, *Bono*, 137). Driven by compassion, conviction, and a sense of moral duty, U2 has consistently used albums, concerts, and special appearances to inform, inspire, and call fans to action, reflecting the band's deep commitment to shalom, as well as a call to be peacemakers.

While U2 has spent a career highlighting troubled spots around the globe, its innovative focus on Africa—especially through the ONE Campaign—has transformed Bono, on behalf of the band, into a global activist concerned with issues of poverty, inequity, fair trade, AIDS, and debt relief. The model of "new activism" Bono is largely responsible for creating has been both commendable and debatable, receiving praise and condemnation from fans and critics alike. Though Bono's high-visibility work as an activist has even been a point of contention for the band members themselves, all of the members contribute to a number of philanthropic projects. Reflecting foundational values of faith and justice, U2 has both shaped and been shaped by the cultural issues it has engaged throughout its forty-year mission.

A JOURNEY TOWARD JUSTICE

A young U2 probably couldn't imagine how long and difficult the journey of change would be, but the idea of social engagement infused the DNA of the group from the beginning. As they sat in manager Paul McGuinness's apartment and shaped their first plans to conquer the world—even before they had a record contract—U2's concert schedule began to reflect an interest in philanthropic events. In the fall of 1978, only a few months after Steve Averill gave them their iconic name, Bono, Adam, Larry, and Edge played for the Contraception Action Campaign at a controversial gig promoting the free distribution of condoms in Ireland. And even though it was a taboo activity strictly prohibited by the dominant Catholic culture, U2 continued supporting the Irish Family Planning Association throughout the coming decade. In another effort, later that same month, the band joined other punk musicians and artists to protest sexism in the rock music community. A local paper ran the advertisement: "Rock Against Sexism, an organization which certainly has its work cut out for it, is running a gig in the Magnet, Dublin, on August 28th with the very promising young Dublin band, U2, topping the bill" (www.atu2.com). However, the publicity didn't help much: only about fifty people attended the event. Through the early 1980s, the group played at other benefit concerts, no matter how obscure or small, including the appearance of Bono, Adam, and Larry at the "National Milk Run" in 1980. Eventually, a few more prominent events in 1984 demonstrated U2's growing activist spirit and its ability to work in the mainstream of the social justice movement to a larger audience.

Bob Geldof, lead singer for Irish band the Boomtown Rats, had been increasing his role as an activist and antipoverty crusader throughout the early 1980s and became somewhat of a role model for U2. First performing for an Amnesty International benefit concert in 1981, he was captivated a few years later by the horrific famine that was devastating Ethiopia. Responding to the tragedy, Geldof assembled an unprecedented gathering of musicians to perform and record "Do They Know It's Christmas?" Despite hesitations from Paul McGuinness, Bono and Adam answered Geldof's call and joined the 1984 supergroup Band Aid for the production. Accompanied by a trendsetting, celebrity-filled music video, the song broke several industry records, eventually selling almost twelve million copies worldwide and raising over twelve million dollars for famine relief. Though the song was criticized by some as overly sentimental and poorly written, it became wildly popular and was more successful than even Geldof had foreseen. The "Christmas" collaboration went on to inspire other charitable projects, including "We Are the World" by USA for Africa (written by Michael Jackson and Lionel Richie and produced by Quincy Jones and Michael Omartian) and Comic Relief (a British television event launched from a Sudanese refugee camp in 1985).

Band Aid also inspired Geldof to dream of an entire day of international concerts featuring an unprecedented lineup of popular musicians, all linked together via satellite. This second effort to heighten global awareness and raise funds for Ethiopia was named Live Aid, a first-of-its-kind humanitarian concert phenomenon. In the summer of 1985, U2 took the stage in full force, giving one of the most powerful and memorable performances of its career and demonstrating to a global audience both its passion for music and compassion for the suffering people of Africa. Fresh off of Live Aid, Bono and his wife, Ali Hewson, set out with the international organization World Vision to live in an Ethiopian refugee camp for a month, experiencing the catastrophic famine for themselves while volunteering in an orphanage. The trip was life changing, setting Bono and his band on a course toward activism in Africa that would span the next three decades and become a foundational theme for some of U2's major works, including *The Joshua Tree* (especially "Where the Streets Have No Name"); "Silver and Gold" (a song addressing apartheid in South Africa); multiple humanitarian campaigns such as ONE, Drop the Debt, and DATA; and calls to activism on the Vertigo, 360°, and Innocence + Experience tours.

U2 has also had a long history with Amnesty International, a nongovernmental organization (NGO) that focuses on global human rights and calls for action against systems of oppression and injustice around the world. In 1984, the band supported the still relatively unknown humanitarian agency by playing for a "Stop Torture Week" fund-raiser at Radio City Music Hall in New York. This led to a series of conversations between Amnesty's Jack Healy and U2, finally culminating in a 1986 American tour called A Conspiracy of Hope, promoting the organization's twenty-fifth anniversary as well as recruiting a new generation of members and activists. Healey recalls the moment U2 agreed to perform on the tour: "I knew the human rights movement really changed that day. It really did. No question. I knew what was coming. I knew what was gonna happen. I knew we were gonna grow" (McGee, "It Was 20 Years"). From that point on, Amnesty has been a regular presence with U2, setting up booths at concerts and receiving credit on albums. As a direct result of U2's involvement, the entire demographic of the organization shifted toward twenty- and thirty-year-olds, and Amnesty experienced a rapid and unparalleled period of growth.

The band went on to champion many other humanitarian initiatives, several on behalf of its homeland. In 1986, U2 joined forces with other local artists to promote Self Aid, a Live Aid–styled event designed to highlight the problem of chronic unemployment in Ireland, and secure both pledges for new jobs and funds for job creation. It was the largest concert ever staged in that country. For the Stop Sellafield campaign in 1992, the band took a dangerous ride in a rubber dinghy to the Sellafield nuclear plant on the shores of England in a protest effort to raise awareness about high numbers of Leukemia cases on the east coast of Ireland. In collaboration with other bands, the proceeds from the associated concert went to support the work of Greenpeace, an NGO that has focused on environmental activism since 1970. U2 also used its considerable prowess to support the peace effort in Belfast, hosting a concert and raising support for the Good Friday Agreement, the accord that officially ended the Troubles in 1998. During a heavily criticized and highly controversial photo opportunity, Bono brought David Trimble and John Hume—two opposing leaders in Northern Ireland—on to the stage to shake hands in a moment of mutual compromise. Years later, Larry commented on the importance of U2's own ability to cross sectarian lines, recalling,

> U2 are a living example of the kind of unity of faith and tradition that is possible in Northern Ireland. We all agreed the Yes vote was the only way forward. Getting involved in domestic politics is always dangerous but these were exceptional circumstances. (U2 and McCormick, *U2 by U2*, 285)

The list of charities U2 has been a part of in more recent years is staggering. The band has collaborated multiple times with War Child, an NGO founded in 1993 to assist children experiencing conflict in war-torn countries. For this cause, in 1995 the group donated the proceeds of the single "Miss Sarajevo" and supported Luciano Pavarotti at a benefit concert in Modena, Italy, and in 2013 contributed to the organization's twentieth-anniversary album. Following the lead of Ali, Bono's wife, U2 contributed the profit from its 1998 single "Sweetest Thing" to the Chernobyl Children's Project, a humanitarian agency dedicated to helping families affected by the worst nuclear power plant accident in history. "Walk On," a Grammy Award–winning song from *All That You Can't Leave Behind*, was written about Burmese dissident Aung San Suu Kyi and performed in her honor on multiple tours. Continuing a long history of advocacy for Nelson Mandela, Bono wrote a song with Joe Strummer titled "46664"—the number Mandela wore for much of his imprisonment—and Edge joined him for a concert in Cape Town. The 2003 event both honored Mandela as a civil rights leader and raised awareness of the rapidly spreading AIDS crisis in South Africa. U2 again championed the life of Mandela in 2013 by writing and recording "Ordinary Love," a song commissioned for the biographic film *Mandela: Long Walk to Freedom*. The tune paid tribute to the man that Bono said the band had been working for since he was nineteen years old and was released less than a week before the antiapartheid revolutionary's death. "Ordinary Love" was well received by fans, and in 2014 it went on to win the Golden Globe Award for Best Original Song and was nominated for the Academy Award for Best Original Song (but lost to "Let It Go" from the Disney movie *Frozen*).

While on tour, U2 has used its stage to consistently promote the causes it believes in. In the 1980s, the band denounced the violence of the Troubles and praised those willing to endorse political compromise in Ireland, incurring the anger of the Irish Republican Army (IRA) by speaking out against the organization and deliberately discouraging Irish Americans from making financial contributions to it. Undaunted by the threats of its adversaries, U2 also routinely promoted the nonviolent activism of Martin Luther King, Jr., for which Bono allegedly received a death threat.

Though the band took a break from overt activism during the Zoo TV and PopMart tours, preferring instead a delicate balance of introspection and irony; it confidently resumed using its stage as a pulpit for social causes in the new millennium. On the Elevation tour, U2 used a reinterpretation of "Bullet the Blue Sky" to highlight gun violence and denounce the National Rifle Association (NRA). The segment featured a video montage compiled by Catherine Owens and included graphic images of police actions, shooting victims, and a child playing with a handgun. Noting that more Americans had died in domestic gun disputes than in the bloody Vietnam conflict, Bono targeted the crowd with a high-intensity flashlight—one that even resembled a gun with a trigger—and screamed repeatedly from the stage, "War is over. We don't need your help. America's making war on itself!" Edge later explained, "The song needed something that would contemporize it. We're treading a very fine line between being artists and wanting to lecture Americans about issues that are important. It's basically turning the mirror on the audience" (Eliscu, "U2's Call to Disarm"). In analyzing the band's evolving use of "Bullet" and its ability to contextualize the song, Steve Taylor summarized, "Sampling, the collage-like reappropriation of already-existing elements, is U2's creative approach to using one of its signature songs to try to change a changing world" (Taylor, "'Bullet the Blue Sky,'" 95). In a similar way, throughout the latter half of its career, U2 repeatedly reused standard songs from its catalog but with fresh interpretations and a rekindled sense of purpose. Indeed, culture was challenging and shaping U2's artistic sensibilities at the same time U2 was attempting to influence the culture. This symbiotic relationship between the band and its social context cultivated a unique climate of creativity and relevance, especially in the third and fourth decades of its career.

The Vertigo tour offered a similar approach to issues of social justice, particularly in its "heart of darkness" segment, a somber sequence of songs and media including "Love and Peace or Else," "Sunday Bloody Sunday," "Bullet the Blue Sky," and "Running to Stand Still." As in previous tours, U2 used this section of the concert to challenge societal assumptions, this time tackling the tough issue of terrorism and specifically critiquing the American-led coalition's use of torture as a means to obtain information from Iraqi operatives during the Gulf War. Issuing a call to peace, the band continued its concert with a reading from the Declaration of Human Rights as a backdrop for "Pride (in the Name of Love)," U2's anthemic tribute to the nonviolent resistance of Martin Luther King, Jr.

Closing the main set of its Vertigo show, U2 incorporated a combination of music, images, and interactive technology to call attention to sub-Saharan Africa. During the introduction of "Where the Streets

Have No Name," Bono segued by reinterpreting King's dream of equality in America as a vision for Africa. While the flags of African nations cascaded down the stage's state-of-the-art LED backdrop, Bono challenged audiences by adapting King's message for a new global context: "From the bridge at Selma in Mississippi, to the mouth of the river Nile. From the swamplands of Louisiana, to the high peaks of Kilimanjaro. From Dr. King's America, to Nelson Mandela's Africa, the journey of equality moves on!" (*Vertigo 2005*). Capitalizing on the fevered pitch of its audience, U2 moved from there to an innovative call to action, inviting people to take out their cell phones and join the ONE Campaign immediately. This bold solicitation demonstrated an inventive use of technology, as it brought activism right into the arena on a personal level. Bono challenged concertgoers—specifically naming President Bush, Prime Minister Blair, and other world leaders—reminding them, "We have the technology, we have the resources, we have the know-how to end extreme poverty." He reiterated the ONE Campaign's motto, "We're not looking for your money. We're looking for your voice" (*Vertigo 2005*). Gone were the days of gathering signatures on paper petitions and door-to-door solicitations for charitable causes. U2 was ushering in both new media and a new brand of activism.

The band continued its crusade for an AIDS-free Africa as it supported the 2009 release of *No Line on the Horizon*. Throughout the 360° tour, U2 featured a prerecorded video of a giddy Archbishop Desmond Tutu rejoicing and congratulating audiences for the progress that had been made through their advocacy for his home continent, again invoking and adapting the message of King for the twenty-first century:

> The same people who marched for civil rights in the United States are the same people who protested apartheid in South Africa, who are the same people who worked for peace in Ireland, and are the same people who fought against debt slavery in the jubilee year 2000, who are the same BEAUTIFUL PEOPLE that I see when I look around this place tonight in 360 degrees. WE are those people. WE are the same person. Because our voices were heard millions more of our brothers and sisters are alive thanks to the miracle of AIDS drugs and malaria drugs. . . . They will be doctors, they will be nurses, they will be scientists who will live to solve GREAT problems. Yes, there are many obstacles. Of course, there are always road blocks in the

way of justice. But God will put a wind at our back and a rising road
ahead if we work with each other as ONE . . . ONE! (*U2: 360°*)

The 360° tour also showed U2 and its fans standing in solidarity with
both the nonviolent protesters of the Green Movement in Iran during
"Sunday Bloody Sunday" and the Burmese political dissident and Nobel
Peace Prize winner Aung San Suu Kyi. During "Walk On," a song
dedicated to Suu Kyi, representatives from Amnesty International and
the ONE Campaign filled the platform as they paid tribute to the imprisoned Burmese activist. U2's spaceship-themed stage had transported audiences to Africa, Iran, and Burma in a truly global moment of
activism.

The Innocence + Experience tour called attention once again to the
ongoing fight against AIDS in Africa, this time focusing more closely on
the plight of mothers who inadvertently pass the infection on to their
babies. Using a lullabyesque cover of Paul Simon's "Mother and Child
Reunion," U2 featured Oliver Jeffers's childlike drawings, illustrating
both the continuing problem and the achievements gained since the
360° tour. In a quiet, intimate moment, U2 reminded its audience that
two little pills could prevent the transmission of HIV from mother to
child, thwarting six hundred new cases a day and bringing the goal of an
AIDS-free generation within sight. At the same time, the band promoted Product (RED), the advocacy initiative founded by Bono and
Bobby Shriver in 2006 to create awareness and provide funding for the
fight against AIDS.

The Innocence + Experience tour addressed a few other social concerns as well. During the North American leg in 2015, U2 used "Bullet
the Blue Sky" to highlight police violence against African American
males in highly publicized cases from Florida, Missouri, South Carolina,
Maryland, and New York. In Europe, the focus of "Bullet" shifted toward the refugee crisis as hundreds of thousands of people fled Syria,
Afghanistan, Iraq, and North Africa due to civil unrest and war. In this
segment, U2 invited European audiences to open their borders and
accept the refugees—an unpopular idea in many countries due to the
fear of terrorism. And for a brief time on the tour, U2 also celebrated a
critical piece of legislation in Ireland. In May 2015, Irish citizens voted
overwhelmingly to legalize same-sex marriage and extend a variety of
benefits and privileges to the lesbian, gay, bisexual, and transgender

(LGBT) community, making it the first country in the world to do so by popular vote and marking a rapid and radical shift in the country's attitude toward sexual orientation. Due to its religious conservatism and repressive culture, Ireland had endured a long history of discrimination against those of different sexual orientations, only decriminalizing homosexuality in 1992. The band used "Pride" to promote equality and joked that it was helping put the "gay" back in "Gaelic." As in previous tours, Innocence + Experience continued the tradition of addressing controversial social themes and boldly proclaimed U2's commitment to an ongoing and evolving engagement with current issues.

As a collective organization, U2 has used its vast resources to address topics of social concern throughout its four-decade career. Since the earliest days, long before it was known by anyone other than its local following at the Dandelion Market, the band has demonstrated a commitment to seek justice and equality by appearing at charity events, endorsing humanitarian organizations, and weaving controversial causes and issues into concerts. Historian Alan McPherson notes,

> U2 did not single-handedly "remake" global activism. But it has stood at the vanguard of new trends and strategies in activism since the early 1980s. Equally important, U2's remaking of the world of global activism should be understood as a reaction to their times. (McPherson, *World and U2*, xvi)

Always responding to cultural ebb and flow, the band has both adapted to it and worked as a shaping force in it through music and art. But when not appearing as a band, the individual members of U2 have also invested both money and time in their own personal causes, thus extending their influence beyond the stage. Bono, in fact, nearly made another career out of his advocacy and humanitarian efforts.

A NEW KIND OF ACTIVISM

Though all the members of U2 have been involved in philanthropic projects, neither they, nor any other recording artist, can compare to the role Bono has taken in advocating on behalf of the world's poor. As a band, U2 has supported more than twenty charities and spoken on behalf of over twenty causes, but as an individual Bono has nearly doubled that, setting him apart from other celebrity activists. It's common for celebrities to become activists after they become famous, as activism typically follows celebrity and philanthropic efforts usually culminate in charitable contributions while also providing positive exposure and publicity for the donor. It can be common, too, that well-meaning celebrities never develop a deep understanding of the issues involved and thus can only be helpful up to a certain point. Bono, however, is a completely different type of celebrity philanthropist, engaging in a new kind of activism that partners fame, entrepreneurial spirit, business strategies, government policy, and economic investments in a way that makes a difference on a grand scale. Along with other wealthy and influential figures, including Bill Gates, George Soros, and Bill Clinton, Bono has become what economist Matthew Bishop calls a "hyper-agent" of society because of his ability to effect change on a global level in ways that others cannot. These "philanthrocapitalists" use their wealth and influence to access essential systems such as the White House, Congress, and Wall Street. Another economist explains, "The need for philanthropy to become more like the for-profit capital markets is a common theme among the new philanthropists, especially those who have made their fortune in finance. As they see it, three things are needed for such a philanthropic marketplace to work" ("Birth of Philanthrocapitalism"). Those three things include investment in socially entrepreneurial ventures, an economic infrastructure of banks and markets, and the ability to maximize their return on social investments. Above all, these new socially conscious celebrities are driven by a sense of faith and obligation to help humanity through responsible, efficient, and profitable humanitarian projects. Reacting to the waste and inefficiency of traditional government and nongovernment programs, Noreena Hertz describes this "new activism" as a shift in influence from nation-states to an ethical capitalism that intensifies lobbying, develops academic solutions, and implements business proposals on behalf of the world's poor. Hertz has been a major influence on Bono's own philosophy of philanthropy and was also a primary inspiration for his (RED) campaign.

Bono's interest in global activism has led to a love affair with Africa that can be traced back to two events: his involvement with Live Aid and his trip with the relief agency World Vision to Ethiopia, both in 1985. He emerged from these experiences with a righteous zeal for a land that had largely been forgotten by the rest of the globe. But his passion for the people and his relentless interest in the problems of sub-Saharan Africa also exposed a flaw in his and other's benevolent strategies on behalf of the continent. In hindsight, Live Aid has become a case study in what not to do. While the charitable event eventually raised over $200 million, it was raised so quickly that an effective structure for overseeing and dispensing the funds wasn't in place. As Band Aid and Live Aid channeled money to Ethiopia, various humanitarian agencies welcomed the infusion of cash with a no-strings-attached approach, but some of the funds were manipulated and rerouted to be under the control of Ethiopia's oppressive, abusive dictator Mengistu Haile Mariam. In the end, the aid U2 helped generate benefited health care services, educational resources, and agricultural practices in Ethiopia, but critics point out that lives saved may have been offset by the deaths of thousands under the Mengistu administration. A second inadvertent result of Live Aid also caused organizers to question their charitable tactics. A portion of the money raised went to pay off some of Ethiopia's massive foreign debt, which had ballooned due to corrupt African regimes recklessly borrowing from Western nations. Ironically, some of Live Aid's contributions went to Ethiopia but ended back in the banks of the nations that had loaned the money. This cyclical return of funds revealed a deep systemic flaw in charitable giving.

Ultimately, Bono—and by extension, U2—learned that money wasn't the only way to provide support for Africa. In the twenty-first century, the lead singer was older and wiser, a well-studied version of his younger zealous self. Seeking to hone his own skill as an activist, he befriended and sought the advice and training of influential people such as venture capitalist Bobby Shriver, economist Jeffrey Sachs, and computer magnate Bill Gates. Through the counsel of these successful humanitarians, Bono began to shape a complex, informed, and multi-faceted plan for advocacy on behalf of Africa, including political, economic, and social strategies. Starting with the Jubilee 2000 campaign, an international project that called for the cancellation of third-world debt by the year 2000, Bono embraced a new vocation as spokesperson and activist on behalf of the band. Reflecting on the lessons learned from the marginally successful charitable projects of the mid-1980s, Bono commented, "Here was a chance to revisit that situation, but with more than a Band-Aid, to look at the structure of poverty" ("Can Bono

Save the Third World?"). While campaigning for Jubilee 2000, Bono took on a strategic role as lobbyist in the US Senate, asking politicians to forgive nearly $6 billion in third-world debt and soliciting the support of conservative Republicans who were likely to vote against key legislation. Armed with an arsenal of data and up-to-date information, Bono collaborated with a host of artists, actors, and celebrities; lobbied politicians across the political spectrum; hobnobbed with presidents and prime ministers; and often won over adversaries through smart, articulate, and passionate conversations. Eventually, the campaign resulted in $100 billion of debt relief for thirty-five of the world's poorest countries. In Bono's own words, that's "[n]ot bad take-home for a year's work" ("Can Bono Save the Third World?").

Though the Jubilee 2000 campaign's goals were ambitious and successful in ways that Live Aid could never have anticipated, Bono was just getting started in a career of philanthropy. While campaigning for Jubilee, the lead singer began to understand that his celebrity was a kind of capital in and of itself. And though he had tried in jest to call the White House during concerts on the Zoo TV tour (calls that were always disconnected), his twenty-first-century rock star status nearly guaranteed him entrance to any politician's office, including US president Bill Clinton, British prime minister Tony Blair, German chancellor Gerhard Schroder, and other heads of state such as US treasury secretaries Robert Rubin and Larry Summers, national security advisor Sandy Berger, Federal Reserve chief Paul Volcker, and World Bank president James Wolfensohn. Bono even got an audience with Pope John Paul II, at which time he gave the pope a pair of his sunglasses in return for a rosary. A photo of Bono next to the pope wearing "Fly Shades" has become an iconic image of the rock star's charismatic personality and efficacious activism.

For Bono's next humanitarian effort, he didn't just join an existing campaign, he started his own. In 2002, the front man collaborated with Bobby Shriver and other activists from the Jubilee project to cofound DATA, an acronym for "debt, AIDS, trade, Africa." The purpose of this multinational NGO was to seek equality and justice for poor African nations by advocating for debt relief, fair trade rules, and the eradication of AIDS. The campaign challenged wealthy Western nations to increase funding and adjust policies in ways that would bolster African democracy and independence, but it also placed constraints on African

leaders by requiring governmental transparency in an effort to mini-
mize corruption. DATA's role in advocating for Africa has been multifaceted. First, because many African nations pay more for the mainte-
nance of foreign debt than they do for health care, education, and other
services for their own people, DATA has both lobbied rich countries to
forgive the debt and monitored the follow-through of those nations that
make commitments. Second, when DATA was formed, over thirty million people on the continent were living with AIDS, and sixty-five hundred were dying every day. The NGO has fought to create awareness,
lobby for assistance, ensure that drugs are available, and reverse the
epidemic in sub-Saharan Africa. Third, as it has sought the end of
extreme poverty across the globe, DATA has lobbied foreign governments for development assistance that would finance education, health
care, roads, clean water, technology, and other infrastructure on the
African continent. In 2016, through a partnership with the ONE Campaign, the agency successfully petitioned the US Congress to support
the Electrify Africa Act, a bill providing energy access for parts of Africa
that had previously been without electricity. A fourth premise of DATA
is that economic growth across the continent can only be boosted and
sustained through fair trade practices, resulting in the ability for
Africans to sell their products without being undercut by the United
States and other European nations.

In 2004, Bono helped cofound yet another nonprofit agency. The
ONE Campaign was originally a collaboration of eleven humanitarian
organizations, including DATA, Bread for the Word, Save the Children,
World Vision, and others, with start-up funding from Bill and Melinda
Gates. Focusing on the fight against extreme poverty and global disease,
the goal of ONE has been to mobilize more than seven million members to take action, primarily by pressuring politicians to support global
development through awareness campaigns. "We don't want your money—we want your voice," a popular slogan for ONE, demonstrates the
organization's emphasis on "getting smart policies agreed and implemented, and holding governments accountable" (Elliott, "Money
Counts"). The campaign to "Make Poverty History" merged with
DATA in 2008, while retaining the name ONE, forming a substantial
and formidable humanitarian agency that has routinely and successfully
lobbied governments around the world, specifically focusing on the G8

nations. Aiming to end senseless, extreme poverty by 2030, ONE's global membership continues to press key international governments.

In 2006, Bono joined once again with Bobby Shriver to launch Product (RED). This venture was the culmination of all that Bono and his cadre of influential business associates had learned about the blending of philanthropy and capitalism. Partnering with companies such as Nike, Apple, Coca-Cola, Starbucks, Converse, and many others, (RED) differed from Bono's previous policy-oriented projects by being unabashedly revenue driven. Following a new and innovative business model, affiliate companies from the private sector created specially branded products and donated a portion of the profit from their sales to the Global Fund, an organization established to raise money in the fight against AIDs, tuberculosis, and malaria. By 2016, on its tenth anniversary, (RED) had contributed more than $350 million to the Global Fund and positively impacted sixty million people in multiple African countries, primarily focusing on the distribution of lifesaving antiretroviral (ARV) drugs and the prevention of mother-to-child transmission of HIV. Blending ethical consumerism and performance-based funding, (RED) demonstrated that corporations and major label brands could be both competitive in capitalist markets and benevolent with their profits.

In 2016, after returning from a fact-gathering tour of Middle Eastern and African countries that were struggling to deal with the escalating refugee crisis, Bono appeared before a US Senate Appropriations subcommittee on "The Causes and Consequences of Violent Extremism and the Role of Foreign Assistance." In his testimony, he continued his advocacy for Africa and other conflicted countries such as Jordan and Syria, making the case that foreign aid is not just a nice gesture but an essential weapon in the battle against terrorism. He argued,

> For too long, aid has been seen as charity—a nice thing to do when we can afford it. But this is a moment to reimagine what we mean by aid. Aid in 2016 is not just charity—it is national security. Though of course we know that aid alone is not the answer, it is also true that when aid is structured properly, with a focus on fighting poverty and improving governance, it could just be the best bulwark we have against the extremism of our age. (United States Senate, "Hearing on Violent Extremism")

Just two weeks later, while speaking to Willow Creek Community Church via a prerecorded video, he reminded the congregation, "Jesus was a displaced person—his family fleeing to Egypt for fear of the life of their firstborn child. Yep, Jesus was a refugee." Signaling the importance of welcoming refugees, he continued, "'Love thy neighbor' is not advice, it's a command" (Bono, "Celebration of Hope"). Much more than a lead singer in a rock band, Bono has been respected and valued as an authoritative voice of philanthropy, a compassionate humanitarian, a smart and articulate consultant on foreign policy, and an experienced venture capitalist, resulting in a trusted reputation unlike any rock star before him.

Bono has also partnered with his wife, Ali, an activist who is equally articulate and informed on issues in sub-Saharan Africa. In 2005, the couple founded Edun, a fashion brand established to promote trade by using African labor and products. Edun's emphasis on fair business practices exhibited a commitment to African economies not through financial contributions and direct aid but by creating business partnerships that offered locally sourced products and maintained just and sustainable working conditions. The company—whose name spelled backwards is "nude" and also sounds like the idyllic garden of Eden—models a socially conscious ethic uncommon in an industry known for exploiting child labor and manufacturing products in sweatshops. Ali explained, "We wanted to show that you can make a for-profit business where everybody in the chain is treated well" ("Even Better"). The mission-driven fashion company initially produced most of its products in Africa, but the business model became untenable when African suppliers and manufacturers lacked the infrastructure to complete orders in a timely manner. As a result, the company lost millions of dollars in 2007 and 2008, requiring Bono and Ali to invest their own money and eventually merge the brand with another fashion company. Through the failure, the couple learned a hard lesson: their noble mission was worthless without an efficient business plan. In a corrective move, a portion of the manufacturing had to be outsourced to China for a while, but Edun began moving more and more of its production back to Africa as techniques and relationships evolved. Bono and Ali's investment in a new fashion brand and a revolutionary business model once again demonstrated their commitment to economic development in Africa, fair trade practices, and also to a posture of lifelong learning.

At the height of his humanitarian efforts, Bono visited Africa on yet another information-gathering tour in 2002. While in Addis Ababa, Ethiopia, the lead singer gave a closing address to the African Development Bank meetings, and reflected on how his own understanding of philanthropy had changed since the days of Live Aid. Martin Wroe reported and commented on Bono's words:

> "Seventeen years ago, I came to Ethiopia on a wave of tears and compassion, flowing from the rich countries to the poor, from soccer stadiums taken over by musicians to refugee camps taken over by the starving people of Ethiopia. The brilliant Bob Geldof taught me the importance of being focused, angry, persistent. We raised $200 million, and we thought we'd cracked it. It was a great moment, it was a great feeling." But they hadn't cracked it. The poor world, it turned out, needed political change more than loose change. "I discovered," adds Bono, "that Africa spends $20 million every five days repaying old debts. Tears were obviously not enough." (Wroe, "Tears Are Not Enough")

Determined to create change, Bono committed a substantial amount of his own time, resources, and money to political advocacy, social awareness, and transformational practices on behalf of the poorest of African nations. For his humanitarian efforts, Bono was named "Person of the Year" (along with Bill and Melinda Gates) in 2005 by *Time* magazine, nominated for a Nobel Peace Prize three times, and awarded honorary British knighthood, among many other distinguished accolades. President Bill Clinton has offered his highest praise, reflecting, "I love this man because he has a mind and heart. He can say words, but he knows deeds mean so much more. . . . To Bono, there is no 'them,' there is only 'us.' We should follow him" (Varga, "Part-Time Rocker"). Speaking before dignitaries at the National Prayer Breakfast in Washington, DC, in 2006, Bono summed up his own thoughts on Africa and activism:

> And finally . . . this is not about charity after all, is it? It's about justice. . . . I just want to repeat that: This is not about charity, it's about justice. And that's too bad. Because we're good at charity. Americans, Irish people, are good at charity. We like to give, and we give a lot, even those who can't afford it. But justice is a higher standard. Africa makes a fool of our idea of justice; it makes a farce of

our idea of equality. It mocks our pieties, it doubts our concern, and it questions our commitment. (Bono, *On the Move*)

Indeed, Bono's relentless pursuit of justice and equality helped position him as a new kind of activist—one that leveraged celebrity, lobbied politicians, launched awareness campaigns, and initiated socially ethical business ventures. As he accepted the NAACP Chairman's Award in 2007—along with a thunderous standing ovation from a theater full of America's most influential African American leaders—Bono once again pointed to a deep and stirring personal faith as the impetus for his work:

And to those in the church who still sit in judgment on the AIDS emergency, let me climb into the pulpit for just one moment. Because whatever thoughts we have about God, who He is, or even if God exists, most will agree that God has a special place for the poor. The poor are where God lives. God is in the slums, in the cardboard boxes where the poor play house. God is where the opportunity is lost and lives are shattered. God is with the mother who has infected her child with a virus that will take both their lives. God is under the rubble in the cries we hear during wartime. God, my friends, is with the poor. And God is with us if we are with them. This is not a burden, this is an adventure. Don't let anyone tell you it cannot be done. We can be the generation that ends extreme poverty. (Bono, "Bono at NAACP Awards")

Throughout the third and fourth decades of U2's industrious career, it has been easy to spot Bono's passionate and evocative activism. But other members of the group have also contributed in both public and private ways. Edge made a major commitment to philanthropy in 2005. As New Orleans—a city known for a long and rich musical legacy, especially with Dixieland and jazz—recovered from the catastrophic effects of Hurricane Katrina, the U2 guitarist cofounded Music Rising. Originally a campaign to replace the instruments of musicians who lost everything in the storm and ensuing flood, the charity has also provided grants, promoted music education, and offered aid to other musical communities affected by natural disasters. As part of the effort, U2 joined with Green Day in a historic performance during a New Orleans Saints football game at the reopening of the Superdome. The two groups collaborated to cover "The Saints Are Coming" and donated all proceeds from sales of the live recording to Music Rising. An accompanying music video sparked controversy as it depicted a fictional scenario in which President George W. Bush recalled troops stationed in Iraq to help victims of Katrina. It was a bold commentary on the US government's lack of response to the disaster and a perfect complement to Edge's humanitarian work.

Edge has also given significant time and resource to the fight against cancer, a relevant topic because of his own daughter's battle with the disease. In 2016, he took part in the Third International Conference on the Progress of Regenerative Medicine at the Vatican. Focusing on an intersection of science, philanthropy, faith, and culture, the pope, US vice president Joe Biden, and others heightened the need for ongoing cancer research in the pursuit of a cure. A highlight of the conference included Edge's performance—the first ever for a contemporary musician—in the Sistine Chapel in front of a distinguished audience. In 2010, Edge participated in the Stand Up to Cancer telethon, and in 2007 he joined the board of the Angiogenesis Foundation, an organization focusing on cancer treatment. Always smart and articulate, Edge summarizes, "Angiogenesis is a study of a process which is common to over 40 human diseases, which is the development of new blood vessels" (Fegan, "Brush with Disease"). An issue of close personal significance, Edge has continued to study, learn, and support the fight against cancer.

Adam has often been known as the shy, reserved member of U2, but in 2012 he became an ambassador for Walk in My Shoes, an initiative from St. Patrick's University Hospital in Dublin. The charity's mission is to provide positive mental health for young people, and the hospital was a favorite cause supported by Adam's mother before she passed away. Picking up where she left off, Adam stated, "I think it is essential to take care of people with mental health problems. Money raised will be used to help put young people back on the road to mental health" ("Get on Your Boots"). Adam has continued to raise funds and awareness for services to young adults and has worked hard to remove the stigma of mental health issues.

WEATHERING CONTENTION AND CRITICISMS

U2's foray into activism has not come without controversy, especially when considering Bono's ambitious efforts. And while critics have always been a part of the U2 story, sometimes the criticisms have come from within the band itself. Larry, Adam, and Edge were particularly concerned when Bono's busy activist schedule seemed to take precedence over his involvement in U2. Just after the turn of the new millennium, the lead singer found himself in a bit of a paradox: his role as front man had propelled him into the international spotlight, giving him entrance into elite legislatures and parliaments across the globe, but he jeopardized the very success that gave him his credibility by spending more time as a philanthropist than as a musician.

In fact, Bono spent so much time and energy on Jubilee 2000 that it created tension during the production of *All That You Can't Leave Behind*. Paul McGuinness recognized the dilemma: "It could be irritating for [the other members of U2], as much as they supported him in what he was doing. He was sometimes a little careless of other people's time and there were certainly strains on Principle Management and strains on the band" (U2 and McCormick, *U2 by U2*, 293). Larry concurred, "Bono was spending more and more time on the phone, talking to world leaders, arranging to meet the Pope. There was some grumbling about the amount of time it was taking up, and Brian [Eno] and Danny [Lanois] were very frustrated" (U2 and McCormick, *U2 by U2*, 293). Bono's humanitarian efforts also delayed production of *How to Dismantle an Atomic Bomb* while he was developing DATA. Paul McGuinness again noted, "He takes far too much on, I think, but it is hard to criticize him because his political achievements are very real. But there are times when it makes the rest of the band feel that they're taking second place. I suspect they think U2 should be more important to him than it sometimes is" (U2 and McCormick, *U2 by U2*, 314). Even Bono himself realized his exploits had jeopardized the record, recalling, "I do think at one point U2 wanted to get an album out really quickly. It is fair to say the DATA work derailed that" (U2 and McCormick, *U2 by U2*, 317). Though bolstered by the support and affirmation of his bandmates, Bono's relentless activism caused tension within U2 and its management, resulting in unavoidable but, in the end, manageable internal conflict.

Aside from some contentions from within the band, there are at least four reasons why critics have blasted Bono and his band for their philanthropic efforts. First, this new activism, especially as it's demonstrated by (RED), could be viewed as a convenient collusion with corporations. Critics have charged that philanthrocapitalists use the rhetoric of being "socially responsible" for their own personal gain. They also argue that consumers of (RED) merchandise continue to perpetuate and justify rampant materialism and greed, buying products at inflated prices at the expense of poor Africans. Detractors contend that this new activism is equal to a fresh exploitation of a people who have long been subservient to powerful Western economies. When confronted with accusations of compromise and collusion, Bono has responded, "I don't see this as selling out. I see this as ganging up on the problem. . . . For those people [whose lives are saved], my motivation or our (RED) motivation is irrelevant" (Bono, "Bono, Guest Editor"). The lead singer has consistently rebutted his accusers, both in concert and in press conferences, by pointing out that Africans who receive antiretroviral pills don't care whether the medicine comes through private donations or corporate contributions, they are just thankful for the lifesaving drugs.

A second criticism often levied against U2's brand of activism relates to a historic pattern of condescending and demeaning attitudes in the West. Many would argue that Bono's advocacy on behalf of the poor simply updates and maintains a nineteenth-century "white man's burden" mentality, an ideology carried over from the colonizing and partitioning of the African continent, in which North American and European powers felt a moral obligation to "save" Africa. The problem lies in the idea that advocacy is often patronizing and paternalistic, leaving those that are being helped out of the planning and facilitation. Critics argue that while the white West arrogantly assumes it has all the answers, Africans themselves must be allowed and empowered to solve their own problems through education and expanded trade. A celebrity philanthropist, they contend, is nothing more than an egocentric crusader with a messiah complex. Labeling Bono's activism as "the Rock Star's Burden," author Phil Theroux retorted, "The impression that Africa is fatally troubled and can be saved only by outside help—not to mention celebrities and charity concerts—is a destructive and misleading conceit" (Theroux, "Rock Star's Burden"). As Bono, Bill Gates, Jeffrey Sachs, Warren Buffett, George Soros, and others speak for the poor, some believe the poor themselves are not being invited to speak.

A third accusation made against U2 is that the band has compromised its core values by allying with the very political powers it once castigated. Many loyal fans recoiled in dismay in the early 2000s as Bono conducted photo ops with Republican president George W. Bush, schmoozed with neoconservative strategist Paul Wolfowitz, entertained the staunchly conservative senator Jesse Helms, and traveled to Africa with Republican US treasury secretary Paul O'Neill. Even worse (from the perspective of his critics), Bono gained the support of US churches, contemporary Christian musicians, and the Vatican while praising the virtues of capitalism as the answer for Africa's desperate situation. Nonetheless, though fans were stunned—and sometimes repulsed— Bono was having a positive effect in Congress, and U2 was swaying audiences in concert. Success was most succinctly seen in 2003, when the conservative Bush administration authorized an astounding $15 billion for the President's Emergency Plan for AIDS Relief (PEPFAR), an amount that grew to $60 billion by 2016. Many commentators had to admit that Bono played a significant part in this and several successive funding schemes. Drawing on the example of Martin Luther King, Jr., the lead singer learned to turn enemies into allies by appealing to a value or interest that motivates them and advises, "When you have a person who may appear rigidly opposed to something, look for ways to widen the aperture of their narrow idealistic view" (McGirt, "Bono"). Often criticized for his conciliatory role, even Bono recognized his own change in attitude toward the people he had once rebuked: "You grow up with this idea of us and them, that all politicians are full of s—t. Now I see their life is the art of the possible" ("Can Bono Save the Third World?").

A fourth, though surely not final, critique of U2 is related to the band's own corporate strategies. In 2006, the franchise shifted a portion of its complex business affairs from Ireland to the Netherlands in an effort to avoid paying high tax rates. The move was chastised by both media pundits and fans alike as hypocritical. Throughout its career, U2 had routinely championed Ireland, advocated for its workers, and declared a singular loyalty, proclaiming that the group would forever be based in Dublin. Though other musical acts fled the republic at the first signs of success, U2 endured, even remaining steadfast and hopeful during a bleak economic recession. But Bono's loud and unambiguous call for debt relief, fair trade, and ethical business practices in Africa seemed at odds with the band's behavior at home. In defense, Bono called its move a normal and reasonable financial strategy, maintaining that many of the band's investments were still headquartered in Ireland and that it was, indeed, still paying a fair amount of taxes. Edge responded, "So much of our business is outside Ireland. It's ridiculous to sort of make a big deal about the fact that we operate outside of Ireland" (Gayle, "Bono Defends"). Nonetheless, though U2 perceived it as a "smart" decision, critics of the band saw the controversial transaction as just another in a long string of insincere activities.

A WORLD OF CHANGE

Throughout four decades of making music, U2 has consistently and passionately engaged in a complex web of activism and advocacy on behalf of those without power, position, or influence, delighting fans and fueling critics. While the goal of traditional activism has been to rally the masses and promote common activities such as protesting, letter writing, and signing petitions, Bono's new brand of megaphilanthropy targeted the major stakeholders of key systems, including business moguls, politicians, religious leaders, and community activists. Driven by faith and a strong desire to make a difference in the world, Larry, Adam, Edge, and Bono have used albums, concerts, and special causes to develop not only their musical ability but also a benevolent sensibility about the world in which they live. McPherson summarizes U2's core traits and evolution this way:

> Community, faith, and action: such are the lessons—the pillars—of U2's activism. They have run through every period of their lives, even if at times they were lying in wait or explicitly hidden from the press. In later decades, all three lessons became explicit and allowed four teenagers from Ireland to feel confident that their values and good works rested on sound moral foundations. (McPhearson, *World and U2*, xxvi)

Can U2 change the world? Does rock 'n' roll really make a difference? Perhaps Bono's own words from a commencement address he gave at the University of Pennsylvania in 2004 give us a partial answer:

I didn't expect change to come so slow, so agonizingly slow. I didn't realize that the biggest obstacle to political and social progress wasn't the Free Masons, or the Establishment, or the boot heal [sic] of whatever you consider "the Man" to be, it was something much more subtle. [It was] a combination of our own indifference and the Kafkaesque labyrinth of "no"s you encounter as people vanish down the corridors of bureaucracy. (Bono, "Because We Can")

A much younger and less patient Bono from 1989—the zealous preacher that nearly hung himself on the cross of a Joshua tree—also dared to ponder out loud about his band's role in culture: "Can those dreams, can records, can music really challenge entrenched power? I don't know. I don't think so. It can effect change. It can be a catalyst for change. How? It can be a voice of dissent" (Block, "Bono Bites Back"). A still younger Bono—just twenty-three years old in 1983, with a full mullet hairdo—announced his vision for the coming decade:

The sixties was a period where idealism ruled, and I'm proud of idealism. I think it was diluted, it was turned into escapism by drugs and people just going over the top, but now in the '80s, we're trying to change that, we're trying to say, "Hold on a second. We can do something. Music can change the world because it can change people." Maybe that's naïve, I don't care, let me be on record as saying that. (Bono, "Bono Interview")

Wondering whether U2 has changed the world is a legitimate question worthy of pursuit, but perhaps it's only half of a larger inquiry, the flipside of which is has the world changed U2? With forty-plus years of activity to examine, the answers are yes and yes. U2 offers a marvelously intriguing case study of the dynamic interplay between artist and culture, where each influences and responds to the other, as two dancers embrace to move across the floor in one fluid motion. U2 is one of the few rock bands to have engaged its culture on such a large scale, and among its peers is the only one that has done so by continuing to produce new material to popular and critical acclaim and consistently inventive and successful methods for delivering its art.

Bono concluded his address to the University of Pennsylvania graduates with a final comment—a piece of advice that seems representative
of U2's long and vibrant journey: "My point is that the world is more
malleable than you think and it's waiting for you to hammer it into
shape" (Bono, "Because We Can"). Sometimes the sculptors, sometimes the stones, the members of U2—four dreamers who continue to
be transformed by the world they set out to conquer—have shown us
again and again that they, too, are more malleable than we might think.

FURTHER READING

"25 of the Greatest Gigs Ever." *Guardian*, 20 Jan. 2007. Accessed 10 Sep. 2015.

"43rd Grammy Awards Highlights." Grammy.com, 21 Feb. 2001. Accessed 15 Aug. 2015.

"Advocate of the Week: Sheila Roche." *Archetypes*, 3 June 2013. Accessed 5 Nov. 2015.

"Apple Introduces the U2 iPod." Apple. Apple Press Release, 26 Oct. 2004. Accessed 8 Mar. 2015.

Assayas, Michka. *Bono*. New York: Riverhead, 2005. In this informal and intimate book-length conversation with journalist Michka Assayas, Bono talks about family, faith, politics, global poverty, social justice, the music industry, and every U2 album to date. This is a seminal work and a must-read for anyone wanting to understand how Bono's own ideologies contribute to the band.

Atu2 (www.atu2.com). "Here's a scan about U2's Rock against Sexism Gig on August 28, 1979 http://twitpic.com/675nza." Twitter, 16 Aug. 2011, 1:23 p.m.

"The Birth of Philanthrocapitalism." *Economist*, 25 Feb. 2006. Accessed 27 Feb. 2016.

Block, Adam. "Bono Bites Back." *Mother Jones*, 1 May 1989. Accessed 16 June 2015. A classic interview with Bono from 1989, just after the release of *Rattle and Hum*, revealing thoughts about religion, drugs, hopes and dreams, musical influences, and the use of irony.

Bono. "Audio. Bono, August 1979, RTÉ Radio, Ireland." YouTube, 1 June 2008. Accessed 24 Apr. 2015.

Bono. "Because We Can, We Must." *Almanac*, 19 May 2004. Accessed 3 Apr. 2016. Bono's inspiring commencement address on May 17, 2004, to the University of Pennsylvania, challenging a new generation to combat and eliminate senseless poverty.

Bono. "Bono at NAACP Awards." YouTube, 4 Mar. 2007. Accessed 14 Mar. 2016. This is a video clip of Bono receiving the Chairman's Award, during which he sounds more like a gospel preacher than a rock star, advocating for Africa and the elimination of AIDS.

Bono. "Bono, Guest Editor: I Am a Witness. What Can I Do?" *Independent*, 15 May 2006. Accessed 25 Feb. 2016. An editorial by Bono reflecting on his visits to Africa, the devastating impact of AIDS, and the development of (RED) as a tool for generating revenue to combat the virus.

Bono. "Bono Interview at US Festival 1983 U2." YouTube, 23 Sept. 2013. Accessed 7 Mar. 2016.

Bono. "Bono's Teenage Kicks." Interview by Cormac McSherry. *Guardian*, 16 June 2007. Accessed 10 Mar. 2015.

Bono. "Celebration of Hope: A Word from Bono." Willowcreek.tv, 24 Apr. 2016. Accessed 24 Apr. 2016.

Bono. *On the Move*. Nashville: Thomas Nelson, 2006. A beautiful presentation of Bono's speech to the National Prayer Breakfast on February 2, 2006, that also includes photographs Bono took on his first trip to Ethiopia in 1985.

Bono. "Psalm Like It Hot." *Guardian*, 30 Oct. 1999. Accessed 27 Aug. 2015. The full text of Bono's introduction to Pocket Canons's translation of Psalms in 1999.

Bono. "The *Rolling Stone* Interview: Bono." Interview by Jann S. Wenner. JannSWenner. com, 3 Nov. 2005. Accessed 10 Sept. 2015. Hours of candid, broad, and articulate archival recordings from Wenner's interview with Bono for a feature article in *Rolling Stone*.

Bono and Elton John. "Bono, Elton John & Chuck D Talk about Joe Strummer/the Clash." Interview. *Epitaph*, 25 Nov. 2003. Accessed 25 Apr. 2015.

Bono and Eugene Peterson. "Bono & Eugene Peterson on the Psalms." Interview by David Taylor. *Fuller Studio*, 2016. Accessed 26 Apr. 2016.

"Bono." *Charlie Rose*, 16 May 2013. An in depth, feature television interview with Bono by news journalist and anchor Charlie Rose.

Boyd, Brian. "Bono's Dublin: 'A Long Way from Where I Live.'" *Irish Times*, 13 Sept. 2014. Accessed 9 Mar. 2015.

Boyd, Brian. "Meet the Bomb Squad." *Irish Times*, 23 Dec. 2004. Accessed 16 Apr. 2015.

Boyd, Brian. *U2 Experience*. London: Carlton Books, 2015. This interactive book includes replications of memorabilia that tell the story and span the career of U2.

Byrne, Andrea. "The Rock 'n' Roll Graduates." Independent.ie, 13 July 2008. Accessed 10 Nov. 2015.

Calhoun, Scott D., ed. *Exploring U2: Is This Rock 'n' Roll? Essays on the Music, Work, and Influence of U2*. Lanham, MD: Scarecrow Press, 2012. A seminal academic work, this is a collection of essays from the very first U2 studies conference in 2009 and is a good reference for both scholars and avid fans.

Calhoun, Scott D., ed. *U2 Above, Across, and Beyond: Interdisciplinary Assessments*. Lanham, MD: Lexington Books, 2015. A collection of interdisciplinary essays from the second U2 studies conference in 2013, featuring topics such as communication, music theory, literary studies, religion, and cultural studies, written to academics and informed fans.

"Can Bono Save the Third World?" *Newsweek*, 23 Jan. 2000. Accessed 19 Feb. 2016. A classic *Newsweek* article describing the relentless activism of Bono at the turn of the millennium.

Clarke, Donald. "How Did U2 That?" *Irish Times*, 22 Feb. 2008. Accessed 11 Dec. 2015.

Eliscu, Jenny. "U2's Call to Disarm." *Rolling Stone*, 3 July, 2001. Accessed 20 Dec. 2015.

Elliott, Michael. "Money Counts." ONE.org, 14 Apr. 2015. Accessed 9 Mar. 2016.

Espen, Hal. "U2 Interview: Oscar Hopes, That Unfinished Album, Anxiety about Staying Relevant." *Hollywood Reporter*, 12 Feb. 2014. Accessed 06 Jan. 2016.

"Even Better than the Real Bling." *Time*, 14 Feb. 2005. Accessed 28 Feb. 2016.

Fegan, Catherine. "Brush with Disease Changed U2 Star's Life." *Daily Mail*, 3 Mar. 2009. Archived at Atu2.com. Accessed 4 May 2016.

Flanagan, Bill. *U2: At the End of the World*. New York: Dell Publishing, 1995. Written by music journalist Bill Flanagan, this is an authorized and in depth recounting of U2 in the early 1990s, focusing specifically on the band's global activities during its three-year-long Zoo TV tour.

Gayle, Damien. "Bono Defends U2's Tax Arrangements as 'Sensible.'" *Guardian*, 15 May 2015. Accessed 19 Mar. 2016.

"Get on Your Boots: Adam Steps into Limelight for Charity-Independent.ie." Independent. ie, 21 Mar. 2012. Accessed 15 Mar. 2016.

Gittins, Ian. *U2: The Best of Propaganda: 20 Years of the Official U2 Magazine*. New York: Thunder's Mouth, 2003. A collection of selected features from U2's official fan club magazine, which ran between 1986 and 2000.

Graham, Bill. "Battling through a Hail of Spittle." *North Side Story: U2 in Dublin 1978–1983*. Edited by Niall Stokes, 41. Dublin: Hot Press, 2013.

Graham, Bill. "Revolver, U2." *North Side Story: U2 in Dublin 1978-1983*. Edited by Niall Stokes, 28. Dublin: Hot Press, 2013.

Graham, Bill. "Trinity Buttery & McGonagles Matinee." *North Side Story: U2 in Dublin 1978–1983.* Edited by Niall Stokes, 28. Dublin: Hot Press, 2013.

Graham, Bill, and Caroline van Oosten de Boer. *U2: The Complete Guide to Their Music.* London: Omnibus, 2004. A concise overview of U2's music from two authors who have known the band from the beginning.

Hammond, Pete. "Oscars: U2 Writes One from the Heart for Nelson Mandela; Interview with Bono and the Edge." *Deadline,* 6 Jan. 2014.

Henke, James. "Here Comes the Next Big Thing." U2.com, 17 Feb. 2003. Accessed 10 Aug. 2015. Henke is the curator of the Rock and Roll Hall of Fame and has covered the band from its earliest days, beginning with *Rolling Stone* in 1980.

Hurtgen, John. "U2's Use of Antilanguage." *Exploring U2: Is This Rock 'n' Roll? Essays on the Music, Work, and Influence of U2.* Edited by Scott Calhoun, 219–20. Lanham, MD: Scarecrow Press, 2012.

King, Wayne. "The Fire Within: An Interview with U2's Bono." *Record Magazine,* 1 Mar. 1985. Archived at Atu2.com. Accessed 10 Aug. 2015.

"A Kind of Family . . ." U2.com, 28 May 2015. Accessed 29 Sept. 2015.

Kokkoris, Tassoula. "William Blake and the Inspiration behind U2's *Songs of Innocence.*" Atu2.com, 28 July 2015. Accessed 9 Apr. 2016. Atu2.com contains a vast archive of news stories as well as its own original reporting and analysis of U2's work.

Lawrence, Sherry. "Bono Returns to Willow Creek." Atu2.com, 9 Aug. 2009. Accessed 13 July 2015.

Lawrence, Sherry. "The Musical Holy Trinity in Songs of Innocence." Atu2.com, 16 Sept. 2014. Accessed 21 Sept. 2015.

Lawrence, Sherry. "Preaching to the Converted." Atu2.com, 20 Aug. 2006. Accessed 13 July 2015.

LePage, Mark. "Bass Notes: U2's Adam Clayton on Geography, Spirituality and Rock 'n' Roll." *Montreal Gazette,* 26 May 2001. Archived at Atu2.com. Accessed 28 July 2015.

Lewis, C. S. *The Screwtape Letters.* San Francisco: Harper San Francisco, 2001, 118. Bono is a big fan of Lewis and has often referenced the author's work, especially *The Screwtape Letters,* while creating the Fly persona for Zoo TV.

Mann, Sol O. "U2: For Those Who Have Ears to Hear." *Rock Rebel,* 22 Oct. 2001. Archived at Atu2.com. Accessed 17 Feb. 2016.

McCormick, Neil. "Boy to Man: A Dublin-Shaped Band." *Exploring U2: Is This Rock 'n' Roll? Essays on the Music, Work, and Influence of U2.* Edited by Scott Calhoun, 3–22. Lanham, MD: Scarecrow Press, 2012.

McCormick, Neil. *Killing Bono.* New York: Pocket, 2004. McCormick is a veteran music journalist and an authoritative voice on U2 who was there with the band as it formed.

McGee, Matt. "It Was 20 Years Ago Today: Remembering the Conspiracy of Hope Tour." Atu2.com, 4 June 2006. Accessed 14 Dec. 2015.

McGee, Matt. *U2: A Diary.* London: Omnibus, 2008. This book provides the most detailed account of U2's history and is a must-read for the avid fan.

McGirt, Ellen. "Bono: I Will Follow." *Fortune,* 24 Mar. 2016. Accessed 24 Mar. 2016. A thorough feature article outlining the financial and business details of Bono's many philanthropic projects.

McPherson, Alan L. *The World and U2: One Band's Remaking of Global Activism.* Lanham, MD: Rowman & Littlefield, 2015. A great, thoroughly documented summary of U2's social activism throughout its career.

Mulrooney, Deirdre. "Vertigo Vision." *Irish Times,* 19 Mar. 2005. Accessed 26 Nov. 2015.

Myers, Becky. "A Conversation with Catherine Owens." Atu2.com. Accessed 22 Dec. 2011.

Newman, Jason. "9 Biggest Revelations in Bono's 'BBC' Interview about U2." *Rolling Stone,* 3 Feb. 2014. Accessed 20 Dec. 2015.

Nietzsche, Friedrich. *Beyond Good and Evil.* Translated by Helen Zimmern. In *The Complete Works of Friedrich Nietzsche.* 1909–1913. Reprint by Project Gutenberg, 2009. Accessed 17 July 2015.

"Noreena and Bono Discuss (RED)." Noreena.com, 25 Sept. 2005. Accessed 5 June 2006.

"North American Media Comment on U2's Super Bowl Performance." Atu2.com, 7 Feb. 2002. Accessed 28 July 2015.

O'Hagan, Andrew. "Imaginary Spaces: Es Devlin and the Psychology of the Stage." *New Yorker*, 28 Mar. 2016. Accessed 28 Mar. 2016.

O'Hagan, Sean. "From Fez to Dublin and Beyond, via Presidents and Royalty, Sean O'Hagan Charts the Making of the New U2 Album." *Guardian*, 14 Feb. 2009. Accessed 2 Nov. 2015.

Robinson, Valerie. "'I Nearly Quit U2 before We Found Fame' Says Bono." *Irish News*, 26 June 2013. Accessed 11 Jan. 2016.

Sandberg, Marian. "Willie Williams on U2's Innocence + Experience, Part 1." *Live Design*, 3 June 2015. Accessed 3 June 2015.

Stockman, Steve. *Walk On: The Spiritual Journey of U2*. Orlando: Relevant, 2005. The best overview of U2's unique perspective on faith and spirituality, tracing the infusion of Christianity in the band's music and activism.

Stokes, Niall, ed. *North Side Story: U2 in Dublin 1978–1983*. Dublin: Hot Press, 2013. A remarkable anthology of *Hot Press* articles from 1978 to 1983, detailing the birth of U2. This book was only released as a gift to U2.com subscribers.

Stokes, Niall. *U2: The Stories behind Every U2 Song*. London: Carlton, 2009. The *Hot Press* journalist discusses the origin and inspiration for every song up to and including *No Line on the Horizon*.

"Stories about Boys." *Hot Press*, 30 Mar. 2011. Accessed 10 Aug. 2015.

Takiff, Jonathan. "From 'Good Voice' to 'Great Voice.'" Atu2.com, 30 Sept. 2007. Accessed 30 Dec. 2015.

Tanner, Kenneth. "Courageous Crooners." *National Review Online*, 23 Nov. 2004. Accessed 29 Jan. 2016.

Taylor, Steve. "'Bullet the Blue Sky' as an Evolving Performance." *Exploring U2: Is This Rock 'n' Roll? Essays on the Music, Work, and Influence of U2*. Edited by Scott Calhoun, 84–97. Lanham, MD: Scarecrow Press, 2012.

Theroux, Paul. "The Rock Star's Burden." *New York Times*, 15 Dec. 2005. Accessed 7 Mar. 2016. An often-cited piece offering a heavy critique of Bono's unique blend of philanthropy and capitalism.

Thyret, Andre, and Melanie Dohle. *Cedarwood*. Herten, Germany: H. Buschhausen GmbH, 2015. This is a charming children's book, with beautiful illustrations, portraying a young U2 in a story of friendship. All proceeds from this German publication are being donated to (RED).

U2: 360° at the Rose Bowl. Directed by Tom Krueger. Performed by U2. Interscope, 2010. DVD.

U2 and Neil McCormick. *U2 by U2*. New York: HarperCollins, 2006. The definitive, authorized account of U2, told by the members themselves.

U2 Go Home: Live from Slane Castle. Directed by Hamish Hamilton and Maurice Linnane. Performed by U2. Interscope Records, 2003. DVD.

U2. "Jack Heaslip/Bono: U2 Elevation Tour Prayer/Blessing." YouTube, 31 May 2008. Accessed 19 Sept. 2015.

"U2 May Be the Band of Tomorrow." *Grand Rapids Press*, 7 Dec. 1981. Archived at U2tours.com. Accessed 12 Apr. 2016.

U2: Rattle and Hum. Directed by Phil Joanou. Performed by U2. Paramount, 1999. DVD.

"U2's 'Songs of Innocence': A Track-by-Track Guide." *Rolling Stone*, 9 Sept. 2014. Accessed 9 Mar. 2015.

U2's Vision. Littlehampton, England: Dream Depot, 2005. CD. This is a CD that was briefly made available in 2006 and is a recording of Bono, Edge, and Larry speaking at a Christian musicians conference in 1981.

U2. "Transcript: The People in Our Rock 'n' Roll Hall of Fame." U2.com, 21 Mar. 2005. Accessed 19 Nov. 2015.

U2. "U2 Live Lovetown Tour—30 December 1989—Point Depot Dublin." YouTube, 1 Mar. 2013. Accessed. 8 Jun. 2015.

U2. "U2 Live Lovetown Tour—Point Depot Dublin 31 December 1989." YouTube, 27 May 2013. Accessed 8 Jun. 2015.

U2. "U2 October Interview 1982." YouTube, 20 Oct. 2011. Accessed 24 Apr. 2015.

U2. "U2—Sunday Bloody Sunday/Bad (Live Aid 1985) HD DVD Quality." YouTube, 10 Aug. 2014. Accessed 23 Apr. 2015.

"U2 Use Concert to Call for 'Leadership' over Refugee Crisis." *Guardian*, 5 Sept. 2015. Accessed 8 Mar. 2016.

U2: Zoo TV Live from Sydney. Directed by David Mallet. Performed by U2. Island, 1994. DVD.

United States Senate. Appropriations Subcommittee on State, Foreign Operations, and Related Programs. "Hearing on Violent Extremism & the Role of Foreign Assistance." United States Senate Committee on Appropriations, 12 Apr. 2016. Accessed 12 Apr. 2016. A transcript of Bono's full testimony before the Senate subcommittee in which he argues for increased assistance to countries suffering from the effects of the ongoing refugee crisis.

Vagacs, Robert. *Religious Nuts, Political Fanatics: U2 in Theological Perspective*. Eugene, OR: Cascade, 2005. A brief but insightful presentation of the theology inherent in U2's music and activism.

Varga, George. "Part-Time Rocker, Full-Time Humanitarian: Bill Clinton, Others Sing Bono's Praises." *Union-Tribune*, 2 Mar. 2003. Archived at U2interference.com. Accessed 3 Apr. 2016.

Vertigo 2005: Live from Chicago. Directed by Hamish Hamilton. Performed by U2. Island/Interscope, 2005. DVD.

Whiteley, Raewynne J., and Beth Maynard, eds. *Get Up Off Your Knees: Preaching the U2 Catalog*. Cambridge: Cowley Publications, 2003. An inspiring compendium of sermons based on the songs of U2.

Wroe, Martin. "Tears Are Not Enough." *Express On Sunday*, 2 December, 2002. Archived at Atu2.com. Accessed 15 Dec. 2015.

FURTHER LISTENING

The following is a list of U2's popular recordings (arranged chronologically), most of which are readily available for purchase. In addition to the band's studio albums, I have noted several corollary projects, as well as live concert films/videos in separate sections. The list of collections, rare editions, and fan club compilations over U2's forty-year career is far too large to inventory here, but readers can explore the fascinating depth of the band's entire catalog through a variety of Internet resources, including U2.com, atu2.com, and u2songs.com.

STUDIO ALBUMS

Boy. Island, 1980. The band's debut studio album reflects on the innocence and idealism of adolescence. It was well received and produced the hit "I Will Follow," a standard that U2 continues to use in concert.

October. Island, 1981. With a heavy religious subtext, this second album reflects Bono, Edge, and Larry's involvement in a Christian commune. Though not as acclaimed by critics as the earlier record, its opening track, "Gloria," was a huge hit and received lots of airplay on the new cable channel MTV.

War. Island, 1983. The third album is a well-developed, "grown-up" version of *Boy*. The shift to more overt political themes is clearly evidenced in the hits "New Year's Day" and "Sunday Bloody Sunday."

The Unforgettable Fire. Island, 1984. With its fourth album, U2 made a significant shift in style, moving toward a more ambient and experimental sound, and also began tackling social themes, including heroin addiction in "Bad" and the assassination of Martin Luther King, Jr. in "Pride (in the Name of Love)."

The Joshua Tree. Island, 1987. U2's fifth album landed them global status as superstars, resulting in multiple award-winning singles, including "With or Without You," "I Still Haven't Found What I'm Looking For," and "Where the Streets Have No Name."

Rattle and Hum. Island, 1988. The sixth album combined live recordings with new studio tunes and also had a companion film of the same name. It was not received well by critics but still produced several chart-topping singles with "Desire," "Angel of Harlem," and "All I Want Is You."

Achtung Baby. Island, 1991. U2 launched into a new decade with a redefined image on its seventh album, this time featuring a more industrial sound and provocative themes. Though the band was conflicted and unsure of its future while producing the record, it contains some of U2's best-loved songs: "One," "The Fly," "Mysterious Ways," and "Even Better than the Real Thing."

Zooropa. Island, 1993. The group's eighth album picked up where the previous one left off with wild sonic experiments and earned U2 a Grammy Award for Best Alternative Music Album, demonstrating the band's ability to create relevant, up-to-date music.

Pop. Island, 1997. On its ninth album, U2 mixed rock with the progressive sounds of the European dance and electronica scenes. One of the band's least selling records—potentially due to the hurried pace of its final stages of production—it was a bit of disappointment for a group accustomed to awards and honors.

All That You Can't Leave Behind. Interscope, 2000. As the band entered a new millennium, its tenth album once again helped redefine U2's image, this time focusing on familiar sounds and themes. The record produced award-winning tunes, including "Beautiful Day," "Elevation," and "Walk On."

How to Dismantle an Atomic Bomb. Interscope, 2004. U2's eleventh album reinforced the direction of the one before it with driving rock anthems and deep spirituality, resulting in the smash hit "Vertigo," which also represented a promotional partnership with Apple.

No Line on the Horizon. Interscope, 2009. With a long gap between its last album and this one, U2's twelfth veered toward the experimental once again. Nuanced with African music, complex rhythms, lavish harmonies, and rich theology, the record underperformed yet produced the largest supporting tour of the band's career.

Songs of Innocence. Interscope, 2014. Suffering from a bit of an identity crisis, U2 took longer than it ever had—five years—to complete a new project. The result was its thirteenth record, a retrospective that reflected back on the band's earliest days. Partnering again with Apple, the album was released digitally as a gift to all iTunes subscribers.

OTHER SIGNIFICANT ALBUMS

Under a Blood Red Sky. Island, 1983. Featuring several concerts while the members of U2 were in their early twenties, the album introduced U2 to an American audience.

Passengers: Original Soundtracks. Island, 1995. Under the pseudonym Passengers, U2 teamed up with Brian Eno on an album that allowed them to create music not intended for the mass market.

The Best of 1980–1990. Island, 1998. This greatest hits collection from U2's first decade also included "Sweetest Thing," a new single that charted in Top 10 lists around the world.

The Million Dollar Hotel: Music from the Motion Picture. Interscope, 2000. In collaboration with Daniel Lanois, Brian Eno, and other artists, this album features music by U2 for the film *The Million Dollar Hotel*, which Bono helped write and produce.

The Best of 1990–2000. Interscope, 2002. A compilation of hits from the band's second decade, this album includes several tracks not previously available on U2 albums, including the single "Electrical Storm," as well as "The Hands That Built America," "Hold Me, Thrill Me, Kiss Me, Kill Me," and "Miss Sarajevo."

U218 Singles. Interscope, 2006. A third compilation album, this time containing sixteen of the band's all-time greatest hits, plus "The Saints Are Coming" and "Window in the Skies."

Spider-Man: Turn Off the Dark. Interscope, 2011. This is the sound track to the Broadway musical for which Bono and Edge wrote the music and lyrics.

CONCERT FILMS

U2 Live at Red Rocks: Under a Blood Red Sky. Island, 1984. This concert features the
   historic performance by U2 at Red Rocks Amphitheatre in Colorado on June 5, 1983, and
   also helped solidify the band's reputation as a remarkable live act, especially in America.
Rattle and Hum. Paramount Pictures, 1988. Filmed at several locations in 1987 while on the
   Joshua Tree tour, this feature movie appeared in cinemas and showed behind-the-scenes
   footage of U2 at play in America as well as in concert.
Zoo TV: Live from Sydney. Island, 1994. This performance from May 17, 1993, features the
   Zoo TV tour and illustrates U2's stunning use of theatrics, irony, and stage personae while
   supporting both *Achtung Baby* and *Zooropa*.
PopMart: Live from Mexico City. Island, 1998. In conjunction with the album *Pop*, U2's
   PopMart concert from November 22, 1998, intentionally presented gargantuan represen-
   tations of the kitschiest icons from a 1990s consumerist culture.
Elevation 2001: Live from Boston. Island, 2001. Supporting *All That You Can't Leave Behind*, this video was filmed over three nights in June 2001 and features a simpler,
   stripped-down version of U2 while still becoming one of the band's best-selling live
   performances.
Vertigo 2005: Live from Chicago. Island, 2005. This concert film tapped into the fears of the
   times, especially with regard to terrorism and the Middle Eastern conflict, and supported
   the album *How to Dismantle an Atomic Bomb*.
U2: 360° at the Rose Bowl. Interscope, 2010. This October 25, 2009, concert promoted the
   album *No Line on the Horizon*, featured the biggest stage ever built, and was broadcast
   live on YouTube.
U2: iNNOCENCE + eXPERIENCE Live in Paris. HBO, 2015. This performance, originally
   planned for Nov. 14, 2015 but then rescheduled for December 7 due to the terrorist
   attacks in Paris, showcases state-of-the-art technology as well as a retrospective on U2's
   earliest days as a band and was broadcast exclusively on HBO.

INDEX

ABOUT THE AUTHOR

Timothy D. Neufeld is a professor at Fresno Pacific University where he is chair of the biblical and religious studies department and teaches practical theology. One of his favorite classes to teach is Theology, Culture, and U2, a course he designed in 2006 as an effort to help students think theologically about current global issues. He has presented papers, chaired panels, and published articles related to U2 for the Pop Culture Association National Conference, two U2 studies conferences, the North American Association of Christians in Social Work, and the *Pacific Journal*, as well as other academic and popular organizations. He is a frequent blogger and a news writer for @U2 (www.atu2.com), the longest-running fansite on the Internet, and is also the creator and host of a U2 fan community on Periscope called the Crystal Ballroom. Tim is a licensed pastor and lives in Fresno, California, with his wife and two sons.

Tim invites you to join him on social media:

Website: timothyneufeld.com
Facebook and Instagram: timothyneufeld
Twitter and Periscope: timneufeld